21st Century
DISCIPLINE

Teaching Students
Responsibility & Self-Management

Second Edition

by Jane Bluestein, Ph.D.

Fearon Teacher Aids
A Division of Frank Schaffer Publications, Inc.

The first edition of the present work was published by Scholastic Inc., 1988, and revised by I.S.S. Publications, 1998.

Cover and Interior Design: Good Neighbor Press, Grand Junction, CO

Fearon Teacher Aids products were formerly manufactured and distributed by American Teaching Aids, Inc., a subsidiary of Silver Burdett Ginn, and are now manufactured and distributed by Frank Schaffer Publications, Inc. FEARON, FEARON TEACHER AIDS, and the FEARON balloon logo are marks used under license from Simon & Schuster, Inc.

© **Fearon Teacher Aids**
A Division of Frank Schaffer Publications, Inc.
23740 Hawthorne Boulevard
Torrance, CA 90505-5927

Contents

Foreword: Welcome to the Second Edition

It's hard for me to believe that it's been nearly a decade since I wrote the first edition of this book. Back then, the 21st century seemed like it was still a long way off. Not so today.

In many ways, discipline issues haven't changed much since I first started writing about them. Kids still come to class unprepared, forget to put materials away, don't turn their homework in on time and lack skills needed to succeed with the curriculum we're supposed to teach them. Bad attitudes, lack of initiative, poor impulse control, passive learning, indifference, power struggles and, in many instances, verbal or physical violence are a reality in many classrooms. I've seen increasing impatience and disillusionment with traditional practices and ineffective techniques that simply do not address the most fundamental component of any educational experience, that is, the relationship between teacher and student.

The good news is this: There is a better way. In the time in which this book has been in print, I've gotten feedback from countless teachers, counselors, administrators and other school personnel who have made changes suggested in *21st Century Discipline* with great success, often as a last resort. I've seen educators year after year at conferences who make a point of coming back to tell me, "It works!"

As a result, I am more positive than ever that the changes we say we want are not going to come from stricter enforcement of punitive discipline codes. I am convinced that these changes will come, instead, from our efforts to develop relationships with our students that can indeed accommodate their needs—particularly their needs for autonomy and power within clear, definite limits in an emotionally safe environment.

During the past ten years, I have concentrated my efforts on refining the language, conceptual foundation and techniques of a 21st century approach. I've borrowed from other fields and have learned much from educators throughout the world with whom I've worked. This revision incorporates research, observations, personal experiences and information that account for several small but significant changes.

For example, one of the barriers I run into whenever I talk about discipline is a rather persistent negative connotation. Ask anyone involved in the lives of children what the word means to them and nearly every response equates discipline with punishment or, at very least, a negative reaction to a student's misbehavior. In the original text of this book, I worked hard to reframe the concept of discipline, to redefine the term to emphasize the development of relationships and classroom environments in which many typical discipline problems simply do not occur (or occur much more infrequently and much less disruptively). Despite my confidence in the effectiveness and appropriateness of the motivation and reinforcement techniques I originally presented, I was not entirely satisfied with the intervention strategies for dealing with mis-behaviors. There were just too many similarities—both in concept and implementation—to the dynamics of using punishments. Yes, I accentuated prevention, but even putting the most positive spin on the pattern of using rules and consequences could not pull this approach out of its negative and reactive tradition.

In the second edition, I have shifted from using rules and negative consequences to setting boundaries, emphasizing contingent access to positive outcomes instead. I have found that this model afforded me a context, not only for intervening disruptive and nondisruptive off-task behavior, but also for using the original techniques for motivating and reinforcing cooperation without relying on power, threats or conditional teacher approval. The change is subtle but the difference is powerful. As a result, the relationship dynamics are a great deal "cleaner" and less power-oriented, all without losing their effectiveness. Since rules are a fact of life in educational institutions, the term appears occasionally in this revision. Nonetheless, my preference for using boundaries stands, as well as my belief in their effectiveness and compatibility with win-win objectives.

Another change was in the area of internal and external motivation. These terms seemed a lot less ambiguous when I first started writing about them: Internal motivation came from inside, external motivation from something or someone else. I've seen a lot of teachers upset or confused by these terms and I have experienced a great deal of frustration with this language myself. What I've come to is this: All motivation is internal. Whether we do something for the joy of doing it, to please someone, to get it out of the way, to feel a sense of pride or accomplishment, to fulfill a commitment or responsibility, to avoid a penalty or punishment, to keep from disappointing or annoying someone, to get a grade or a paycheck (or some other token) or so that we can do something we really enjoy once we've finished, we are satisfying some internal need. Always.

In this revision, I differentiate instead between motivators and reinforcers which rely on the reaction of another person (or jeopardize emotional safety with conditional approval) and those which do not. I will occasionally use the word "internal" to refer to motivators that are not dependent on pleasing or appeasing another person, even if the motivator is neither related to the task nor connected with some intrinsic pleasure involved in the task itself. As far as I'm concerned, doing what the teacher wants so you can do a fun enrichment activity, check off a task you've completed or go help out in the library is just as "internal" (and, quite frankly, as reasonable) as cooperating because you happen to love a particular subject area. In creating a safe emotional environment, I'm far more concerned about using motivators and reinforcers that teach kids to constantly look outside themselves, to base their decisions on anticipated reactions of other people or build dependence on outside approval. I will occasionally refer to these instances as examples of "external" motivation, even though, quite frankly, the need to avoid rejection or anger is just as internal as anything else.

Finally, in the first edition, I frequently described student misbehavior as a matter of "poor choosing." My thinking has shifted somewhat in this area, too. I no longer believe that there is a such thing as a "bad choice" because all choices afford us opportunities to learn, sometimes the seemingly bad choices most of all. I have tried to minimize the use of this expression. Any reference to "poor choices (or choosing)" simply refers to choices less favored or desired by the teacher.

It is my hope that these changes will make the entire matter of restructuring power dynamics and creating win-win authority relationships with kids a bit more clear and accessible, and will make your journey in this direction simpler, smoother and more enjoyable.

Jane Bluestein
Albuquerque, New Mexico

Preface

A few years ago, after meeting the student teachers and first-year teaching interns I was to supervise, I asked about the topics and concerns they wanted to explore during the year we were to work together. The question was barely out of my mouth before I heard a unanimous response: Discipline. They had dozens of questions, mostly about how to get the kids to do something—or stop doing something. "What if they don't listen?" "What if there's a fight?" "What if they won't do their work?" "What if . . . ?"

Since then, I've run across thousands of teachers whose questions and primary concerns have sounded remarkably similar. And over the years I've discovered few simple answers to questions about specific behaviors—or misbehaviors. Instead, I've found it far more useful to back up and talk about seemingly unrelated issues: goals, needs, relationships, cooperation, motivation, success, classroom climate and responsibility, to name a few. Without addressing these issues, most advice is short-term, ineffective and out of the context of the classroom relationships in which the problems occur.

In the context of creating healthy, positive and mutually-respectful relationships between teachers and students, discipline becomes a set of preventative techniques that encourage student self-management and self-control while reducing the number of conflicts anticipated by the vast majority of "what if" questions.

My second discovery was the fact that any discussion of student behavior ultimately leads back to teacher behavior. Motivating cooperation from our students usually means modifying our own behaviors, learning new interaction skills and letting go of ineffective or destructive techniques. Whenever we're not happy with how students are behaving, the next question for us is this: "What can I do differently?" Because for better or worse, they don't change until we change.

This news can be rather disconcerting: it's always easier to want the other person to change. Even with firm commitments to positive interaction strategies, avoiding the pitfalls of our own negative programming can be quite a challenge. Learning to motivate students to adjust their behavior is a process on every level—not just for us, but for our students as well.

As with any change, the prospect of restructuring relationships may seem confusing and overwhelming, so let's start with where you are. A preassessment follows to help you examine your beliefs and the behaviors that are working for you, as well as those that may be keeping you from reaching your goals. The rest of this book will offer some constructive alternatives, along with a number of self-evaluation and reflection questions to help you assess the progress you're making.

And always, best wishes for continued success and happiness throughout your journey.

Date_____

Preassessment

In each pair of statements, mark the one you identify with most strongly. The sole purpose of this activity is to establish a basis for tracking your own growth and development.

_____ I try to build a positive emotional climate in the classroom.

_____ I prefer to focus on academics. The students are there to learn.

_____ I try to give each student a chance to feel successful by meeting his or her individual needs.

_____ All students have an opportunity to feel successful if they listen and stay caught up.

_____ Whether or not my students cooperate, I communicate my acceptance of them as people.

_____ When my students cooperate, I communicate my approval.

_____ It's possible to have fun with your students and still keep their attention.

_____ Students will probably take advantage of a teacher who tries to have fun with them.

_____ I have a variety of classroom materials out and available for my students to take as needed.

_____ Most of the time, I dispense materials.

_____ I want my students to be cooperative.

_____ I want my students to be obedient.

_____ I may not accept a student's misbehavior, but I can still accept the student.

_____ I cannot accept a student who is misbehaving.

_____ I want my students to listen to me, and I try to make it need-fulfilling for them to do so.

_____ I want my students to listen to me, and I punish them when they do not.

_____ Students can choose responsibly and still not choose what I would like.

_____ I am reluctant to let my kids make decisions because they might not choose what I want them to.

_____ I allow students to experience the natural consequences of misbehavior.

_____ Misbehavior should be punished.

_____ The best negative consequence is the absence of a positive consequence.

_____ A negative consequence has to be punitive, painful or embarrassing to be effective.

_____ "Johnny, you really got ready in a hurry today!"

_____ "I like the way Johnny got ready today!"

_____ My students are cooperative because they choose to be.

_____ My students are cooperative because I do not allow them to misbehave.

_____ My students can manage OK even if I'm not there.

_____ My students behave as long as I don't turn my back on them.

_____ I treat my students the way I would like to be treated.

_____ I really have to blow up at my students from time to time.

_____ "Please put the lid on the paste so it won't dry out."

_____ "Please put the lid on the paste because I said so."

_____ I try to find something positive to say about every paper I get.

_____ I normally mark only mistakes or incorrect answers.

_____ I try to speak to my students the way I like to be spoken to.

_____ I sometimes talk to my students in ways I would never speak to another adult.

_____ My students know I care about them even if they are driving me crazy.

_____ I cannot accept them when they act up.

_____ I like my job most of the time.

_____ I dislike my job most of the time.

_____ I like to call parents when my students are doing well.

_____ I rarely call parents unless my students really mess up.

_____ I give my students reasons for doing things.

_____ Students should do what they're told, period.

_____ I work for my students' respect.

_____ Students should respect me because I'm their teacher.

_____ It's possible for students to have power in the classroom without disrupting the class or hurting anyone.

_____ Give them an inch and they'll take a yard.

_____ I immediately withdraw privileges when my students misbehave (or violate boundaries).

_____ I frequently give my students warnings and reminders when they misbehave (or violate boundaries).

_____ I know I'm doing a great job when I'm prepared and doing my best, even if my students don't respond.

_____ It's hard for me to feel successful or effective unless my students are busy learning and excited about their work.

_____ When my students behave, it is because they are working for positive consequences.

_____ When my students behave, it is because they want to avoid punishment.

_____ Even the best teachers are limited as to what they can control.

_____ Good teachers are in control of their classrooms.

_____ Everyone works better when there is a payoff.

_____ Students should not have to be rewarded for good behavior or performance.

_____ My students cooperate because they find cooperation personally rewarding.

_____ My students cooperate because they want to please me.

_____ I like to joke with my students.

_____ I rarely joke with my students.

_____ I want my students to care about me.

_____ I do not care if my students like me as long as they behave and do their work.

_____ I encourage my students to help with administrative details.

_____ I take care of most of the administrative details in my classroom.

_____ I like to let my students check their own work.

_____ I rarely allow my students access to my answer keys.

_____ I sometimes ask my students to choose which assignments they would like to do first.

_____ My students do their work in a specific sequence.

_____ My students sometimes choose which problems or assignments they want to do.

_____ I determine the assignments for my students.

_____ I sometimes ask my students for input about which topics or concepts they would like to study.

_____ I determine what we cover in my classroom.

_____ "You can go out for recess as soon as you finish your work."

_____ "If you don't get your work done, you won't be able to go to recess."

_____ "If you're quiet in the hall, we'll be able to get to lunch quickly."

_____ "If you're noisy in the hall, we'll have to come back here."

_____ "Please pick up those marbles so that no one will slip and fall."

_____ "Would you pick up those marbles for me, please?"

_____ I try very hard to treat my students with respect, even when I am responding to their negative behavior.

_____ It's sometimes necessary to criticize or humiliate a student.

_____ I have a number of unrelated, non-destructive diversions to relieve work-related stress.

_____ Most of my out-of-school time is devoted to my work.

The first statement in each pair reflects the discipline philosophy described in this book. If you have checked a majority of these statements, this book will help you enhance what you're already doing. The second statement in the pair reflects a more traditional authoritarian approach to dealing with children. If you checked many of these statements, you're certainly in good company. This is, for the most part, the model most of us grew up seeing and the way many of us were trained to work with children in a classroom. Read on; you'll find more positive alternatives. If you had a difficult time choosing between the two statements in a particular pair, this book can point out the differences between the two discipline strategies, which are actually very different and generally exclusive of one another.

Introduction

My interest in classroom discipline began before I ever encountered my first group of students. My training (and confidence) had been geared to lesson plans, bulletin boards and color-coded task cards. In terms of preparation, I could not have been outdone. Yet the thought of facing a roomful of children somehow wasn't relieved by my skill with the laminator. Throughout my methods courses one question persistently nagged: "But what do I do with the kids?"

I did not get many answers, and those I did hear were not particularly satisfying. More often than not my question was answered with a warning: "Keep them busy and make sure you look like you're in charge."

Great.

At the time, the university stressed freedom and creativity in the classroom. The undercurrent from the schools, however, warned that control was the goal. To that end, some veterans confessed to having students copy their science books because, when observed, the kids were quiet and looked busy. Is that what I wanted? Was there a way to strike a balance between nurturer and storm trooper?

I went into my classroom armed with the best bulletin boards in the district and a handful of cliches: Be tough. Be consistent. Be clever. Don't smile before Christmas.

Yet very quickly I realized there was something missing, and I spent the next several years looking for the magic that got kids moving, kept them busy, attracted their attention and generated responsible, caring attitudes and behaviors.

My first few months in the classroom were painful, to say the least. My attempts at power were, for the most part, unimpressive and unheeded. My students, though equipped with street smarts and savvy, could not make simple decisions or get from one side of the room to the other without direction. I was so busy nagging, reminding and policing that I never seemed to do any teaching.

During that time, I learned that love, dedication and my own creativity would not be enough. I learned that expectations alone did not generate cooperation, that powering alienates and ultimately impedes growth, and that heeding the advice to not smile for any length of time left little room to enjoy being a teacher.

But I also learned that there are tricks that work—most of the time, with most of the kids—and that the success of these tricks is closely tied to the quality of the classroom atmosphere that's been created and the interactions that occur. I slowly discovered alternatives to blaming other teachers, the system or parents, and eventually I found ways to meet the students' needs without sacrificing my own.

Over the years, I've had the privilege of meeting and working with thousands of teachers worldwide. I've learned much from my observations and conversations and in these pages, I present, along with anecdotes from my own teaching experience, many stories and examples that these other teachers graciously shared with me. This book details what I've learned, both as a classroom teacher and as a teacher educator, about which teacher behaviors work best in which situations, about encouraging student commitment and responsibility, and about creating a positive and preventive interactive framework so that teaching time is spent as it was intended—devoted to instruction, not discipline.

Acknowledgements

Revising this book took me back through a great deal of my history, allowing me to relive, in particular, much of my teacher training as well as those first weeks and years in the classroom. To be sure, each story and example presented here has faces and feelings attached, each of them a part of who I am today, both personally and professionally. Much water, many bridges, as a friend once said.

Certain individuals bear mention, as their influence on my knowledge, beliefs, confidence, skills and understanding of how people learn and interact successfully has been immense. For example, I never would have survived my first year without the constant support of Marian Morris, the site coordinator of the Intern Program in which I was enrolled, and the other beginning teachers fumbling and stumbling along with me.

Various professors throughout my graduate training at the University of Pittsburgh also left their respective marks. My thanks to John Morgan, Horton Southworth, Jeanne Winsand, Janice Gibson, Dave Champagne, Larry Knolle and Dave Campbell. All of these individuals could somehow see me beyond where I was when I came into their lives; each in his or her own way planted seeds for an unfoldment I could not have imagined.

I would also like to acknowledge the students and teachers with whom I worded at Arlington Heights, Sterrett School and Chartiers Elementary in Pittsburgh, as well as the Student Teachers and Interns I supervised at the University of New Mexico. Much of what I know I learned from you.

I am particularly grateful to Peggy Bielen for sharing with me her idea of agreeing with criticism and judgments. I find statements like "You could be right" to be a healthy alternative to explanations and defensiveness. I'm sure that my sharing her ideas has helped others as well.

I am also indebted to the hundreds of workshop participants throughout the United States, Canada and Europe who generously shared their stories and experiences with me and to the many friends and associates who have touched my life and my heart.

And finally, and extra-special thank-you to Jerry Tereszkiewicz, who came into my life as I was starting out in my first classroom—and has hung with me ever since.

Section One

You and Your Students

1

What You Want

Before talking about the whys and hows of discipline and classroom management, let's make sure we're headed in the same direction.

Right now, it's fantasy time. Imagine you have an ideal class of perfect students who behave exactly the way you want, all the time. How do they act? Think about those classroom behaviors that you perceive as ideal. Consider what you want and need as a classroom teacher, and what your students need to succeed in your class.

Regardless of how your students actually behave, imagine each statement below as behavior you can indeed elicit. If you could have anything you want, how strongly would you want to see the behaviors in each statement—for your students' benefit and your own?

Use the following scale to complete the survey:

5 = Yes, very much! (Where do I sign up?)

3 = Not crucial, but would be nice.

1 = No big deal.

Survey

Date:_____

I want my students to:

____ respect school and class limits, standards and rules.

____ be good decision makers, be able to evaluate options and predict outcomes.

____ take care of materials, put things back, keep work area neat.

____ make cooperative choices within the limits I define.

____ be committed to their own learning.

____ take risks with their learning; try new things.

____ exhibit responsibility, accountability and independence.

____ interact cooperatively with each other.

____ solve their own problems constructively.

____ come to class prepared.

____ listen and follow directions—the first time.

____ participate enthusiastically in activities and discussions.

____ take initiative for their work and learning.

____ stay on task and make good use of class time.

____ turn in work on time (with their names on their papers).

____ demonstrate self-control; avoid disruptiveness.

____ feel good about themselves.

____ manage frustration or setbacks; control aggression and rebelliousness.

____ enjoy working with me and with each other.

____ enjoy school and learning in general.

You have the choice of accomplishing your instructional goals either by spending your time engaged positively or negatively.

Discipline is more than simply getting kids to do what you want.

Now total your ratings. If your score is low (that is, closer to 20 than 100), either your discipline goals are significantly different from those expressed in this book or your imagination was not adequately cranked. (Try again. Be good to yourself!) In either case, consider the following: you have the choice of accomplishing your instructional goals either by spending your time engaged positively (teaching, observing, recognizing) or negatively (nagging, threatening, criticizing). Which would you prefer?

The statements in the survey present a definition of discipline that will be used throughout this book. When your students are demonstrating these behaviors, class time can be devoted to instruction and positive interactions. These behaviors do not evolve in a vacuum, however, and the remainder of this book is devoted to helping you create the kind of classroom environment in which students do what you ask, come prepared, interact cooperatively, act responsibly, feel good about themselves *and* remember to put the caps back on the markers!

The position presented in this book is that discipline is more than simply getting kids to do what you want, and certainly more than reacting to what you don't want. The behaviors described in the survey are important, because when your kids exhibit them, your job will be significantly easier and more pleasant. More importantly, students who acquire these skills tend to be able to function more successfully in and out of the classroom, during their school years and later in life.

For most of us, it's much easier to agree that these behaviors are important and valuable than it is to actually bring them about. In fact, even teachers with the deepest devotion to encouraging independence, responsibility, cooperation, social skills and all of the other skills described, may inadvertently choose teaching behaviors and interactive strategies that actually prevent these skills from developing.

The next chapter examines how we have fallen into this trap. The rest of the book shows the way out.

2

The Discipline Trap: Catching up to the 21st Century

If you're old enough to remember the television family sit-coms of the 1950's, you may recall how, regardless of the show, the family structures and values were remarkably similar. These were the values of suburban, middle-class America at the peak of the post-war industrial era. During this period, as so clearly reflected in the television programming of the time, uniformity was the goal; innovation and initiative were viewed as odd or eccentric, if not downright threatening.

These values were clear in the workplace and the classroom, where authority relationships were typically power-oriented. Competitive goal structures limited the number who could succeed and behavior was governed by fairly rigid expectations. In the industrial era, success, recognition and advancement depended on obedience, dedication, persistence and the ability to avoid making waves.

With the continuing technological developments of the past few decades, America has changed from an industrial to an information society. This new economy demands a different set of work skills than those required by a factory economy, particularly in areas, such as interaction, innovation, negotiation and communication.* With a need for different work skills comes a gradual shift in what is valued in the workplace. While the worker of the industrial age may have looked for security

and permanence, workers in the current economy are showing a marked preference for individuality, personal empowerment and potential for growth.

That's the good news.

The bad news is that while our systems of education have, in many instances, made strides in the curriculum to accommodate technological developments, behaviorally, they are still, for the most part, set up to crank out factory workers. Present-day businesses, which lean more toward networking, cooperation, negotiation, flexibility, creativity and divergence than their industrial-era counterparts, often attract students schooled in a system that values factory-era skills and behaviors. These students may have difficulty making the transition to an information-age workplace. Even when individual teachers recognize these needs and make a commitment to build toward the future, we are so much a product of win-lose, competitive goal structures that our teaching and interaction skills may lack congruence between well-intentioned goals and our ability to carry them out.

For example, many of us have vowed, at one time or another, never to act or sound like an authoritarian teacher we did not like when we were in school. Yet how many of us have actually kept that promise? Part of the problem is that the person whose behavior we disliked

Our teaching and interaction skills may lack congruence between well-intentioned goals and our ability to carry them out.

The behaviors we observed are the ones we tend to adopt.

---

*For more information about the change from an industrial society to an information society, read John Naisbitt's *Megatrends*. New York: Warner Books, 1982.

Conflict situations are inevitable when we attempt to motivate or teach information-age children with industrial-age strategies.

was one of our role models. We grew up with this behavior; and, though it might be difficult to admit, it's easy to repeat behaviors that are most familiar.

The value system of the industrial era seeped into all authority relationships, shaping the behavior of our parents and teachers, who used strategies necessary to help us function in a factory society. The model was rigid and power-oriented, perhaps by necessity; like it or not, this was how most factories operated. There existed an unquestioned *should* or *for-your-own-good* mentality, as well as a belief that control and punishment were essential and ultimately effective, particularly with regard to raising and educating children.

It's doubtful that parents, teachers or employers of this era were deliberately abusive; more likely, they were unskilled in the interactive dimensions of their roles and probably believed themselves to be short on options. Whether or not they actually liked the model, most people accepted it and followed the precedents set by their own parents, teachers and bosses, probably without much thought. In this context, it's easy to see how information-age priorities, such as individuality, independence, intrinsic motivation and self-control would pose quite a threat to an autocratic, conformity-oriented value system or institution.

If we grew up with power-based, win-lose authority relationships, the behaviors we observed are the ones we tend to adopt. However, when we apply industrial-age techniques, we interfere with our students' ability to develop the skills they will need in an economy structured on a different set of needs and values—often the very skills we're trying to inspire. Therein lies the confusion and frustration.

When everything is going along well, we have no need to fear the demons of our upbringing. It is the conflict situation that

21st Century Discipline means taking time to learn new techniques to teach responsible learning skills

elicits the words and behaviors we had sworn to avoid. And conflict situations are inevitable when we attempt to motivate or teach information-age children with industrial-age strategies.

Discrepancies can exist between what we want and what we know best. The world has gotten considerably larger for children than it was even a few years ago. No longer do kids depend on a handful of significant adults to let them know what's going on. Simply regretting the simplicity of the idealized "good old days" will not help kids rise to the demands of contemporary realities. What worked for our teachers not only may not work for us, it may actually work against us. We need a new game plan.

21st Century Discipline means examining attitudes, beliefs and behavior patterns we often revert to automatically. It requires rethinking goals and priorities and, in some instances, letting go of industrial-era values that are no longer effective. It involves reframing the concept of discipline from a set of punitive behaviors which emphasize reactions to what kids are doing wrong, to a set of preventative behaviors which emphasize relationship building to avoid conflicts and disruptions in the first place. It calls for taking time to learn new techniques to teach responsible learning skills, avoid conflict or even restructuring entire relationships in order to achieve desired results.

Fortunately, the means to reaching these goals are specific, learnable skills that work in and outside the classroom for children and adults. You probably already know many of these skills and use them in successful adult relationships. Now, with the 21st century upon us, we have a context for applying them in the classroom.

Industrial Age

(Traditional Classroom)

Values, Priorities, and Motivators

- Uniformity, sameness; fitting in.
- Stability, permanence, security (rigid roles)
- Competitive
- Motivation for cooperation: pleasing authority (approval-seeking), avoiding punishment, humiliation, rejection, disapproval; oriented to adult and adult's reaction
- Outcome or product orientation
- Pleasing others regardless of personal needs
- Perfectionism
- Black-and-white thinking (or all-or-nothing thinking, dualism); tunnel vision
- Past or future orientation
- Personal worth is dependent on achievement, appearance, wealth, performance, etc.

Skills: Student Behaviors that are Encouraged or Reinforced

- Following orders, obedience, people-pleasing, asking permission, compliance, dependence
- Listening
- Respecting authority relationship while protecting existing hierarchy or power structure
- Avoiding conflict; peace at any price
- Self-sacrifice, self-abandonment; putting others first even at cost to self
- Not making waves; maintaining status quo
- Ability to "stuff" feelings, appear "fine;" impression management; blaming, making others responsible for how you feel
- Dependence on leader (credit or blame)

Information Age

(The 21st Century Discipline Classroom)

Values, Priorities and Motivators

- Growth potential, personal fulfillment; diversity, personal unfoldment
- Flexibility, choices, personal control, (variable roles, expectations)
- Cooperation
- Motivation for cooperation: personal satisfaction; curiosity; positive consequences or outcomes that are unrelated to adult's reaction; oriented to student
- Process or person orientation
- Self-care; doing for others with regard for personal needs
- Mistakes seen as a necessary and valuable part of growth
- Many options and alternatives; ability to see various points of view
- Personal worth is unconditional, regardless of achievement, appearance, wealth, performance, etc.

Skills: Student Behaviors that are Encouraged or Reinforced

- Taking initiative, making decisions within limits of rules or boundaries; self-caring choices
- Communicating
- Respecting authority relationship while networking, negotiating
- Personal integrity
- Self-care; maintaining personal boundaries; service and consideration with respect to personal needs
- Taking risks, trying new things; innovating
- Expressing feelings honestly, responsibly and non-disruptively
- Operating according to a personal value system as long as no one's rights or boundaries are violated
- Assuming personal responsibility; team-work

Authority Relationships

- Reactive

- Power-oriented; punitive

- Win-Lose (powering or permissive)

- Command-oriented; demands; few choices offered

- Teacher sets limits and determines what is and is not negotiable; enforces rules

- Student empowerment discouraged; initiative often punished or criticized; perceived as a threat to adult authority

- Manipulative

- Purpose for rules and boundaries power-based: "Because I said so;" not explained to students

- Teacher responsible for students' behavior

- Tendency to take students' behavior or misbehavior personally; vulnerability of self-worth or sense of adequacy to how kids act

- Rescuing behavior is common; warnings, inappropriate second chances; denying or making excuses for students' misbehavior; protecting students from non-life-threatening consequences of poor choosing

- Rules and boundaries established to protect teacher power

- Mistrust; belief that students are "always trying to get away with something" and will behave only in presence of authority they fear

- Teachers frightened by or uncomfortable with students' expressions of feelings (especially anger, sadness or fear); denial of feelings; judgment, criticism, blaming, distracting or shaming students for their feelings

- Approval of students conditional on students' cooperative, teacher-pleasing behavior

- Arrogance, self-centeredness, self-righteousness; "shoulds;" focus on teacher needs

- Double standards for adults and children; certain language, behaviors or attitudes teachers model are not tolerated (and punished) when students do the same things

Authority Relationships

- Proactive, preventative

- Goal- or consequence-oriented (positive or negative)

- Win-win (cooperative)

- Negotiation-oriented; many choices may be offered

- Teacher sets limits and determines what is and is not negotiable; encourages self-enforcement

- Student empowerment and initiative encouraged within limits that respect everyone's rights

- Direct

- Purpose for rules and boundaries is consequence-based, explained to students

- Students responsible for their own behavior

- Greater detachment from personal impact of students' behavior (affect of students' behavior on self-worth or adequacy of teacher) without loss of caring

- Students allowed to experience non-life-threatening consequences of poor choosing

- Rules or boundaries established to protect everyone's rights, consider everyone's needs

- Trust; belief that students will make responsible choices if given the opportunity (and reason) to do so; trust in students' ability to function even in absence of authority

- Teachers accept and encourage students to feel feelings and express them constructively (without hurting others or themselves); students accepted regardless of their feelings

- Acceptance of students regardless of their behavior

- No need to make student "wrong" in order for teacher to be right; respect for students' needs

- Absence of double standards; teachers model behaviors they want children to exhibit

Discipline Goal: Controlling Students, Disempowerment

- Students make few decisions, have few opportunities to act independently

- Independence seen as threatening to power, undermining teacher's role as authority disciplinarian

- Punishment for infractions (often long-term and severe); rarely opportunities for self-correction (although remorse, shame and contrition may be accepted)

- Confusion of student behavior and worth

- Praise of student for cooperation, achievement, teacher-pleasing behavior (connecting student's "goodness" to positive choices); emphasis on student, not deed and value of student's choice to teacher

- Critical, judgmental; focus on negative

- Warnings, lectures, delayed consequences

- Problems with students often referred to outside authority for punishment (principal, counselor, coach, parent)

- Greater rigidity and uniformity in assignments, rewards; evaluation tends to be comparative (based on the performance of others)

Discipline Goal: Student Self-Control

- Students have opportunities to make decisions, act independently

- Independence seen as supporting cooperative relationship; frees teacher for instruction, guidance, facilitation

- Consequences for infractions (often the absence of positive consequences until behavior changes); self-correction encouraged; objective is improved behavior (remorse, shame, and contrition are not necessary).

- Separation of student behavior and worth

- Recognition of student cooperation or achievement without judging; emphasis on deed, not student (student's worth is not an issue) and value of student's choice to student.

- Focus on positive

- Immediate consequences (or removal of privilege)

- Personal responsibility for problems with students; teachers may contact outside authority as a resource, for ideas or support, or simply to let them know what's going on and how they are going to handle the problem

- Greater diversity and flexibility in assignments, rewards; evaluation based on individual performance and ability

Becoming more effective in our interactions with students involves a number of processes: clarifying goals, examining our own habits and values, and learning and applying new behaviors. The activities presented throughout this book will help direct you on this journey.

Date_____

Activity

Refer to the information on the previous pages to answer the following:
In what ways did your own experiences as a student reflect the values, skills and relationships of the Industrial Age?

In what ways did your own experiences as a student reflect the values, skills and relationships of the Information Age?

In what ways have your experiences affected your values and priorities as a teacher?

How do your teaching behaviors reflect your values and priorities?

What do you want out of teaching? Which needs does teaching fulfill for you? Which needs can teaching fulfill for you?

3

The Obedient Student

Talk to any nostalgic veteran and you're likely to hear about the good old days when teachers were respected just for being teachers, when kids were obedient and easy to control, and when the threat of a bad grade or a phone call to the home could usually keep the worst of the lot in line.

It's true that teacher-student relationships aren't the same as they were even a generation ago. Today's children have greater mobility and access to more resources and information than ever before. Often, they have more responsibility and independence at earlier ages. While their basic needs are the same as any other group of children in times past, the means for satisfying these needs have changed, and motivators and deterrents that were effective in the past may not work with many of our students.

The autocratic, competitive strategies of factory-era management appear attractive. They are, after all, familiar and well supported by tradition. They seem effective and promise results. And they don't challenge people to question, much less change their behavior. But the outcomes of these strategies are inconsistent with the values and demands of our information-oriented society. Obedience may have been the ultimate discipline goal of the past industrial age; in the information era, obedience can be a liability.

We've heard that a good teacher is one whose students listen and do as they're told—the more obedient the children, the better the reflection on the teacher. And we've been raised to believe that the obedient child is the one best able to assume his or her place as a responsible member of society. While that assumption certainly held true in an industrial society, there is a great deal of evidence that children who are too obedient may have difficulty functioning as independent, responsible individuals in today's world.

And yet, to some, the mere idea of questioning the sanctity of obedience stirs visions of anarchy, or at least permissiveness. *21st Century Discipline*, however, is not remotely in favor of either. Your classroom, like any group or institution, needs the structure of boundaries and limits in order to function. And to function effectively requires cooperation within that structure. So the question is not whether to have structure, but what is the best way to motivate cooperation within that structure?

To answer, let's first look at the difference between obedience and cooperation. On the outside they often look the same. To illustrate, imagine that your supervisor has planned to observe your class later today. You know she's a stickler for time on task so you want to keep your second graders busy, at least while your supervisor is in the room.

Just before she's scheduled to arrive, you divide your class into three groups and take the

The question is not whether to have structure, but what is the best way to motivate cooperation within that structure?

first one aside. "Now listen," you threaten, "If you don't do your work, you can forget about recess for the rest of your lives." These students live for playground time; they get busy.

You take the next group aside and coo, "You know boys and girls, I just love it when you finish your work for me."* You know this group, too. Your love and approval is very important; they get right down to work.

Now, the kids in group three just love television: "If your work is done by 2:00 you can watch the show on jungle animals." They want to see the show so they get right down to work.

Your supervisor comes in and what does she see? Everyone is busy working. The outcome behavior is obvious; the motivation is not.

Your first group complies because the students are more attached to their free time than to not doing the work. This is an example of motivating through fear. This strategy depends on the students' fear of the teacher's anger or power, of the possibility of deprivation (in this case, loss of recess), humiliation or punishment. The message to students: "Please me and I won't hurt you." This approach suggests the students' emotional (and, in some settings, physical) safety is contingent upon their ability to do what someone else wants.

The students in group two want your approval more than they want to avoid doing their work, so they, too, comply. This, too, is an example of motivation through fear, only in this case, it is the fear of abandonment that elicited a response. This strategy relies on the students' fear of the teacher's potential to withdraw approval or affection, to stop caring or even start disliking the child. The message to students: "Please me and I won't stop liking you." Again, the students' emotional safety and worth is at the mercy of their ability to do what someone else wants. (Even secondary teachers who would never in a million years talk to students like the teacher in this example,

Conditional love, in whatever form it is expressed, implies conditional rejection.

There's a big difference between obedience to beliefs and obedience to people.

still have ways of communicating that their feelings for the students depend on how the students are acting. Conditional love, in whatever form it is expressed, implies conditional rejection, and is punitive and fear-producing. The subtlety is deceptive.)

The students in the third group probably did not find the assignments any more compelling than the rest of the class, but they did want to watch that show. The big difference between this example and the other two is that, in this group, there was no stress on the students' relationship with the teacher. Their emotional safety was never at stake. In fact, the only thing at stake was their access to the television. They were not at all distracted by the need to avoid the teacher's wrath or withdrawal because the teacher's reaction was never an issue.

You may be wondering, "What difference does it make—the teacher got what she wanted and so did the kids?" Put yourself in the students' place. Which motivation strategy would you prefer? Which would create less stress in your world? Which approach best enhances the learning environment and is the least likely to compromise the emotional climate of the classroom? And as a teacher with a choice of motivators, which would you prefer that your students respond to?

Many of us grew up hearing obedience touted as a great virtue, and certainly, if we're talking about obedience to a set of values or principles, in most instances, you'll get no argument from me. But there's a big difference between obedience to beliefs and obedience to people—which is what we're talking about in this book.

Lots of teachers get very nervous when facing the prospect of obedience being problematic. A pattern called all-or-nothing thinking (sometimes referred to as dualism or black-and-white thinking) kicks in, bringing with it the assumption that if children aren't

---

*In case it's not obvious, these examples are offered to make a point and are neither recommended nor suggested as motivational strategies.

obedient, they must be disobedient. Not so! Disobedience would hardly create an ideal learning environment and wouldn't be much fun for anyone.

There is another option, however, and that is cooperation. *21st Century Discipline* is characterized by responsible cooperation— behavior choices motivated by something besides the anticipated reaction of another person. Even though the three groups in the example looked the same, and even though the outcome behavior (in this case, doing the assignment) was identical in all three groups, the third group was not being obedient. They were neither responding to nor trying to control another person's reaction or behavior. They were cooperating with the teacher in order to gain access to a more need-fulfilling outcome (the TV show), one that had nothing to do with teacher's power or affection.

Do your goals include wanting your students to be self-motivated, to be able to think and make decisions in their own best interests, to resist peer pressure, and to have enough faith in their safety and security that they are willing to take risks necessary for learning new things? If so, then you probably don't want to use strategies that teach kids to constantly look outside themselves (or over their shoulders) and base their choices on the possible reactions of someone important or more powerful.

There can be great danger in teaching children to simply do what they're told, especially without questioning or evaluating what's being asked of them. Perhaps the most benign consequences of obedience is evident from common complaints from teachers of obedient students: "Sure they do what I tell them, but that's all they do!" These children are so used to doing what they're told that they are likely to wait for instructions and then take them more literally than they were intended.

A kindergarten teacher discovered three bewildered students wandering around the room with their hands full of papers because she had told them to pick up the scraps without explaining what to do with them afterwards. When an entire group of fifth-grade students forgot to use capital letters on a punctuation review, the teacher, they claimed, was to blame: "You didn't remind us." These students were not independent thinkers!

We often use external validation and approval to generate obedience, reinforcing with love and praise those behaviors that we want. As a result, children become conditioned to believe that their worth and safety depend on their ability to please someone else. This tendency may be hard to avoid: Let's face it— as teachers we love to be pleased now and then. But if we give positive feedback to our students only when they do what we want, we are, inadvertently, conditioning them to become people-pleasers, thinking of the needs of others before or instead of their own.

It is possible that in certain situations or groups, these students can lose their ability to think and act in their own best interests, and may endanger or compromise their own safety, health or long-term happiness in favor of peer approval. As long as you're the one doing the ordering and reinforcing, there may be no problem—after all, you have your students' safety and well-being at heart. But obedient children will obey anyone whose love, friendship or approval is important to them, no matter how often caring adults tell them to *just say no*. (Watch your students as peer pressure gains importance in their lives. Imagine saying "no" to invitations to get high, cut school or become sexually active when you believe that you are only loveable or safe when you just say *yes*.)

Obedient children typically have difficulty expressing or maintaining boundaries. They may have difficulty making choices, because they are constantly juggling outside requests and possible reactions with their own preferences and need for approval. By defining themselves from an external frame of reference, their self-image is at the mercy of anyone with whom they interact. These

Responsible cooperation characterizes **21st Century Discipline:** *behavior choices motivated by something besides the anticipated reaction of another person.*

Children can become conditioned to believe that their worth and safety depend on their ability to please others.

factors reinforce dependence, low self-confidence and poor self-esteem, regardless of the praise or approval we offer.

Because children raised with "Do as you're told!" do not have many opportunities to make decisions, they may also have difficulty solving problems and anticipating the probable outcome of the choices they make. Obedient children may have difficulty seeing the connection between what they do and what happens as a result of their behavior. They are likely to shift responsibility for their choices, blaming people or forces outside of themselves for anything—good or bad—that goes on in their lives. (How often do you hear, "It wasn't my fault," "He started it," or "She made me do it"? One high school teacher related a conversation in which a student expelled for arson claimed, "Hey, I just lit the match. I didn't know the building would burn down.")

Finally, obedience is generally a win-lose proposition that depends upon the powerlessness of the person who obeys. The authority relationship that encourages

obedience also reinforces victim behavior, disempowerment and limitations, and may provoke passivity, paralysis, passive-aggressiveness or even rebelliousness under the strain of conflicting demands from different people. Thus obedient children tend to face life with a narrow range of responses to negative situations: continue to suffer or hurt someone else.

Obedience is often a deterrent to responsibility and independence. And while this reality may appear grim (or at least unnerving), take heart. It is possible not only to get the same kind of cooperation that obedience promises but also to build responsible learning and living skills along the way!

As adults working with children, teachers are in an excellent position to help students acquire tools to encourage personal empowerment with regard to boundaries and to inspire a positive self-concept, based not on the opinions of others, but on self-knowledge and confidence.

The Obedient Student*

- Motivated by external factors, such as the need to please authority and experience extrinsic approval (fear of conflict, disapproval or abandonment)

- Follows orders

- May lack confidence in ability to function in absence of authority; lacks initiative; waits for orders or instructions

- Creates safety by keeping others happy (regardless of cost to self)

- Self-esteem is defined externally (worthwhile when getting approval)

- Self-abandoning; focus on needs of others

- "I am my behavior (and somebody else probably made me this way)"

- Interaction tools include being "nice," perfectionism, doing what everyone expects, achievement, recognition, tears, guilt, passive-aggressiveness

- Difficulty seeing connection between behavior and consequence

- Difficulty seeing options or choices available; difficulty making decisions

- Helpless and teacher-dependence common; disempowered; sees self as having few choices

- Operates from external value system (often that of someone important to him or her) which may not be personally relevant and could even be harmful or destructive

- Obeys, may think; complies with requests fairly automatically, often without questioning the appropriateness of the request or considering the long- or short-term effects of compliance

- Lacks confidence in personal instincts and ability to act in own self-interest

- Difficulty predicting outcomes or consequences

The Responsible Student

- Motivated by internal factors, such as the need to weigh choices, experience positive consequences unrelated to others' reactions (getting needs met with a minimum of conflict and inconvenience for others)

- Makes choices

- More confident in ability to function in absence of authority; takes initiative

- Creates safety by identifying and expressing needs; taking care of self

- Self-esteem is defined internally (worthwhile with or without approval, or even with disapproval)

- Self-caring; focus on personal needs, respects needs of others as well

- "I am not my behavior, although I am responsible for how I behave."

- Interaction tools include negotiating, compromise; ability to identify and communicate personal needs; self-expression; ability to make you a deal you can't refuse

- Better able to see the connection between behavior and consequence

- Better able to see options or choices available, able to make decisions

- Personal empowerment and independence common; sees self as having choices and power of choice

- Operates from internal value system (what is best or safest for him or her), considering needs and values of others

- Thinks, may obey; will evaluate requests made by others and consider the effects of compliance before choosing to cooperate

- Confidence in personal instincts and ability to act in own self-interest

- Better able to predict outcomes or consequences

---

*Adapted from *Parents in a Pressure Cooker*, Bluestein, J. & Collins, L. Rosemont, NJ: Programs for Education, Inc., 1988.

- Difficulty understanding or expressing personal needs
- Limited ability to get needs met without hurting self or others
- Limited negotiation skills; orientation is "You win, I lose" (or "I win by giving you what you want"); gives power away
- Compliant
- Commitment to avoid conflict or punishment, "keeping teacher off my back"
- May experience conflict between internal and external needs (what student wants vs. what teacher wants); stress may manifest as guilt or rebelliousness
- May make poor choices to avoid disapproval, ridicule or abandonment ("... so my friends will like me more")

- Better able to understand and express personal needs
- Better able to get own needs met without hurting self or others
- Better-developed negotiation skills; orientation is "You win, I win;" shares power
- Cooperative
- Commitment to task, experiencing personal outcome of cooperation
- Better able to resolve conflict between internal and external needs (what student wants vs. what teacher wants); less inclined toward guilt or rebelliousness
- May make poor choices to satisfy curiosity or from poor judgment or lack of experience

Teacher Behaviors, Beliefs and Attitudes that Encourage Obedience*

- Judgmental, authoritative, critical
- Often inconsistent; likely to have a double standard for adult and student behaviors
- Outcome oriented
- Criteria for requests based on teacher power: "Because I TOLD you!" demands
- Orders, tells; the choices offered to students are rarely more than "Do it or else!"
- May offer choices between "good" and "bad" options, creating pressure on student to make the "right" choice (choose a particular option) to please teacher
- Likely to mistrust student's ability to decide in own best interests; may mistrust student's motivation
- Makes decisions for students: "I know what's best for you."

Teacher Behaviors, Beliefs and Attitudes that Encourage Responsibility

- More positive orientation to student; accepting
- Tries to be consistent; commitment to modeling behaviors requested of students
- Process oriented
- Criteria for requests based on consequences or outcomes: "Put the lid on the paste so it won't dry out."
- Requests, asks; choices are task oriented
- All options offered are equal (no "good" and "bad" choices); no pressure for students to choose particular option to stay in teacher's good graces
- Trusts student's ability to make decisions; likely to understand that student is motivated by own needs

---

*Adapted from *Parents in a Pressure Cooker*, Bluestein, J. & Collins, L. Rosemont, NJ: Programs for Education, Inc., 1988.

- Offers few opportunities for students to practice decision making

- States contingencies negatively (as threats): "If you don't . . ."

- Punishment oriented

- Believes that teacher's needs are more important than student's needs; may disregard student's needs or preferences

- Likely to be threatened by student's independence and initiative; may discourage or prevent both types of behavior; protective; has difficulty allowing students to experience negative consequences of poor decisions or mistakes; more likely to cover for student's poor choosing; inclined toward rescuing, giving warnings or making excuses, not holding student accountable

- Takes responsibility for student's behavior and consequences: If student forgets library book, "I have to remind you every week."

- Avoids making decisions for student; will give student information and encourage decision making based on that information; guides, helps

- Can still feel needed by independent student; encourages independence and initiative (does not need to disempower to feel powerful)

- States contingencies positively (as promises): "If you do . . ."

- Reward oriented

- Teacher's needs are equally important to student's needs; respects student's needs and often attempts to accommodate preferences

- May have difficulty allowing student to experience negative consequences but is willing to hold student accountable and allow him or her to make and learn from mistakes (except in life-threatening situations); resists inclination to rescue, warn or make excuses; can feel powerful and important without solving student's problems or protecting student from unpleasant outcomes of choices

- Leaves responsibility for student's behavior and consequences: Student forgets library book because of poor decision made by student.

Date_____

Activity

Look at the descriptions of the obedient student and the responsible student.
In what ways are the characteristics of the obedient student consistent with the behaviors you would like to encounter or encourage in your own students?

Are there any characteristics that concern you? For what reason?

In what ways are the characteristics of the responsible student consistent with the behaviors you would like to encounter or encourage in your own students?

Are there any characteristics that concern you? For what reason?

From a personal standpoint, to which characteristics do you best relate?

What have been the positive outcomes of these characteristics for you as a student (or child) and as a teacher (or adult)?

In what ways have these characteristics created obstacles in your interactions, particularly as an adult?

Look at the lists of teacher behaviors that encourage obedient or responsible behavior.

As a student, which characteristics did you encounter or observe most frequently in your teachers or other adults in your life?

What was the impact of these behaviors on your own attitudes, behavior, motivation and self-concept as a student (or child) or as a teacher (or adult)?

Which characteristics best describe your own teaching behaviors and attitudes?

Choose any three characteristics you'd like to adopt or improve. What are they?

Why have you chosen those characteristics?

What do you plan to do to make improvements in these areas?

4

The Teacher-Student Relationship

The whole point of 21st century discipline is to create a climate in which the teaching and learning of content can occur with little or no interference from disruptive student behavior.

Up until the moment we face our first class, the bulk of our attention is focused on what and how we're going to teach. Chances are, we've learned the how-to's of explaining fractions, introducing new reading vocabulary or demonstrating condensation. We've learned to prepare transparencies, assemble a unit test, create manipulatives and decorate bulletin boards.

With all this concentration on content, it's easy to become consumed with getting through the books. It's understandable when new teachers get nervous if students aren't in reading groups by the second week of school or if the other third grade teacher gets a few pages ahead in math. In departmentalized and secondary classes, limited contact with large numbers of students adds to the pressure. Curriculum guides loom overwhelmingly, and of course there are always the pressing expectations of principals, parents and the students themselves.

Content-related pressures, real or self-imposed, exist in every teaching situation and with the most ideal students. When your students lack the learning, social or self-management skills necessary for school success, even your best lessons and instructional skills will fall flat. When student behavior interferes with learning or teaching, the pressure to cover content can become unbearable.

The whole point of 21st century discipline is to create a climate in which the teaching and learning of content can occur with little or no interference from disruptive student behavior. This goal translates to a variety of skills and attitudes, but at the heart of this approach is a teacher-student relationship that fosters student commitment and cooperation. All behavior, including learning, occurs in this context. As teachers, we learn to adopt specific language and behaviors to elicit a positive behavior where none exists, to reinforce and maintain cooperation as it occurs and to intervene in disruptive behavior. The types of strategies we employ will have a strong influence—positive or negative—on the nature and quality of the relationship we establish with our students.

Unfortunately, the traditional emphasis on content and control may make it difficult to see what relationships have to do with education. I've often heard teachers complain, "I've got so much to cover this year and my kids are already behind. Who has time for relationships?" (This is especially common among secondary teachers who face 160 students or more every day.) And yet, the teacher-student relationship forms the basis for a classroom climate in which learning—and, indeed, catching up—can occur. The positive climate creates an instructional environment that encourages risk taking, initiative and personal commitment necessary for learning.

The success of our instructional interactions with our students depends, to a large degree, on the relationship and climate we develop. Working to build a positive classroom climate— even if temporarily at the expense of the curriculum—can help us avoid being sabotaged by negative attitudes, weak learning behaviors and unrealistic self-expectations as well.

Finally, because teaching is an interactive experience, a positive teacher-student relationship increases the likelihood that the time students and teachers spend together will be more effective and enjoyable for all concerned.

Date_____

Activity

Describe the characteristics of an ideal teacher-student relationship.

How can these characteristics contribute to a positive classroom climate?

How can these characteristics contribute to the students' growth and learning?

How can they encourage responsible, cooperative student behavior (as opposed to fear-based obedience)?

How will establishing a positive classroom climate help you achieve the goals you identified as important in the survey in Chapter 1?

If you are currently teaching, what are you doing to build a positive classroom climate?

What else can you do to improve or enhance the climate as it currently exists?

If you are not yet teaching, what do you plan to do to build a positive classroom climate?

5

Needs and Interactions

It's late Friday morning, the only time the VCR was free all week. You are setting up a video that introduces material your students will need for a follow-up assignment as well as most of next week's lessons and activities. The video has to go out to another school at the end of the day.

In the meantime, it's the first nice day in nearly three weeks. There's a school festival this weekend and the anticipation has captured the attention and enthusiasm of the entire class. Not surprisingly, you're having a hard time getting the students to settle down for the video.

This story illustrates a frequent occurrence in any group: needs in conflict.* You need to show this video. The content is important and presents resources you otherwise do not have access to. You also need to avoid, if at all possible, having to restructure the majority of next week's well-sequenced plans.

At the same time, your students need some time to play, plan, run and interact.

Both you and the kids think your own needs are important. Although they normally enjoy seeing videos, they can't see why this one

is such a big deal. And even though you might understand their distraction, showing this video is a high priority for you.

You have several ways of reacting to this situation. While your needs may not determine your specific response, your response is certainly related to your needs, particularly in the context of the relationship you've established with this group. Before attempting to resolve this specific problem, let's back up a bit and look at how the process works.

All behavior is motivated by needs. When facing different options, our choice is determined—consciously or not—by the strongest current need and the option that will best fulfill that need. As another example, perhaps later that same day you have a chance to stay after school to finish up your lesson plans for next week. Doing so will satisfy a number of needs: Your weekend will be free for other things, you won't have to drag home all your planning materials and your principal did ask you to turn in your plans by the end of the day. Those needs are important.

But if you leave immediately, you can meet some friends and unwind after a terribly long

*There are at least a few people who believe that I use the term "needs" somewhat loosely. They are those individuals who insist that the only real needs we have are the basic needs like air, food and water, and that anything else is a "want." I suppose that if your goal is simple survival, that's probably true. But most of us are interested in far more than survival–for ourselves and for the children in our lives. In this book, I use the term "needs" to refer to something that is wanted, desired or required. As far as "basic needs" go, I'd like to include my vote for things like dignity, belonging, emotional safety, success and empowerment. I see these as far more than "wants," and believe that meeting these needs is crucial to healthy growth and development.

All behavior is motivated by needs.

When facing different options, our choice is determined by the strongest current need and the option that will best fulfill that need.

week. If these needs are more important to you at the time you make your decision, you will choose to fulfill them instead, regardless of whatever benefits you might experience by staying late and finishing your work. You will take all your stuff home, set aside some planning time during the weekend and promise your principal a copy of your plans first thing Monday morning.

It's one thing to struggle with conflicting personal needs, as in the example above. But what happens when your needs clash with someone else's? Generally needs in conflict are resolved by one of three approaches: power (my needs overshadow yours), permissive (your needs overshadow mine), or cooperative (both sets of needs are considered and, whenever possible, both are accommodated).

Let's go back to the video problem. If your relationship with your student is power-oriented, you may not even be thinking about their needs: You are the teacher; they are there to work. A powering response might sound something like this: "Everybody settle down right now. We are watching this video today. One more word about that festival and you can write about it during recess."

If your approach is permissive, you probably give up your plans, though you're likely to resent the students' lack of appreciation for all your effort in getting that video. You may also become increasingly angry at the difficulties this change will present in your planning and instruction.

However, if you have established a cooperative atmosphere, you will assert your need to show the video, describe the payoff for their patience and cooperation, and offer an early recess or perhaps some time for quiet talk as soon as they have their work finished. You might consider requiring a portion of the follow-up assignment instead of the whole

thing (offering the rest for homework or even holding off until Monday). You set limits by announcing that you'll run the video as long as you have their attention. This approach, although clearly the more positive of the three, will only motivate cooperation if the outcome—in this case, the extra time to interact with one another later—is more meaningful and need-fulfilling than talking now (or avoiding the video.) It is also likely to work best if you've already established an atmosphere of mutual consideration and respect, one in which your students know that although you've got your agenda, you also care about them getting what they want.

We may use different approaches for different situations, in different settings or with different students. Each approach has pluses and minuses, as well as fairly predictable outcomes. Each varies also in its ability to reinforce cooperation over obedience, build responsible learning behaviors and increase commitment and time on task.

Although nearly everyone has used or experienced each approach, each of us tends to favor one predominant model in our interactions with any given individual or group. The approach we choose in our interactions with our students is the product of a number of factors, including our values and attitudes, previous experiences with authority relationships, the behaviors of other teachers in the school and the way we think we should respond. In examining our responses to situations in which our needs are in conflict with others, we may find that we are not actually using the approach we prefer or intended, or even the one we think we are using! For this reason, each approach is worth a second look. The charts on the following pages clarify each of the three different approaches to needs in conflict.

Generally, needs in conflict are resolved by one of three approaches: powering, permissiveness or cooperation.

Cooperation works best in an atmosphere of mutual consideration and respect.

Powering Approach (Win-Lose)*

Interaction dynamic:

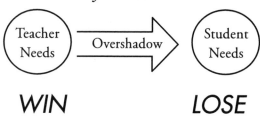

Description:

- Demanding, power-based; authoritarian, inflexible.

- Probably the most familiar model of interaction between adults and children.

  Very often, the teacher may hold a powering attitude and not realize it.

- Payoff to student for cooperating includes avoidance of punishment, criticism, negative involvement with teacher.

- Little or no distinction between student behavior and student worth; equates student's poor choosing with character flaw (bad choice, bad person).

- Does not respect nor accommodate students' needs for power and autonomy.

- Basic belief: "Students won't do anything right unless they are forced to."

- Competitive goal structure (nearly always, some students fail).

- General focus is negative (on what student has done wrong or cannot do); may offer conditional approval (as long as students are doing what teacher wants); pushes for perfection.

- Outcome oriented, usually at expense of process, geared to getting immediate results.

- Teacher makes decisions; student rarely has opportunity to offer input or make decisions (besides "do it or else").

Strategies:

- Threatening emotional safety: humiliating, expressing contempt, condemning or attacking student's behavior, attitude and values; loss of dignity, violation of self-worth; criticizing, shaming; verbal or emotional violence, yelling, intimidating, threatening, sarcasm; controlling, manipulating, punishing; conditional approval or love; threat of emotional abandonment

- Threat to physical safety, physical violence

- Punitive or reactive deprivation of meaningful privilege or activity (for example, recess, eligibility, graduation)

Communicates to students:

- "I'm the boss here! What I says goes!"

- "I know what's best for you."

- "My needs are more important than yours."

- "I do not respect what is important to you."

- "I can get what I want because I am bigger (or more powerful or more important) than you."

Sounds like:

- "Because I said so."

- "Get in your seat this minute."

- "You keep your locker like a pigsty."

- "I told you to get to work."

- "If you don't do what I want, I will punish (hurt, deprive) you."

Boundary Issues:

Does not respect students' boundaries or their need for power or autonomy; violates students' boundaries.

Overall Effectiveness:

Can be effective in getting short-term cooperation from compliant students. Cost to emotional environment and quality of relationship between teacher and student is high.

---

*Originally adapted from *Parents in a Pressure Cooker*, Bluestein, J. & Collins, L. Rosemont, NJ: Programs for Education, Inc., 1988.

Outcomes (Advantages):

- The model is familiar and well-supported by tradition.

- May get you what you want (satisfy your needs)

- Most effective with students who respond to authority, fear of punishment or deprivation, or need for teacher approval.

Outcomes (Disadvantages):

- Reinforces obedience, teacher dependence, need for external validation (dependent on doing what teacher wants).

- May generate superficial compliance, not commitment; passive learning.

- Encourages students to focus on keeping teacher happy or keeping teacher "off my back."

- Seemingly positive results tend to be temporary and not self-sustaining (requires monitoring, policing to continue).

- May generate resentment or rebellion from the student; does not accommodate students' need for personal control.

- Does not teach decision-making or responsible, self-managing behavior.

- Discourages personal empowerment (actually disempowers, inhibits initiative).

- Consequences of students' choices related to teacher reaction rather than to intrinsic benefit to student (other than protecting personal safety)

- Teaches students to use power (bullying, hurting, deprivation) to get what they want in life; does not model compromise, negotiating, cooperation or mutual respect.

- Depends on students' fear of teacher's power, anger or reaction which may be limited or undermined by indifference, overconfidence or competition for power (the need to win or "save face"); can inspire rebelliousness, power struggles.

- Control-oriented relationships with students can be exhausting, stressful, and unfulfilling; frustration and burnout possible.

Permissive Approach (Lose-Win)

Interaction dynamic:

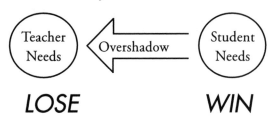

LOSE   WIN

Description:

- Frequently (and incorrectly) seen as the only alternative to powering; may be employed by teachers who do not perceive themselves as having power, who find the powering model distasteful or who are afraid of alienating students by expressing limits and needs.

- Basic belief: "If they care enough, they'll do it (for me)."

- Does not respect nor accommodate student's needs for limits and structure.

- Indirect communications; specific needs of teacher unclear or rarely expressed; lack of clarity or inconsistency may require "mind reading" from student.

- Dishonest and unpredictable; teacher frequently minimizes personal needs, then later expresses criticism or disappointment for student's lack of cooperation.

- Teacher rarely willing to take responsibility for own needs; may offer freedoms with little structure and few limits, expecting student to self-monitor in appreciation.

- Teacher may offer choices to test student's loyalty or ability to guess correct choice.

- Teacher may make decisions and not stand by them; inconsistent in limits, boundaries, tolerances, rewards, consequences and follow-through.

- Little or no distinction between student behavior and student worth (or self-worth); apt to take student behavior (positive or negative) personally; disappointment and hopelessness common.

- Offers conditional approval (as long as student is doing what teacher wants); praise, when offered, is given for pleasing teacher.

Strategies:

- Allowing students to behave in ways that can create problems for the teacher or others

- Letting kids have their way to avoid their outbursts, tantrums, resentment, contempt or other conflicts.

- Letting kids do something they want in order to obligate them to cooperate; attempt to motivate cooperation through guilt or being "nice".

- Manipulating cooperation with conditional approval, disappointment, withdrawal, disengaging; with victim behavior, self-pity, martyrdom or appealing to students' sense of guilt; or with potential for resentment behaviors, such as blaming, condemning, sarcasm, indirect (or implied) attack on student behavior, attitudes and values, "blowing up."

- Resistance to holding kids accountable, enabling, rescuing, giving warnings, asking for excuses, solving problems for the student

- Giving up; perception of having less influence or control than is true

Communicates to Students:

- "Your needs are more important than mine."

- "My needs are important, but so what?"

- "My needs to avoid conflict or your negative reaction are more important than my teaching objectives."

- "External approval is more important than self-care."

- "I'm not very good at this."

Sounds like:

- "I'm so sick of picking up after you kids."

- "Oh, forget it." (or "It just doesn't matter," "It's easier to do it myself.")

- "I like the way Susie is sitting quietly."

- "What's your excuse?"

- "Well, OK. Just this once . . ."

Boundary Issues:

General lack of boundaries, unclear boundaries based on differences between teacher's understanding and students' understanding ("Be good." "Write neatly."), ambiguous boundaries or boundaries with built-in loopholes (using warnings, asking for excuses); teacher tolerates violation of his or her boundaries by students.

Overall Effectiveness:

Minimal; usually kids know that they don't have to listen until the teacher starts screaming, for example. Lack of limits and predictability make cost to the emotional environment and quality of teacher-student relationship high.

Outcomes (Advantages):

- May get the teacher what he or she wants (i.e., satisfy your needs).

- Supports desire to feel self-righteous; validates attachment to victimization, disempowerment and chaos.

- Most effective with students who respond to guilt, fear of abandonment or need for teacher approval.

Outcomes (Disadvantages):

- Least effective means of motivating cooperation from students, although it may get results from students who require teacher approval, respond to guilt or need to please the teacher.

- Reinforces obedience, teacher dependence, need for external validation.

- Generates compliance (if anything), not commitment.

- Often chaotic; lack of structure and consistency can be overwhelming, even for students with best intentions; may cause resentment and insecurity.

- Consequences of students' choices related to teacher reaction rather than to intrinsic benefit to student (other than protecting personal safety)

- Does not teach decision-making or responsibility; can interfere with development of student self-managing behavior; disempowers through lack of structure.

- Encourages kids to push the limits.

- Teaches students to use victim behavior (helplessness, manipulation) to get what they want in life (win by losing); does not model compromise, negotiating, cooperation or mutual respect.

- Apt to take student behavior (positive or negative) personally; disappointment and hopelessness common.

- Failure of this approach frequently reverts to powering approach when teacher reaches personal limit; frustration, unpredictable "blowups" likely; may also lead to quick burnout and desire to leave profession.

Cooperative Approach (Win-Win)

Interaction dynamic:

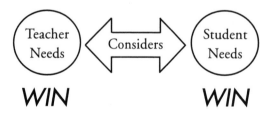

Description:
- Teacher takes responsibility for own needs while considering needs of students.

- Characterized by direct, honest communication; teacher requests specific behavior or input.

- Teacher considers student input in final decision (or gives students specific guidelines or limits for making the decision themselves); respects and attempts to

accommodate student's needs for power within limits.

- Cooperative goal structure; possible for all students to succeed.

- Teacher focuses on positive, building on what students can do; recognizes positive behavior by connecting cooperative choice to benefit to student (positive outcome not related to teacher).

- Payoff for student cooperation: may include access to specific activities, materials, structured free time, or greater range of choices, freedoms, and responsibilities; payoff is not related to reaction of teacher.

- Teacher leaves consequences of choosing (positive and negative) with students; students retain responsibility for personal choices and behavior.

- Non-life-threatening consequences to poor choices allowed as learning experience; teacher resists temptation to rescue but remains available to provide information and help students rethink goals and strategies and try again.

- Greater consistency in teacher behavior and beliefs than in other two models.

- Process oriented; allows students to learn from consequences of choosing.

- Teacher differentiates between student's worth and behavior; teacher is better able to accept student as a person, even if his or her behavior is unacceptable.

- Basic belief: "Even if I can't always accommodate them, the students' needs are as valuable and important as my own."

- Limits exist in the context of the group (not the teacher's power).

Strategies:
- Identifying, communicating and maintaining boundaries; having excellent (consistent and predictable) follow-through; allowing rewards and privileges only when student has done what teacher requests.

- Offering positive outcomes which may include access to meaningful activities, such as going to a center, self-selection, use of certain equipment, games, extra free time, time with adult, working with a friend, drawing, running an errand, choosing where to sit or which assignment to do, a chance to help in another classroom or other privileges important or valuable to the student.

- Offering positive outcomes which may include good grades (motivating for students who find grades meaningful) or progress in a particular subject area (moving on to the next skill, page, chapter).

- Offering positive outcomes which may include other meaningful rewards such as a "good note" home or a night off from homework.

- Willingness to listen, support, guide, inform and accept.

- Using promises instead of threats.

- Making success possible for all.

- Encouraging self-correction.

Communicates to Students:

- "Both our needs are important."

- "How can we both get what we want?"

- "Win-win is possible."

- "You are valuable (and safe), even if you mess up."

- "It's possible to get what you want without hurting anyone (or misbehaving or using unpleasant or annoying behaviors)."

Sounds like:

- "I will continue reading you this story as soon as it gets quiet again."

- "Please work independently so that I can finish with this group."

- "I see you forgot your book. How are you going to do your work this period?"

- "You got your work done early. Now you can go to the enrichment center."

- "You can choose any ten problems on this page."

- "You can have the jump rope back as soon as you both decide how you intend to share it."

Boundary Issues:

None. Boundaries are clearly communicated and upheld. Teacher boundaries are maintained (follow-through) and student boundaries are respected.

Overall Effectiveness:

Best possibility for success of all configurations of authority relationships, especially if your goals include encouraging responsibility, independence, accountability, mutual consideration and respect, and self-management. Actually builds and supports the development of positive classroom relationships and protects emotional safety of all concerned.

Outcomes (Advantages):

- Preventative, proactive; uses clearly-communicated contingencies, boundaries, limits or guidelines before students have a chance to misbehave.

- Reduces conflict and stress, minimizes power struggles, need or occasion for teacher reactivity.

- Discourages resentment and rebelliousness; students recognize that their needs are heard and considered.

- Reinforces responsible, cooperative behavior without depending on teacher's reaction, fear of teacher's power or need for approval; allows teacher to maintain authority without disempowering students.

- Can accommodate student's need for control and structure without interfering with the needs of the teacher or other students.

- Does not compromise or threaten emotional safety.

- Discourages teacher dependence, helplessness, need for external validation.

- Helps students make connection between "what I do" and "what happens to me as a result of what I do" at an internal level.

- Consequences of students' choices related to intrinsic benefit to student (positive outcome not externally based or referenced in someone else's behavior or reaction)

- Builds personal empowerment, enhances student self-concept and reinforces responsibility for personal choices and behavior.

- Generates commitment; students have a stake in choosing cooperatively and in the success of the classroom.

- Encourages students to focus on personal needs within set limits, considering the needs of the teacher and other students.

- Results tend to be long-term and self-sustaining; do not require constant monitoring from teacher, although reinforcement helps.

- Teaches decision making and responsible, self-managing behavior.

- Models compromise, negotiating, cooperation and mutual respect.

- Teaches students that it is possible and desirable to get what you want in life without hurting or depriving anyone else.

Outcomes (Disadvantages):

- Because this method is process-oriented, it may take longer.

- Building student self-management may require teaching students specific learning (non-content) skills and allowing them to practice.

- Less familiar than the other two models; often requires learning new interaction, self-care and self-expression skills; may require restructuring perception of authority relationships.

- May be perceived as permissive by people who favor powering model (or do not know anything else); may not receive support or acceptance from administration or other teachers (until they see the results).

Activity

Relate the activities on the next few pages to actual personal experiences. If your teaching experience is limited, you can complete this exercise by substituting the word "child," "sibling," "co-worker," "employer," "parent," "roommate" or "partner," for example, in place of the word "student." You will find the dynamics to be remarkably similar. If possible, try to keep the same reference group for all three activities.

Think of a time you used the powering approach in an interaction with a student (or group of students).

• Describe the situation:

• Your needs:

• Your students' needs:

• Your reaction (behavior, language):

• Short-term (immediate) outcome:

• Long-term outcome:

• What you learned:

• Alternate reaction (behavior, language):

• How could this alternative accommodate both sets of needs more effectively?

Think of a time you used the permissive approach in an interaction with a student (or group of students).

• Describe the situation:

• Your needs:

• Your students' needs:

- Your reaction (behavior, language):

- Short-term (immediate) outcome:

- Long-term outcome:

- What you learned:

- Alternate reaction (behavior, language):

- How could this alternative accommodate both sets of needs more effectively?

Think of a time you used the cooperative approach in an interaction with a student (or group of students).

- Describe the situation:

- Your needs:

- Your students' needs:

- Your reaction (behavior, language):

- Short-term (immediate) outcome:

- Long-term outcome:

- What you learned:

- Alternate reaction (behavior, language):

- How could this alternative accommodate both sets of needs more effectively?

6

Rules and Boundaries

When I started teaching, I had some reservations about being completely in charge and responsible for the rules, so I tried involving the students in this task. Part of my intention was an honest stab at building a positive, win-win classroom environment, wanting to acknowledge the students' needs for input and control. I also believed, or at least hoped, that their input would magically inspire self-management. I was wrong. This exercise killed the entire morning and produced about 478 "don'ts," nearly a quarter of which had to do with a range of objects the students felt they should not throw in the classroom. I quickly realized that the brunt of enforcement would ultimately rest on my shoulders, and with nearly 500 rules, their list would have certainly kept me hopping, putting me more in the role of policing these children than teaching them.

This was my first inkling that there were some serious problems with rules, at least as we know them best. I found this revelation extremely disconcerting: It was obvious that no class could succeed without some kind of structure and authority, but were rules the best tool for establishing them? Rules certainly were familiar! But there were simply too many places where the methods and dynamics of rule-making and enforcing just didn't fit in with my idea of win-win. What else was there? Was there a way for teachers to truly get what they wanted from their students without creating additional conflicts, resorting to power

or somehow compromising the emotional climate of the classroom?

I started looking for techniques that worked, strategies that were not only effective in classroom and behavior management, but also in creating the kind of climate that would support the goals and values of the 21st century classroom. I had noticed that certain "if . . . then" statements were more positive, more effective and less power-oriented than rules. I discovered that the promise of positive outcomes was less destructive than the threat of negative consequences. And I found that the most successful teachers were those who were able to ask for what they wanted with clarity, assertiveness and great respect for the needs, preferences and dignity of their students. Additionally, research and experience in fields that included business management, child development, counseling and addiction (family systems as well as chemical dependency) gave me a few more critical ingredients to throw in this stew. The result involved reframing rules as boundaries and suddenly the whole process fell into place.

Now I'm hardly the first person to write about boundary setting (although not all definitions include the characteristics I believe to be essential) and quite frankly, the idea is, in many ways, not all that different from more common terms like limits, contingencies or, in some ways, rules. But the interaction patterns involved in this technique are quite different

The most successful teachers were those who were able to ask for what they wanted with clarity, assertiveness, and great respect for their students.

from those used with rules, and they're still pretty uncommon in most educational settings.

During the past two decades, I've had the good fortune of visiting hundreds of educational institutions throughout the world. Among the features common to most of these vastly different environments were the inevitable lists of "Class Rules" (or, sometimes "School Rules"). In some settings the Rules were displayed in every classroom, in others, in just a handful. Some schools had imposing signs to greet students, staff and visitors as they entered the building; others had more covert documents with formidable titles like "School Discipline Code."

Regardless of format or conveyance, these lists were invariably negative. Often the rule itself was stated negatively: "No hitting," "Don't call out," "Eating in class is prohibited." However, even when the rule was stated positively ("Turn in work on time," "Speak respectfully," "Raise your hand to speak"), the result of an infraction was always negative. In some instances, the punishments—often called "consequences"—were listed right along with the rules. Frequently, to my amusement, the list included consequences for the first infraction, the fifth infraction, the thirtieth infraction . . . . OK, so maybe they didn't go up quite that high, but think about it: If you've got plans (and expectations) for second, third, fourth or whatever occasions to catch kids doing something wrong, clearly something is not working. In many cases the consequences of the first several transgressions were so inconsequential that the message to the students was clear: "You can break this rule so-many times before anything serious happens to you. You don't need to change your behavior until right before you really get in trouble!"

There are subtle differences, in process and focus, between encouraging cooperative behavior and discouraging uncooperative behavior. Rules and penalties depend on the students' fear of the negative consequences. If the child is afraid of a bad grade, missing recess or having her name written on the board

(which, incidentally, simply reinforces attention-getting behavior for most kids) then she may do what you want, at a cost to her emotional safety. But how many kids aren't fazed by even the most severe negative consequences? (Indifference is a great tool for creating safety in an otherwise unsafe environment.) Either way, if you're committed to 21st century priorities, and you're relying on rules, you lose.

Boundaries do not rely on fear or power, other than the teacher's power to allow a positive consequence to occur when the students have done their part. This positivity represents an important characteristic of a boundary, as well as a significant difference between boundaries and rules. As a management tool in a win-win setting, boundaries are always stated positively, as promises rather than threats. Likewise, boundaries offer a refreshing change from punishment-oriented strategies to a reward-oriented approach to behavior management. Boundaries allow us to think of consequences as the good things students get (or get to do) as a result of their cooperation, changing the prevailing connotation of the word "consequence" from negative to positive.

In addition to being positive, boundaries support win-win power dynamics because they are themselves win-win. Even the most reasonable rules are oriented to the power needs of the adult, providing information for the students on how not to "lose." Rarely do rules communicate how students can "win" in any other, more positive way. Boundaries, on the other hand, take into consideration the desires and needs of the students they attempt to motivate.

Additionally, boundaries are proactive, attempting to prevent problems in positive ways. Rules typically focus on the negative or punitive reaction of the teacher (or the system) when a student gets caught. Both rules and boundaries can prevent misbehavior, but because with rules the payoff to students for compliance is simply avoiding a negative

Boundaries take into consideration the desires and needs of the students they attempt to motivate.

consequence, the process of enforcement becomes unavoidably reactive. (This is why simply posting a bunch of rules, penalties or punishments before kids misbehave is proactive only in forewarning of impending reactivity!) With a boundary, a positive outcome simply does not happen unless the desired behavior occurs. The absence of the positive outcome—pending the student's cooperation—is, in most cases, the only "teacher reaction" necessary. (Other characteristics of boundaries, such as clarity and follow-through, as well as implementation details, are described in later chapters.)

The subtlety of the differences between boundaries and rules makes it easy to discount the impact each can have on the emotional climate in a classroom and the quality of the relationship between teachers and students. However, teachers who endeavored to shift from the win-lose familiarity of rules to the win-win prospects of boundaries report a significant decrease in conflicts and power struggles in their classes, and far greater success in reaching kids previously deemed difficult, unmotivated or, in some instances, even dangerous, than with any strategy previously attempted.

Characteristics of a Good Boundary*

Clarity

Communicates clearly what students are being asked to do and what they get or get to do as a result of cooperating: "I'll know that you're ready for dismissal when your desks are clear." "You can receive credit for your work as long as it's on my desk by the 3:00 bell." "'Done' means complete and legible."

Win-Win

Accommodates students' need for power within limits teacher defines. Communicates how students can get what they want by doing what the teacher wants: "You can do any ten problems on page 83." "Do the morning activities in any order you choose." "If you need extra credit, you can create a 1-minute demonstration of one of the simple machines described in Chapter 6." "You can sit anywhere you'd like as long as you don't block the fire exits or interfere with anyone else's learning."

Proactivity

Focuses on prevention. Most effective when students' and teacher's needs, specific demands of a particular situation and any possibilities for misunderstandings or mistakes are anticipated: "You will be able to take new books home next week as long as you return the ones you borrow today." "You're welcome to join this after-school activity group as long as you'll be able to stay late on Wednesdays and take the special training this Saturday morning."

Positivity

Reward-oriented, offering access to a positive consequence under certain conditions or after students fulfill certain requirements or responsibilities. Stated positively, as a promise emphasizing positive outcomes: "I'll read the story as long as there's no talking." "You can work on the puzzles after you finish your workbook pages." "If we finish early, we'll have time for an extra 15 minutes of recess."

Follow-through

Essential for boundary setting to be effective, this characteristic requires a willingness to insist on students doing what we've asked, within the constraints or requirements previously described, before allowing access to positive consequences (or before allowing access to continue). See Chapter 17 for more information.

Simply posting a bunch of rules, penalties and punishments is proactive only in forewarning of impending reactivity!

*Adapted from *The Parent's Little Book of Lists: Do's and Don'ts of Effective Parenting* by Jane Bluestein, Ph.D. Deerfield Beach, FL: Health Communications, Inc., 1997.

How Boundaries Work*

- Boundaries allow teachers to express limits and to communicate the conditions or availability of certain privileges students desire.

- Boundaries prevent conflict and build win-win power structures. They help teachers take care of themselves while attempting to accommodate their students' needs or desires as well.

- Boundaries build a reward-oriented classroom environment. They emphasize positive consequences—desirable outcomes available with cooperation.

- Boundaries create less stress and fewer power struggles than rules and demands (which are typically win-lose and often focus on punishments or negative outcomes for noncompliance).

- Boundaries build mutual consideration and respect, and do not threaten or violate students' emotional safety.

- Boundaries do not rely on the fear of teachers' reactions (such as anger or disapproval) to help teachers get what they want.

- Boundaries allow positive and negative consequences to occur in a nonpunitive environment (negative consequences simply being the absence of positive consequences). As long as teachers only allow positive consequences to occur when students have done their part, boundaries build student responsibility and accountability.

- Boundaries invite students to change their behavior in order to get their needs met. While rules or threats emphasize the penalties for misbehavior, boundaries focus on the ability to make more constructive choices.

*Adapted from *The Parent's Little Book of Lists: Do's and Don'ts of Effective Parenting* by Jane Bluestein, Ph.D. Deerfield Beach, FL: Health Communications, Inc., 1997.

Activity

Date_____

Listed below and on the following page are several scenarios. For each, think through what you want the students to be doing and what your needs are; specify these as your objective. Then identify what the student wants (or wants to avoid) in each situation. Finally, develop a powering response, a permissive response and a win-win, or cooperative, response (a boundary). To construct a boundary, consider the positive outcomes available or possible in your classroom. Write the responses as quotations.

Jasmine's work area is a mess. You nearly tripped over the pile of papers when you walked past her chair.

• Objective (what you want, your needs):

• Student needs:

• Powering response:

• Permissive response:

• Cooperative response (Boundary):

Lamont and David want to sit together during independent work time.

• Objective:

• Student needs:

• Powering response:

• Permissive response:

• Cooperative response (Boundary):

You've assigned three worksheets but your students would prefer to work on the word search puzzle they got in another class earlier today.

- Objective:

- Student needs:

- Powering response:

- Permissive response:

- Cooperative response (Boundary):

Adrian spent the entire library period absorbed in a new adventure book. At the end of class, she pleads with you to allow her to check out the book so she can finish it at home. Adrian has not returned the books she borrowed four weeks ago.

- Objective:

- Student needs:

- Powering response:

- Permissive response:

- Cooperative response (Boundary):

7

The "Win-Win" Classroom

In previous chapters, we saw that attempts to control students have two main drawbacks. First of all, whether we try to control directly, through powering, or indirectly, through manipulation, we run full tilt into a fact of human nature: people generally do not like to be controlled. We resist other people's attempts to tell us how to act, what to wear, and so on. (What's your first reaction when you see a "Wet Paint! Do not Touch!" sign? Even the most responsible, self-managing adults report sometimes being tempted to "touch," either out of curiosity or defiance.)

Further, we can see how attempting to control students not only eats up a lot of our time and energy, but also deprives them of opportunities to develop responsibility, decision-making capabilities, self-confidence, self-esteem and important self-management characteristics and skills.

We all need to feel a sense of control in our lives, whether or not our classrooms are set up to accommodate this reality. In developmentally-normal human beings, this desire for autonomy typically emerges around the age of 18 to 24 months. (This is where two-year-olds got the reputation for being "terrible"!) At the same time, each of us needs a certain degree of structure in order to exercise control in a constructive manner. Helping students develop responsibility and self-management skills requires that we offer

students a little of both. Powering hampers the students' sense of control; permissiveness denies them adequate structure.

Students who cannot satisfy their need for power in positive, healthy ways will undoubtedly create ways to have this need met. Young children may throw tantrums or simply counter requests or demands with the word "no!" As they get older, they may rebel, shut down, fight back, refuse to listen, swear, threaten, or act sarcastic, rude or contemptuous. They may become aggressive or abusive, act bossy, controlling, mean or hurtful, especially with younger or smaller children. They may physically hurt others or themselves, break things or destroy property. They may drop out, get high, become sexually active or make other dangerous or destructive choices simply to prove that they aren't controlled by some adult.

Strangely, even abdicating personal responsibility can be a way of creating a sense of control. For example, students who seem to act helpless, procrastinate, deliberately underperform, quit before they finish or "forget" something they had agreed to do, are often successful at gaining attention or minimizing expectations or demands adults place on them. Students who seem to enjoy or require being controlled may do so to limit the amount of responsibility they will have to take for their behaviors. (If someone else is calling

Attempting to control students not only eats up a lot of our time and energy, but also deprives them of opportunities to develop important self-management characteristics and skills.

all the shots and can be blamed for everything, a student has to assume very little responsibility.) There's an odd sense of power in the suffering and self-righteousness of individuals who believe that the things that don't work out for them aren't their fault—after all, they didn't have a choice in the matter. In some cases, allowing others to control them allows some children the illusion of controlling the way the controller treats them: "If I do what they want they won't make fun of me or stop being my friends."

These are all things that we, as teachers committed to building a win-win classroom environment, would surely like to avoid. Clearly, the issue is not whether to empower students, but how! Fortunately, it is not only possible to allow kids in our classrooms to experience control in their lives without having them interfere with the safety and welfare of anyone else, it is also possible to accommodate students' need for structure without preventing them from learning to think.

A win-win classroom is characterized by clear and specific limits with opportunities to make choices and experience power within those limits.

A win-win classroom is characterized by clear and specific limits with opportunities to make choices and experience power within those limits. Everyone is offered a stake in the success of the classroom and everyone has a chance to succeed. Each student is encouraged to be responsible for his own behavior and consequences are tied to the choices each individual makes.

In a win-win classroom, the teacher is on the same side as the students and the students know it.

In a win-win classroom, the teacher is on the same side as the students and the students know it. Everyone's needs and feelings are valued and, although it may frequently be impossible for everyone to win, there is usually room for flexibility, negotiation and compromise. No one needs to win at the expense of anyone else. As the cooperative climate develops, resistance and rebellion become increasingly pointless. Attention shifts from teacher-control to student self-control, and from discipline to instruction.

The notion of win-win classroom management can be a bit disconcerting at first,

especially to power-oriented teachers. Considering the tradition of an autocratic teaching role, the expectations of administrators, pressures from parents, needs of students, and demands of curriculum and content, how does this model fit?

As long as teachers are held accountable for what goes on in their classrooms, authority relationships will exist between teachers and students. Both win-win and win-lose approaches demand an element of power (authority) on the part of the teacher, because the teacher is the adult. Teachers have the power to set goals, limits and contingencies, and, when necessary, have the final word on what works in the best interests of the group. But in the win-win classroom, the power of the teacher does not connote the force that characterized the win-lose authority relationships of previous eras. The goal of teacher power in a win-win setting is not to assert ourselves as controlling, punitive, severe or authoritarian, nor is it to disempower our students. Instead, power in win-win relationships translates to an ability to empower students within rules and limits that likewise accommodate the needs of the teacher: "We function within a certain set of boundaries, not because I'm bigger or more powerful, not because I'll like you more, but because we all benefit when these boundaries are respected."

The win-lose models familiar to most of us simply cannot strike that balance. We need an entirely new way of working with students to achieve that middle ground between powering and permissiveness. Yet, even with a firm commitment to win-win interactions and power dynamics, it is annoyingly easy to revert back to the other models without even thinking. As with any change, we need a new set of behaviors, the willingness to make a conscious effort, and the patience and faith to practice what we want to set in motion.

The rest of this book looks at the specific behaviors necessary for positively restructuring authority relationships that encourage student self-control and reduce the need for teacher involvement in classroom management and discipline. The next section addresses specific teacher behaviors that will help our students to function successfully—behaviorally and academically—in our classrooms. This success orientation is crucial to the effectiveness of the win-win alternative.

We need an entirely new way of working with students to achieve that middle ground between powering and permissiveness.

Section Two

Success Orientation

8

Expectations and Routines

Most of us enter the teaching profession with all sorts of expectations—conscious and unconscious. Depending on what we believe our students can (or should) do, what we hear from other teachers and our sense of our own capabilities, we construct a mental picture of a classroom that may or may not reflect the reality we encounter.

We have probably heard that teachers who have high expectations end up with students who perform better than teachers with low expectations. Even with evidence to support this assumption, I strongly doubt that it is the expectations themselves that generate high performance. I suspect that teachers with high-performing students have more going for them than high expectations. Instead, I believe that the students' performance is more a function of the teacher's beliefs, behaviors and *self-*expectations. True, we won't get much out of kids we don't ultimately believe in, but believing that students can learn, achieve or cooperate is quite different from *expecting* them to do so.

By way of introducing myself to my first group of students, 39 low-achieving fifth-graders, I presented them with a long list of my expectations: "I expect you to take care of materials." "I expect you to behave respectfully." "I expect you to put your names on your papers." "I expect you to love learning." Imagine my consternation when the students countered my pronouncements with bored looks, eyes rolled to the ceiling and an

Simply expecting does not secure agreement or generate commitment to learning or cooperation.

exasperated chorus, after a few seconds' silence: "So?" This is where I first discovered that all too often, "high expectations" is a metaphor for wishful thinking. Clearly, the only person committed to my expectations was me!

One of the problems with having expectations is the lack of commitment from the person or people on whom we project our expectations. Simply expecting does not secure agreement or generate commitment to learning or cooperation, certainly not as effectively as win-win power dynamics, interactions and relationships or opportunities to experience fun, success, belonging, discovery or power, for example. If anything, expectations generate a commitment to self-protection, with compliance the result of impending anger, punishment or disapproval. ("I expect this . . ." carries an implicit threat of some negative reaction "if you don't comply.")

Second, expectations presume much. A few weeks into that first year, I presented my students with what I believed to be a perfect lesson. I had designed a well-orchestrated environment with elaborate plans, plenty of materials to go around, color-coded direction cards, and enough stimulating activities to keep them all busy until Easter. These kids were in fifth grade, some of them for the third time; certainly they would be able to navigate the work centers under my watchful, nurturing, facilitating care. Right?

Wrong.

For starters, no one at the mural center could agree on a theme. The kids in the media corner were screaming and fighting over who would operate the tape recorder. And all the markers for the art activity mysteriously vanished within the first ten seconds of class. Evidently no one had ever worked with a ruler or used an encyclopedia before. Although I had explained everything inside and out, I had a steady stream of kids tugging on my sleeve asking me what they were supposed to do. I stood in amazement, watching weeks of planning and work go straight down the tubes. In the midst of the chaos, all I could think was: "But I laminated everything!"

I received two shocks that day. I had expected my creativity to carry far more weight than it actually did; instead, it was unappreciated and overwhelming. Second, I had expected the students, who seemed so mature and streetwise, to have already acquired certain responsible learning behaviors that would enable them to complete the assigned tasks. Yet they were unable to work independently in small groups, care for materials or make decisions about their learning. It seemed as though my expectations were actually creating problems. Now what?

During this time, my students were visiting Mr. Grey for art twice a week. When they came back from his class, I would ask them what they had done. Each report detailed monotonous exercises, such as getting the scissors out of a box, putting the lid back on the box, putting the box back in the cabinet, sitting down with the scissors, then putting the scissors back again, and so on. For the first few days of school, the kids did nothing besides practice getting, holding, passing, using, and returning the things they'd need for art class. Period.

I asked Mr. Grey what he was up to. "Don't you have a curriculum to get through this year?"

"I sure do, and it's massive. But if we don't do this first, we'll never get through any of it."

"You mean to tell me that these kids don't know how to get paint jars out of a storage closet?"

"Some do, sure. But most don't. Or at least they don't think about it on their own. This way, there are no questions later about where things go or how I expect them to be used."

There was that word again. "Don't you expect them to know this stuff?"

"It doesn't matter. I can expect all day long and never get what I want. Expecting kids to clean calligraphy pens and put them back in the boxes doesn't teach them how to do it. I still have to show them."

It was true. Few teachers placed higher demands on the kids than Mr. Grey. But it was neither the demands nor Mr. Grey's expectations that turned his classroom into an exciting and productive place. While he may have started with a mental picture of busy, capable, independent and responsible students—and a great deal of faith in their ability to rise to the challenges he'd present to them—he did not leave their behavior to chance. Nor did he forge ahead on a set of assumptions about what these kids should know. If Mr. Grey expected success from his students, he certainly gave them the training necessary to fulfill his objectives.

It is disappointing to discover that entering an inspiring classroom environment does not trigger some magic hormone that enables children to properly use a pencil sharpener, recap the paste, alphabetize resource books or move around the room nondisruptively. Simply expecting certain behaviors does not guarantee they will occur, even if the lessons are well-planned and your mood is positive and enthusiastic. (Besides, if students cooperate only because we expect their cooperation, we're back to eliciting obedient, teacher-pleasing behavior). Without information, instruction and guided practice, we actually doom our students—and ourselves—to failure. Clearly, there is more to generating cooperation than simply expecting or modeling it.

I had expected my creativity to carry far more weight than it actually did.

Expecting kids to clean calligraphy pens and put them back in the boxes doesn't teach them how to do it.

Certainly the expectations we have for ourselves are appropriate, if not essential, for successfully reaching our goals.

There are hidden assumptions and expectations in every lesson we plan. Take nothing for granted.

Don't be afraid to back up when necessary.

Does this mean that expectations are bad? No, not exactly. But let's not overlook their limitations nor assign them more weight than they deserve. Certainly the expectations we have for ourselves are appropriate, if not essential, for successfully reaching our goals. Self-expectations are also easier to control, as the expectation, commitment and action all come from the same place! We run into problems when we have expectations for others, particularly, as is so often the case, when we have not secured agreement or commitment from people who do not share our agendas. Still, we can take these expectations and use them as a means of identifying what we would like from others. In this sense, expectations are simply starting points, great places from which to anticipate what we want to accomplish and what we'll need (or need to do) to achieve our goals.

To make the best use of your expectations, get a clear picture of what you want. What are your objectives? How will your students behave if this lesson or activity goes as planned? Think about any special details or conditions that will be important to you. For example, do you require a certain heading on the papers they turn in? Do you want them to push in their chairs before they leave the room? Will it drive you crazy if someone starts to sharpen a pencil while you're addressing the group? Where do you want the materials put when the students are finished with them?

Numerous problems and conflicts can be avoided by simply expressing what you want, especially if you mention it before the kids have a chance to do it wrong. Make your boundaries and limits clear. Let your kids know what you want and how it will benefit them to head their papers a certain way (they'll get credit for their work, for example), put materials away properly or push their chairs under their desks (they'll be dismissed for lunch when these things are done).

Once you have a clear sense of your objectives and needs, turn your attention to your students. Which behaviors and skills will they need to complete a particular task or function independently and responsibly in your class? There are hidden assumptions and expectations in every lesson we plan. Take nothing for granted. Do they need to know how to handle science equipment? Use a dictionary? Work with a partner? Move to various parts of the room? Follow written directions? Staple papers together? Put their assignments in a particular place? Even if you firmly believe they should know how to do these things, it's likely that at least a few will not.

Identify your students' levels of ability and responsibility. Watch them work—or not work. What happens when you ask them to do something? Can they solve problems on their own or ask a classmate for assistance without disrupting others when you need a few uninterrupted minutes at your desk? Are they bewildered by choices or directions? What do your shelves look like at the end of the day?

Certain routines and procedures may be so basic or obvious that they're easy to overlook, especially for teachers new to the profession or those working with a grade level they haven't had much experience with yet. Don't be afraid to back up when necessary, or leave time for some extra instruction to make it easier for everyone to succeed. Assume nothing other than the fact that your students may not be sure what you want. In fact, it may be most effective to assume the worst—which is not the same as expecting the worst—and start from there. Sure, they probably know how to take care of the books in the classroom library, but they may not know how *you* want them to do it.

Obviously you cannot predict every single need that will arise, but the better you can account for the skills and behaviors your activities demand, the better you can plan for success. Also, the more clear and specific you are in identifying these needs ahead of time, the less likely you are to be undermined by students' confusion, frustration or ineptness.

Finally, set aside some time to fill the gap between what you need and what they can do. Start where they are and build success on success. I once had a group of high-risk eighth graders spend a few minutes practicing putting the caps on felt-tipped markers they enjoyed using but routinely forgot to recap. I could not afford to keep replacing the markers when they dried out, so I did a half-humorous lesson on recapping the pens, making sure that we listened for the click that indicated they were on tight (a trick entirely unfamiliar to most of my students). From that point on, the markers seemed to last forever, and the students became remarkably committed to their care. (This was also, in part, due to my refusal to remind students or replace—or even discuss—markers from that point on.)

Don't hesitate to have your kids walk through daily routines. For example, before you start teaching reading groups, take a few minutes here and there to have the children practice moving from their work areas to their reading groups. Have one small group at a time learn to play a particular game or operate a piece of equipment before they need to use it in a center, a small group activity or on their own. (You often only need to train a handful of kids yourself. Students can learn quickly when given the opportunity to train their classmates once they've mastered the necessary skills.)

Unless you intend to spend your entire year guarding, dispensing and retrieving classroom materials, teach your students how to get, use and return things when they are finished. Put various kids in charge to help

you monitor the care of materials. I once decided the best person to keep track of the cards in our individualized handwriting program was the one third grader who seemed to lose track of them most often. She took her job quite seriously: Not only did she never lose a card after that, but she once kept the entire class from going to lunch until the "Capital R" card turned up!

If you are working with younger children or students who always seem to need your help and attention, have the entire group practice working independently. Assign some seatwork and put yourself off limits while you work at your desk. Make sure the kids have enough to keep them busy, preferably something they can do easily, such as review work, practice drills or a puzzle. Remember, the emphasis here is on building independence—not academic competence. Encourage students to help one another or go on to a different task until you are available to help.

You may need to start with a one- or two-minute interval if necessary and refuse all contact during that time. Gradually increase the amount of time and the complexity of the tasks. As their skills improve, you will become increasingly comfortable working with small groups and assigning tasks that require independent work habits.

Instruction, guidelines and practice make student responsibility and self-management a reality. Combined with meaningful, positive consequences for cooperation and opportunities to succeed, this type of preparation encourages the positive behaviors that our objectives and instructions can inspire.

Unless you intend to spend your entire year guarding classroom materials, teach your students how to get, use, and return things when they are finished.

Activity

Date_____

It's easy to get tripped up by assumptions and expectations. Look at the lessons you've planned for the next day or two and then answer the following questions for each.

Which skills or behaviors will your students need in order to successfully complete the activities you have planned (for example, use a ruler to measure, retrieve materials from a particular place, construct an outline, choose a sequence, work with the computer, clean up after a messy experiment or art activity, and so on)?

Which skills or behaviors have you observed your students successfully performing?

Which of these skills or behaviors have you presented or demonstrated?

Which have your students practiced?

In what way have you addressed the need for these skills or behaviors in your planning?

Activity

Date_____

There are certain behaviors that bother each of us: people who play with their loose change, rock back on their chairs, interrupt others or walk around with their shoelaces untied. What are yours?

Go back and mark (check, circle, highlight) the items in your list that you run into in your classroom. What have you done to try to prevent these things from happening (as opposed to simply punishing them when they happen)? What else might you do?

9

Consistency and Modeling

Well-meaning experts often caution new teachers to be consistent without ever talking about what that term means. Consistency is a very important component of the structure we provide; its absence will provoke student insecurity at best, distrust and chaos at worst. It permeates all levels of teacher behavior, personal and interactive, and involves language, values, expectations, feelings and needs.

Consistency is a very important component of the structure we provide.

Perhaps at the simplest level, we need consistency from one day to the next in our limits and tolerances. For example, if our students are accustomed to working, without censure, at a certain noise level during a particular work time every day, it's not fair to yell at them when the same noise level gets on our nerves. True, our limits vary from time to time: a run-in with a neighbor, congested traffic on the way to work, or finding out the rent check bounced can limit our ability to deal with things that wouldn't ordinarily bother us. We can prevent unnecessary resentment, surprises or conflicts by simply warning the kids ahead of time that at least for today, the rules have changed.

Different situations will also test our consistency. Obviously, we allow different behaviors on a playground than in a library, and special events like field trips or guest speakers may require different restrictions than normal classroom activities. But if we suddenly lash out at previously-accepted behavior just because the principal is in the room, you can be sure that we've also strained the emotional climate in the classroom, violated trust and compromised safety! When different activities, situations or circumstances require a departure from the normal structure, it's only fair that we adequately prepare our students by letting them know beforehand the new limits that apply.

What about consistency between our behavior and the other teachers in the school—particularly other teachers who work with our kids? We can count on our students to lean on us about any inconsistencies that don't work in their behalf: "But Mr. Peterson never gives homework!" The rules and privileges extended by different teachers reflect differences in personalities, tolerances and personal needs. These differences are not inconsistencies. We do not control other people's behaviors. Trying to model their behavior, adopt their limits or imitate their teaching style for the sake of consistency is silly and self-defeating. If we don't need absolute silence in our room, why demand it just because the other Social Studies teachers do? If our kids get their seatwork done while listening to music, if they prefer to work with a partner, or if their chewing gum doesn't get on our nerves (or anywhere else), applying someone else's standards will only work to meet that person's needs—not our own. Additionally, we're more likely to be careless about following through on values, rules or limits that are imposed on us unless those conditions have meaning and importance in our lives.

Setting standards and limits that apply to our personal needs may require our students to shift gears when they go from one class to another. It's likely that our boundaries will demand a slightly different set of behaviors than some other teacher's. Not all teachers are similarly distracted or provoked by noise, movement, gum chewing, lateness, slouching or a student's preference for working on the floor, sitting with a friend or writing with green ink—nor do they need to be! Even very young children are far more flexible than we often give them credit for. (I once saw a two-and-a-half year old, who rarely went a minute without his pacifier at home, unquestioningly spit it out to leave it in the car when he arrived at his nonpacifier preschool.) Besides, our students will certainly encounter a variety of people throughout their school careers (and lives); let's help them to develop the flexibility they'll need to relate to—and succeed with—these different personalities.

Another dimension of consistency involves role modeling. How similar is our behavior to the standards we hold for our students? When we look at the behaviors listed in the survey on pages 15-16 and compare our own performance in each, how do we measure up? What about other behaviors? Are we on time as frequently as we would like our students to be? When we mess up, do we take responsibility for our mistakes, catching ourselves before we make excuses or cast blame? Do our desk, hand-writing and appearance reflect the degree of order, readability and neatness we want our students to demonstrate? If we forbid eating or drinking in the classroom, are we willing to leave our coffee cups or water bottles in the teachers' lounge? These examples make some teachers very uncomfortable, but they're well worth a second look. Our behavior sends powerful messages to the students in our lives, teaching them a great deal about what is appropriate or acceptable in various situations. (One of the most effective motivators for me to

finally quit smoking cigarettes was the sobering discovery that several of my middle-school students had proudly switched to my brand.) It's hard for kids to take us seriously, or respond with the trust and respect we desire, when we aren't willing to "walk the talk," or when we exhibit behaviors we would not encourage or tolerate from them.

In terms of relationship building, consistency in our modeling is also critical with regard to the we way talk to our students. For example, would we accept from our students the same language and tone we use when we talk to them—even when we're angry? How would we feel if someone we cared about talked to us the way we talk to our students? (If we hear ourselves speaking in a way that we would respond to with anger, resentment, shame, fear or embarrassment, it's a safe bet that our students are hearing the same things.) Would we talk to adults the way we talk to our students? Kids can see through a double standard. However a commitment to establish and maintain congruence between what's acceptable for us and what's acceptable for them builds success and win-win.

What about the consistency between what we say and what we do? One first-year teacher asked me to observe how consistently she recognized only those students who had raised their hands. She started by announcing, "We need to take turns in this discussion. From this point on, I'll call on you only if you raise your hand first."

One student reacted, of course without raising his hand: "Really."

"Yes, I mean it," she answered, undermining her own admonition.

Is the comment "I'll only say this once" an introduction to something we repeat all afternoon? Do we spend a lot of time warning, reminding and nagging? Do we interact with students who are at our side seconds after asking them to stay in their seats? These inconsistencies erode our credibility with our students. (I knew I was in trouble once when a student responded to my frustration by

Our behavior sends powerful messages to the students in our lives, teaching them a great deal about what is appropriate or acceptable in various situations.

A commitment to establish and maintain congruence between what's acceptable for us and what's acceptable for them builds success and win-win.

Matching our behaviors to our feelings can be challenging, particularly in high-stress situations.

We need to watch for consistency between what we want and what we say.

Consistency requires consciousness and deliberateness, a willingness to notice and be mindful of the language, behaviors and attitudes we bring to our relationships.

indignantly claiming, "You only told me once!") Breaking out of these self-defeating traps requires awareness and practice. Outside observation and feedback, or personally keeping count of instances in which you do behave consistently, can be helpful. (Consistency in following through will be discussed in greater detail in Chapter 17.)

Other areas of consistency are somewhat tricky and more subtle. They involve the relationships between our feelings, values and language and are crucial to the quality of classroom climate and our relationships with students.

First, let's look at the consistency between our feelings and words. Matching our behaviors to our feelings can be challenging, particularly in high-stress situations. For example, have you ever had a child rock a little too far back in her seat and then come crashing down on the floor? What did you feel at that moment? You were probably startled by the noise and frightened for the child's safety. How did you react? If you're good at this, you might have asked if the child was all right and then said, "Wow! That really startled me! I was afraid you might have been hurt!"

But is that how most of us react? Our fear and frustration may come out instead: "You're so clumsy! You can't even sit in a chair right!"

The danger in this type of inconsistency is that the child tends to hear only the emotion in the words and can misinterpret our reaction. It's highly unlikely that this student will be thinking, "Gee, my teacher must really have been startled. She's only yelling at me because she's having difficulty dealing with her fear for my safety." What she hears is simply another vote for her clumsiness and inadequacy.

Recognizing and modifying inconsistencies between our feelings and language can be a real challenge. Doing so demands that we wait a few seconds to respond—not react—to emotional or high-stress situations; that we think about what we're really feeling before the words come out of our mouths; that we learn to take responsibility

for our anger, fear and frustration without personally attacking the child.

We also need to keep an eye out for consistency between what we want and what we say. For example, asking students to "please pick up the blocks so that no one trips over them" conveys quite clearly that we want the student to clear the floor. Asking them to "please pick up the blocks for me" may get the same results, but for an entirely different reason (teacher-pleasing). If seeing the blocks all over the rug really upsets us, or if we believe our students will only respond if we're highly reactive, we might respond with an attack: "You are so thoughtless and inconsiderate! Get over here and pick up these blocks this instant!" If all we care about is getting those blocks off the floor, then it probably doesn't matter which approach we use. But if we not only want to have the blocks put away but also want to reinforce self-management and preserve emotional safety, then we certainly want to try to avoid the last two examples. Only the first example expresses congruence between our intent to operate within the parameters and dynamics of the 21st century classroom and the behavior and language we select.

Many of the problems in consistency, such as those mentioned above, may be the natural result of a larger, deeper gap between information-age values (such as independence, initiative, decision-making and self-management) and industrial-age behaviors (ordering, punishing, disempowering and offering few options). Bridging this gap begins with an awareness of and commitment to win-win objectives. From that point on, we have a standard against which we can check the behaviors and language we're tempted to choose. For example, we can examine our own behaviors and ask if the particular feedback and structure we have provided reinforces independence, encourages self-management, and promotes empowerment and self-esteem.

The words and actions we choose will either help us achieve what we say we want or create obstacles for reaching our goals.

Consistency requires of each of us, as adults working with children, a certain degree of consciousness and deliberateness, a willingness to notice and be mindful of the language, behaviors and attitudes we bring to our relationships. Over time it gets easier, and each attempt brings us closer to the positive, cooperative climate of a 21st century classroom.

Activity

Date_____

In the space below, list five or more behaviors you want your students to demonstrate.

In the list above, evaluate your own consistency on the same behaviors. Rate yourself on a scale of 1 (rarely) to 5 (almost always). For example, if you've listed "be on time" or "come prepared," how frequently are you on time and prepared?

Date_____

Describe an instance in which you were challenged to maintain consistency between what you expect of your students and your own behavior.

How was that situation resolved?

What are you doing to maintain consistency at this level?

Date_____

Describe an instance in which you were challenged to maintain consistency from one day to the next.

How was that situation resolved?

What are you doing to maintain consistency at this level?

Date_____

Describe an instance in which you were challenged to maintain consistency between your feelings and your language (words, tone, facial expression).

How was that situation resolved?

What are you doing to maintain consistency at this level?

Activity   Date_____

Describe an instance in which you were challenged to maintain consistency between your language (requests, directions, feedback) and 21st century objectives (such as student responsibility, initiative, internal motivation or self-management).

How was that situation resolved?

What are you doing to maintain consistency at this level?

Activity   Date_____

If your students seem to have a hard time with differences in the needs, limits, or tolerances from one teacher to the next, you might want to involve them in various discussions about individual differences and similarities, not only about their teachers, but also, perhaps, about their siblings and friends. Some possible discussion starters might include:

Tell me something you really like about each one of your teachers.

What are you allowed to do at home that you can't do in school?

In what ways are your friends alike?

How are they different?

What else can you do to help students understand differences in standards, values and freedoms from one teacher or situation to the next?

10

Focus and Feedback

A large number of our interactions with our students involve giving them feedback and information on their performance in our classroom. The type and quality of feedback we offer reflects the focus of our perceptions. Choosing a success-oriented focus can have an exceptionally positive impact on these interactions.

We have a tremendous amount of control over the way we look at any given person, event, item or experience. For example, as you're reading this, you're probably sitting or lying on some piece of furniture. Notice as much as you can about whatever piece of furniture you've selected—what it looks like, how it feels, where it is in the room. See if you can find five things wrong with it.

Let's assume your body is being supported by a chair. Maybe it's too hard. An ugly, dull color. Too heavy. Too far from the window. In a draft. (If you're in a really miserable mood, you can probably go on for an hour).

OK. Now that we know what's wrong with the chair, let's try something else. It may help if you leave the room momentarily and then return. At the very least, shut your eyes for a few seconds and take a deep breath before you try this next part.

Now, look at this wonderful chair! See if you can tell at least five great things about it: It gives fantastic support. It's a wonderfully neutral color. It's sturdy. In a cozy corner. In a well-ventilated space. And so on.

Did the chair change? Probably not, not in the few seconds between paragraphs. The only thing that changed is the way you looked at the chair and what you focused on. (You may have even noticed a slight change in your breathing, your comfort and even your mood.) Consider how powerful a positive perspective can be! The same goes for the way we regard our students. In any given incident, inter-action or assignment, we can find something wrong. But as in the example with the chair, any time we can find something to criticize, we can likewise find something to recognize in a positive way.

To illustrate, a teacher received a paper from one of her second-grade students. The drawing on the paper was little more than an angry black scribble. Instead of a story, there was a sentence fragment without a capital, no punctuation and not one correctly-spelled word. Attempts to erase stray pencil marks had left several holes and the paper had been crumpled at least once in frustration.

The teacher had acknowledged each of the other students' papers with stickers and some positive comment about the work. But this paper was something else! Naturally, the teacher's first instinct was to take out the red pencil and go to town. Her only hesitation

If we can find something to criticize, we can likewise find something to recognize in a positive way.

was not knowing where to start, but that gave her a few seconds to think. Here was a product that had "I can't" written all over it. What would her criticisms contribute?

She made a note to work with this student on capital letters and spelling, and to remember to show him how to use an eraser without mauling the paper. And then, as she had done for the other students, she placed a sticker on the top. Finding something positive was a challenge, although shifting back to that goal enabled her to see the one thing the student had not messed up. She returned his paper marked "Magnificent Margins!"

What did this teacher communicate to the student? At no point was she saying that fragments instead of sentences were OK or that crumpling the paper was acceptable. But instead of seeing these problems as something to criticize, punish or even mark wrong, she chose to see them as skills he simply had not learned yet. This was not a bad student, just one in process. Her primary goal was to encourage this child to continue learning. Simply deducting points for his mistakes would not help him learn the skills he needed in order to move forward in this class. Instead, she started by focusing on what he had done right and developed a plan to teach him the rest.

The student was delighted with his sticker. The positive focus helped him begin to turn his "I can't" perceptions around. Building on the pride and accomplishment of his "magnificent margins," with further instruction, positive feedback on what he was doing right, and a little time, his work improved steadily. He was increasingly willing to take risks and try new things. The shift in the teacher's focus allowed her to break the failure loop that had simply strengthened his "I can't" beliefs.

A success-oriented focus means that the time we take to evaluate our students' work has a greater purpose than simply coming up with numbers to put in little boxes in our grade books. In a success-oriented classroom, it is fundamental to determine what the student knows (or has learned) and what we need to teach next. In most situations, this "greater purpose" challenges traditions in which the feedback students most often receive boils down to a grade—some letter, number or mark. Depending on the task and the teacher, this grade can represent a dispassionate percentage of correct answers or the teacher's opinion of a student's achievement, effort or behavior. We sometimes use grades to motivate students, although most teachers claim that students have become increasingly resistant over the past few decades to this form of motivation. (Grades are, however, still effective with high-achieving students who see high marks as meaningful and accessible, or to students whose self-worth depends upon the approval and validation they derive from good grades. Grades will rarely motivate students with a history of low scores and negative self-perceptions; nor will they inspire students who simply do not care about grades—regardless of their potential or prior achievements.)

In general, our grading practices reflect the intense perfectionism of factory-era standards: only by making no mistakes can students avoid red marks on their papers. (Many teachers report improvements in attitude when they switched from red ink to some other color, but if the focus of the feedback is exclusively negative, that's rather beside the point!) Traditionally, our on-paper responses to students emphasize mistakes, flaws, omissions and deficiencies; most often, the marks on a paper address what the student did incorrectly. So imagine the fate of a student who hands in an assignment done completely wrong! In the win-lose classroom, the teacher probably gives the child a zero and rationalizes, "I already explained this twice," or "Well, she should have been listening." In the win-win classroom, the student can get some credit or acknowledgement for her efforts, remediation for her misunderstanding and a chance to correct her errors.

Grades will rarely motivate students with a history of low scores and negative self-perceptions; nor will they inspire students who simply do not care about grades—regardless of their potential or prior achievements.

I recently surveyed several hundred teachers throughout the United States and abroad, asking them how they typically responded when they discovered that a student lacked a skill necessary to working with content they were about to assign. The majority of these teachers were appalled to realize the frequency with which they automatically or unconsciously reverted to impatience, criticism or shaming: "Why didn't you pay attention last year?" "You should have learned this by now!"

To further illustrate how senseless this reaction could be, I asked if anyone had ever planted a garden. In each group, the majority of hands went up. "Have you ever planted something that didn't grow well?" Of course, the same hands were raised.

"Did you yell?" I asked. And of course, everyone laughs, because it's incongruous for them to imagine standing in their gardens, screaming, "What's wrong with you? I buy the best seeds. I water you. I fertilize you. Look at the beans! They're not wilting and dying! Why can't you be more like them?"

By the same token, children learning to walk rarely get yelled at or punished when they stumble—or one would hope! Indeed, quite the opposite occurs: A first tentative step and out comes the camera or the camcorder to capture the moment; within seconds, we're on the phone to grandparents, neighbors and the media! Helping children learn to walk is a process of pure encouragement and celebration. (If kids learned to read with the same support they receive when they're learning to walk, do you think our culture would have the problem with illiteracy we currently face?) Yelling at a child because he cannot subtract does not improve his math skills. If it teaches him anything, it's only that he's not safe in this classroom, with this teacher—and he's not good at math!

And yet this pattern is so deeply ingrained, that for some teachers, it's hard to imagine that kids will learn without negative or critical feedback! In win-lose classrooms, poor grades may even be used as a powering technique to punish uncooperative students, but again, at what cost?

Legitimate feedback, guidance and instruction are necessary for learning, but how much of these do grades actually offer. As a solitary form of feedback, grades are extremely limited. Unless our criteria for grading each assignment are sharply focused and well communicated, the grades we give tell our students very little about what they know or can do. A grade of B- on a writing assignment says little more than "this is not as good as the one that got the B+." This grade certainly does not tell the student which concepts he misunderstood or where he needs additional work. A grade of 76 tells the student she understood 76 percent of the content on the assignment or that she can do a particular skill 76 percent of the time. What does that mean in terms of learning needs?

For the majority of teachers, grades are a fact of life—like them or not—a familiar tradition that is accepted and understood by parents and administration. Grades work for us because they are far easier to record, communicate and keep track of than descriptive evaluations. But if we have to live with grades, then let them work for the student as well. Let's keep our focus on what the student is doing right. We can use the evaluation process predominantly for noticing areas that need improvement and determining what we need to teach and reinforce. We don't even need to always mark items wrong on the student's paper.

Early in my career, one of my fourth-graders who made a career out of testing me, wrote a long, wonderful story for a writing assignment. One of the criteria for this task was that the final product be presented in cursive handwriting. Although that requirement was an old stand-by, this student handed in three pages in his neatest printing; everything else was fine.

For some teachers, it's hard to imagine that kids will learn without negative or critical feedback!

If we have to live with grades, then let them work for the student as well.

I was at a crossroad—do I lower his grade for printing and disregard all the writing he had done? Or do I ignore the printing? Not comfortable with either option, I read the story, which was excellent, and told him it was a "great first draft!" I'd be happy to accept it when it was completed. He could still turn it in at that point if he didn't mind losing points for printing (although he would get credit for a great story) or he could redo the story in cursive handwriting for full credit. He had a choice; either option was OK with me. I made it clear that I appreciated and enjoyed the work he did and still valued him regardless of his choice.

Offering students the chance to renegotiate a grade puts a great deal of responsibility on the student.

Offering students the chance to renegotiate a grade puts a great deal of responsibility on the student, requiring more time and effort, on their part, devoted to learning, correcting and redoing. (If a student misses a number of items on an assignment and then goes back, after re-explanation, and corrects the errors, what good purpose is served by failing the student for her incorrect first efforts?) This choice leaves the door open for greater success (in terms of deeper understanding, better grades and advancement to new content) while also allowing the student the choice of accepting the grade for the effort he or she made. In this way, grades are simply a reflection of how the student is doing on this particular project so far. This is feedback the student can use in making decisions about personal learning goals.

A positive focus need not be solely reflected in our evaluations of our students' work. A high-school teacher made it a point to individually greet as many of his 150 students each day. He met quite a few at the door as they were coming in and spoke with the others by walking around the room during their independent work time. His comments may not have been terribly elaborate, ranging from a simple "Hi," or "How was your weekend?" to "I really enjoyed reading your essay last night," or even just, "Glad you're

here." Yet he found that connecting with his students helped to improve the overall classroom climate, his relationships with his students and his attitude and feelings about the kids he was teaching. He was able to notice positive qualities in even the most difficult students. He learned to appreciate something in each student and was able to communicate his appreciation for the special contribution each one made. He still had boundaries and required students to operate within the limits he established, and he still corrected errors in work and intervened in the infrequent disruption. But each student felt valued and accepted at the same time.

A positive focus can also help us maintain a certain levity and avoid unnecessary conflicts and confrontations. One day, when I was detained for a minute on my way back from lunch, I returned to thirty-nine loud and disorderly students. Although I had a "get-started" assignment on the board as always, they were completely distracted by a class-wide dispute over who had won the game at recess. They were so wound up they barely noticed me, nor did they hear my request to take their seats and settle down until I finally blew up and yelled at them to sit and put their heads down!

They were quite surprised: This was not my usual way of dealing with this normally cooperative and—by this point in the year—self-managing class. Startled and suddenly quiet, they immediately took their seats. Just as I was beginning to calm down, I noticed that one of the kids still hadn't gotten back yet. That was the clincher! I could feel myself slipping out of control. At that very moment, this student ambled into the class, looked at her classmates with their heads on their arms, and before I had a chance to jump all over her, said, "What are we playing?"

I was on the edge: had I not burst out laughing, I might have later been indicted for murdering an entire fifth grade. To this day, I'm not convinced that the decision was entirely conscious, but it certainly defused the tension. We were able to move on to more important matters—the day's instruction—with a safe and positive climate restored.

Focus also refers to our ability to separate students from their behavior. This task is probably the most difficult aspect of orienting our perceptions and belief patterns to success. When a student (or anyone) does something we find particularly annoying, it can be difficult to see beyond the offending behavior. We forget the nice smile, the great strides in math, the interest in turtles. Suddenly this person is reduced to someone-who-does-not-return-library-books.

Now this is not to suggest that we take time out, while little Joey is torturing the Jade plant, to make a mental list of his great qualities. Our focus does not keep us from intervening negative behaviors (protecting the plant); it simply enables us to remember that Joey is more than the distasteful behavior he is exhibiting at the moment.

Being able to separate the child from his or her behavior has important consequences for our behavior and our relationships with the child. To begin, we are better able to intervene the problem without attacking the child personally. His behavior may be unacceptable or just plain wrong, but he—his self-worth or the essence of who he is—is neither. We are better able, then, to accept the student, even though we do not accept the behavior. We are able to intervene in the problem and still respect and value the person.

There are many times when we find ourselves looking at the hole more often than we notice the doughnut—when we find our comments more negative than positive. This is understandable. Even the warmest adult-child relationships in the industrial era were often marked by criticism and negativity. As society changes, however, the needs of society also change, which is why so many of the old ways which characterized the factory economy cannot work in today's information age.*

Because these patterns may be painfully familiar, a conscious shift toward a more positive focus can pose a real challenge. There are a number of things you can do to help maintain your own positive attitude, from creating a pleasing and comfortable physical environment in your classroom to consciously changing language and behavior. Commit to noticing a student you haven't spent much time with lately. Proclaim a positive period in which your written comments on student papers give feedback only on what they've done correctly. (You may want to extend this positive period indefinitely.) Make a point to recognize something positive in another teacher—and let that person know it. Promise yourself to not complain or make one negative comment about a student, teacher, parent, administrator or administrative policy during your lunch break, in the teachers' lounge or during a faculty meeting. You can even ask your students for feedback on what you're doing well!

One middle-school teacher claimed to have been helped by putting index cards marked with plus signs around her room and at home, on her mirror, in her purse and on her car's dashboard. Not only did the cards serve to remind her that she had a choice, but they even started encouraging her students and her family toward a more positive outlook as well!

Every interaction and event in our lives gives us an opportunity to choose how we're going to respond. Sure, it may be more automatic to blow up, worry or complain, but these reactions cost us—socially, emotionally, even physically. In the midst of an ordinary busy day, a commitment to positivity can quickly disappear. But even in the most stressful situations, we

Commit to noticing a student you haven't spent much time with lately.

Proclaim a positive period in which your written comments on student papers give feedback only on what they've done correctly.

---

*This is also why it's often so difficult to switch to new behaviors, particularly within the generally negative context of a power-based, win-lose model. See Alice Miller's *For Your Own Good.* New York: Farrar, Straus, & Giroux, 1987 or Anne Wilson Schaef's *When Society Becomes an Addict.* San Francisco: Harper & Row, 1987.

always have choices about our own behavior and outlook. (Sometimes pausing for a few seconds can help, not only to avoid doing or saying something that might hurt or alienate, but also to remind us that we have other options.) The more frequently we remember to take the more positive route, the greater the benefits. We can build trust and avoid conflict in our interactions with others, reduce our own stress levels and symptoms, and increase the amount of satisfaction and contentment in our lives as well!

Activity

Date_____

In the *first column* (or on the left-hand side of a separate piece of paper), describe several occasions that evoked or tempted a negative response from you. In the *second column* (or on the right-hand side of the paper), write down a more positive response you could have used instead.

Occasion	Positive Response

In what ways is your verbal feedback to students positively focused and success-oriented?

In what ways is your written feedback to students (grades, items checked on papers, comments on written assignments, essays, tests, and so on) positively focused and success-oriented?

What sort of information do you collect and record to keep track of student progress and performance (letter grades, percentages, anecdotal records or other descriptive data, skill checklists, and so on)?

In what ways does your evaluation of student progress and performance influence your teaching decisions (pacing, materials, review, assignments, and so forth) for individual students in your class?

What opportunities do your students have to change, improve or renegotiate grades?

What have you done to maintain a positive focus in the classroom?

What have you done to encourage your students to maintain a positive focus about themselves, school, their friends, their work and other aspects of their lives?

11

Giving Instructions

I was observing a first-year teacher during the first day of school, as she announced to her kindergarten class that it was time to get in line. A few students stopped and stared; the others started running around the room. It was chaotic. I wondered if "Get in line" was some strange new game until one five year-old came up and asked the teacher, "What's a line?"

We know that our students need clear instructions to succeed at the tasks we set before them, but what could be more clear than "Get in line"? As that new teacher quickly found out, instructions are only clear if the students understand them. The request to "Get in line" assumes they know what a line is, where it starts and ends, which way to face, whether it is single- or double-file, and all other conditions regarding talking, touching and what, if anything, they need to take with them when they get in line. She may as well have given the directions in another language. Imagine the confusion possible with more complex assignments!

The goal of success-oriented instructions goes beyond simply getting the students to correctly do what they need to do. We have a number of choices about the way we give instructions to our students. Depending upon the choices we make, we can either find ourselves setting the students up for failure and confusion or helping to build responsibility and self-management.

Lack of clarity, as in the previous example, is a common problem in giving directions. For the student, not knowing what to do or misunderstanding instructions becomes a source of confusion, helplessness, frustration and feelings of inadequacy. (I once saw an entire class of first graders break down in tears when the teacher innocently announced that they could go home as soon as they "pick up the floor." Another teacher told me that she could barely get her kids to come in out of the rain and mud after telling them they had to "scrape off their feet" first!) Poorly communicated instructions also build teacher-dependence, waste time and often result in reactive or negative feedback from teachers. We can avoid these pitfalls by first, getting very clear, in our own minds, about what we want as well as the components of the task we are asking our students to do. We also need to give students step-by-step directions, using language they are not likely to misconstrue, especially the first time we ask them to do something. It can also help to walk the students through each step of the directions, particularly those involved with routines, the use of equipment or materials, or movement, to increase the likelihood of their success. Remember, if it's important to us, it's worth the time.

To promote clarity, we can also be careful about the adjectives we use. We know what we mean by *good* handwriting, *exciting* characters, *thorough* research and clear presentation. Do they? Do we let students know before their work ends up on our desks how we will evaluate

Poorly communicated instructions also build teacher-dependence, waste time and often result in reactive or negative feedback from teachers.

a project or the particular skills on which our feedback will concentrate? Telling them what we're looking for or grading for helps focus students' efforts and promote success.

Students are bombarded with verbal instructions from teachers and other adults, as well as written instructions from books, the blackboard and assignments. Simple directions, given one at a time, can probably get through to just about any student who happens to be listening. Once students know what you mean by "Clear off your desks," you probably won't need to clarify it further or put it in writing. However, in new or more involved situations, students can benefit by directions provided in as many ways as possible.

For example, announcing that a group is to do the first ten problems on page 86 and any five problems on page 93 might be fine for our auditory learners (if they are really listening), but others students will have greater success with some additional cues. Writing the directions on the board, in a folder or on a task card, can serve as a reminder and a learning aid for these students. Written instructions also free us to move on to other tasks. Once we've given our instructions in oral and written form, the students have recourse to something besides bothering the teacher with questions about "What page?" or "Which problems?" If possible, using codes, cues or illustrations with written directions encourages independence, even among poor readers or very young students.

In addition to being clear, success-oriented instructions are also well-sequenced. I remember an episode of a popular TV series in which the characters were attempting to defuse a bomb according to step-by-step directions read to them. "Unscrew the wing-nut on the end." They do. "Remove the tail assembly." They do. "Cut the wires leading to the timing device." They do. "But first . . ."

The result of unclear sequencing of classroom directions may not be quite as harrowing, but it does present additional opportunities for students to make mistakes. Listing the steps in a specific order is essential,

Success-oriented instructions are clear and well-sequenced.

Ask for their attention and wait. You are worth listening to, aren't you?

particularly with projects that involve a number of steps. Writing and numbering the directions will be particularly helpful for many students.

We can also make success-oriented decisions about when to give instructions. I've seen far too many lessons fail—and far too much time wasted when teachers have to repeat directions over and over—because the teacher did not have the students' attention when directions were given. Sometimes waiting a few seconds until they finish putting things away or get settled in their seats will save time and prevent confusion down the road. Similarly, have you ever gotten your kids busy on some task and suddenly remembered a point you forgot to mention when they were still listening? Did you ask them to stop working before you spoke? If we give information to students without first asking for their attention and, better still—eye contact— we shouldn't be too surprised when the majority get it wrong.

Ask for their attention and wait. Wait until they get their desks cleared. Wait until they are looking at you. Infrequently interrupting their work with a sharp request to "Look at me" can work wonders. The operant word is "infrequent." Any signal—a bell, flashing the lights, clapping hands—or verbal interruption can be very effective at getting your students' attention when they know that some important announcement or meaningful bit of information will follow. Giving directions to inattentive students communicates a lack of self-respect (you *are* worth listening to, aren't you?) and it sets them up to fail as well. Likewise, hold off, if possible, on presenting new or important instructions as kids are getting ready for lunch or dismissal; unless those instructions have fairly immediate relevance, they'll probably be remembered better at another time.

The amount of information we give out at one time will depend on the age and maturity of the students, their experience with our directions and the complexity of the instructions we offer. In giving verbal directions to young students, low-auditory students, attention-deficit or hyperactive students, or students who have not had much practice developing their listening skills, go slowly and give directions a step at a time. If possible, wait until the students are ready for the next step before giving them additional information. (This technique also works well with small groups.)

Some kids simply need a starting point—something concrete from which to depart. These students find a certain security, for example, in writing from a story starter or turning a simple design into a drawing. This initial structure makes it easier for them to eventually face a blank piece of paper, writing their own story starters or beginning drawings by themselves.

We can also provide structure by limiting length (one side of a paper), media (a picture made on the computer), expression (written in the present tense, drawn with only one color of ink), content (using all 20 spelling words, people involved in the women's movement during the 1970's) or any number of criteria. Our ultimate objectives for any assignment will help determine the amount of structure necessary and choices available. Identifying details about tasks to be done or specifying the criteria for a particular assignment can save a great amount of time in reexplaining and help avoid student confusion and mistakes at the same time.

Choices within limits—the anthem of the win-win classroom—applies quite clearly to the directions we give. If the limits are too broad, students of any age can be overwhelmed. Sure, there's usually one person in any group who can take an assignment like "Construct a meaningful learning experience" and run with it successfully. Others, however, will be lost or will get into trouble that could easily have been avoided with more precise directions, greater structure and more specific choices.

It may come as no surprise that the language we choose in giving directions—particularly with regard to our boundaries—can also help us encourage responsible cooperation, avoid reinforcing teacher-dependence and discourage rebelliousness. Since our language and attitude are so closely-linked, changing one will invariably influence the other. As we commit to a positive, win-win focus, we will become increasingly aware of negative tendencies in our words and the tone of our voice. Likewise, as we shift from threats and warnings to promises and positively-stated contingencies, our attitude mirrors that change.

For example, let's say we want our students to remember to put all of the game pieces back in the box before they leave the work area. We can state this boundary by threatening: "If you don't put everything in the box, I'm taking it out of the center." We can also promise: "If you put all the game pieces back in the box, I will leave it in the center." In both cases we give the same basic message, connecting the consequence of their cooperation to the privilege of the game's continual availability. Which would students rather hear? Which would create less tension or stress in the classroom? And, as teachers, which would we rather say?

But there's more to this than just sounding pleasant. Although the threat of having the game removed is clearly implied in the promise to leave the box in the center, the implication of teacher control and responsibility is sharply reduced. In the first example, the game's presence in the center is a function of the teacher's power (external); in the second, it becomes a positive consequence of the student's cooperation (internal).

The difference is subtle, but this shift gives teachers a powerful tool for making students accountable for their behavior. For example, one middle-school teacher reported that her students were disturbed when she changed her boundary from "If you're not quiet in the next 30 seconds, you're not watching the video," to "You can watch the show as soon as you get quiet. This offer is good for 30 seconds." Although the tone and presentation were far more respectful, one student explained her classmates' dismay at the change: "Now if we miss the show, we can't blame you."

Similarly, the reasons for asking for certain behaviors can either work for or against building responsibility and cooperation. In addition to being clearly understood, our instructions and boundaries (which express what we want or need) are most effective when they appear to make sense to our students. In the power-based, authority relationships, the reason for doing something is connected to the power of the authority ("Because I said so") and the punitive consequences of non-compliance (". . . or else"). A statement like "Do it for me" may sound less authoritarian, but the implication of conditional approval actually works in the same manner as "Do it or else."

The win-win classroom operates on the belief that students need not be threatened with deprivation or punitive consequences to be motivated to cooperate. Instead, in 21st century authority relationships, teachers believe the students to be capable of making positive choices even when the outcomes are not directly connected with the power of the teacher. For example, "Please put the lids back on the paint jars so the paint doesn't dry out" communicates much more faith in and respect for students than "Put the lids back on these paint jars or you'll never see them again." There is a clear and sensible reason for putting the lids on the jars; the request in no way compromises the emotional climate in the classroom.

When we ask our students to do something, we usually have a better reason for asking them than "because I said so." The actual, logical and intrinsic reason for a boundary—so the markers don't dry out, so that we don't disturb anyone on our way down the hall, so that no one trips and falls, so that we'll have time to hear the entire story—can help build commitment and cooperation from even rebellious students. These criteria are stated for the benefit of the student and the class as a whole. It has nothing to do with the teacher's needs—although, as part of the group, these needs will be served as well. The fact that this approach clearly focuses on the students' needs (what's in it for them, indi-vidually or as a group) can account for an increase in cooperation. It may take a few extra seconds, but the extra information you provide in giving the students a practical reason for

Giving the students a practical reason for doing what you ask can build responsibility and generate cooperation.

These techniques work best when we can overcome our resistance to having to tell kids things we believe they should already know.

doing what you ask can build responsibility and generate cooperation from a handful of students who otherwise wouldn't bother.

Listen to the way you structure your contingencies and express your boundaries. Are they more frequently stated as promises ("If you do this, then . . .") or threats ("If you don't do this, then . . .")? Practically any threat can be restructured into a promise. (And incidentally, that does not mean: "I *promise* you, if you don't do this, then . . .!") And as we get to know our students better, we can begin connecting what we want to meaningful positive consequences for them.

All of these techniques will work best when we can overcome the resistance to having to tell kids things we believe they should already know. For a long time, I honestly resented having to take time to show fifth graders how to use the pencil sharpener correctly, to demonstrate clicking the caps of felt-tipped markers for eighth grade gang members or to end each of seven classes with a daily reminder to push the chairs under the desks. It was certainly easier to blame the students' parents or previous teachers who either never had bothered to teach these skills to my students, or whose instructions, for whatever reason, just didn't seem to transfer to my room.

And yet when I finally surrendered to these necessities, a few things happened, not the least of which was that my life in school got easier and my relationships—with my students and my job—improved. The few minutes I devoted to these seemingly redundant instructions and my eventual willingness to repeat them significantly increased the likelihood that I would get what I wanted. It reduced the stress of having to react to misbehavior because the focus was on prevention. (After a few weeks, the end-of-class bell would, for the rest of the year, elicit a chorus of students, mockingly reminding everyone to "push in your chairs.") And it helped my students learn the kind of behaviors they could use to function more successfully in my class and elsewhere.

Activity

Date_____

Use the following checklist to plan or evaluate the directions for various activities you assign.

Product and/or Behavior

Objective:

Criteria for successful completion:

Clarity

Skills or behaviors (cognitive, social, motor) required by this activity may be new to the students:

Materials or equipment used to complete this activity that may be unfamiliar to the students:

Other considerations (for example, movement within or outside the classroom, need for other facilities or resources):

Presentation of Instructions (elaborate each that applies):

Verbal:

Written:

Illustrated:

Other (illustrated, taped, signed, other language):

Samples available:

Structure
Limits, starting point or focus:

Choices available:

Other success-oriented features
Getting students' attention:

Time-related*:

Small steps:

Logical sequence:

Evaluation Summary:
In what ways were these directions success-oriented?

In what ways did the students have difficulty with the directions?

In what ways might these directions have been even more success-oriented?

Note to self: Next time, remember to . . .

---

*That is, *not* when they're wound up about something else or too far in advance for them to remember.

Activity

Date_____

In the *first column* (or on the left-hand side of a separate piece of paper folded into three columns), list five or more desired student behaviors.

In *column two,* tell how that behavior will benefit you (make your life easier or your job more pleasant).

In *column three,* tell how that behavior will benefit your students (what's in it for them to cooperate). If possible, please state in terms of positive consequences, rather than as a way to avoid a negative consequence.*

Desired Behaviors	Benefit for Me	Benefit for Student

*If the only benefit for cooperation is to avoid punishment, criticism, anger, ridicule, humiliation or abandonment, the positive behavior is unlikely to occur on its own if the threat (or power) is removed, if the student is competing for power or simply doesn't care. If it's difficult to think positive consequences, it's just because the win-lose power model is so pervasive and familiar. Hang in there.

To what degree have you been successful in announcing limits and criteria before there is a problem or mistake?

Describe a time you did so. In what ways did your behavior contribute to the students' success or positive performance?

To what degree have you been successful in expressing boundaries and directions positively (for example, turning threats into promises)?

Describe a time you did so. In what ways did your behavior contribute to the students' success or positive performance?

12

Planning and Pacing

Success-oriented planning covers everything from making sure there are enough handouts to seeing if our students are conceptually prepared for something new we're about to present. While the importance of appropriate content is indisputable, attention to details, which is easier to take for granted, certainly carries its own weight in instructional planning. Many otherwise well-planned lessons have been doomed by the simplest omissions, timing mistakes or errors in judgment. One first-grade teacher saw a terrific art activity fall apart when she realized she hadn't borrowed enough staplers. Too many kids waiting too long to share too few tools is a consummate formula for disaster.

Consider the plight of the science teacher who planned an entire week's worth of lessons around a shipment of fruit flies that had died in transit or the frustration of the teacher whose plans to have her kids make their own bingo cards faltered from her students' inexperience with rulers.

Good planning is mostly common sense. Sure, emergencies arise. There are times when the media center ships the wrong video or the one available VCR is broken. In these instances, emergency backup plans can avoid disaster. But for the most part, thinking plans through, can prevent monstrous headaches and numerous discipline problems, especially with something new, something we haven't done in a while or

something that's never been tried with this particular group.

Anything we can do to minimize confusion, additional movement, off-task time and interruptions can curtail opportunities for discipline problems to develop. But prevention goes beyond the logistical considerations described above; it actually involves what we teach.

At the end of the summer after my first year of teaching, I was offered a job teaching math to the five upper grades in a K-8 school. The staff greeted me with a warning that the eighth graders might be somewhat difficult: The majority of students in this class had not done well in math in years past and would probably not be eager to come around for one more year of failure and frustration.

The eighth grade text book did nothing to alleviate my concerns: after very few pages of review, the book jumped into complex concepts like multiples, factors, ratio and square roots. These kids were in for a tough year, indeed.

"Well," I thought, "Let's see what these guys remember from seventh grade." I armed myself with a stack of teacher-made diagnostic exercises, sequenced according to district curriculum goals, to greet the students when they first walked through the door.

When they arrived, it was obvious they did not want to be there. Even the presence of a young, enthusiastic teacher did not give them

What kind of behavior could I expect from a group of students who could neither understand the lessons nor do the assignments?

I felt considerable pressure to teach eighth-grade math to eighth-grade students.

I simply wanted them to be better at math at the end of each week than they had been at the beginning—regardless of where we had to start!

much hope: This was still math, and they were still going to fail as they always had. I shut the door and turned to find 38 hostile, hulking beings, arms folded across chests, eyes glaring and suspicious. Fun.

"OK kids, let's see what you can do."

I started with the easy stuff: the first pretest evaluated their skill with counting and number sequence. "No grades—just do the best you can do." Each student did OK with this test (I have since had many who did not), which meant that we went on to the next project, determining who could add whole numbers. I wasn't terribly surprised to learn from this test that nearly half of the class could not work addition problems that required regrouping. They performed even worse on the other whole number operations. The few students who had mastered the basics were tested on more advanced concepts.

As far as planning instruction went, I had only to look at these pretests to imagine how most of this group would do with concepts like multiples or square roots. Do I stick to the book and a curriculum that was years beyond the capabilities of the class, I wondered, or do I back up and start with what they actually can do? And what kind of behavior could I expect from a group of students who could neither understand the lessons nor do the assignments? (This situation was not unique to this particular eighth grade—to somewhat lesser degrees, I faced the same dilemma with the other classes as well.)

I felt considerable pressure to teach eighth-grade math to eighth-grade students, especially since a few of them were chronologically past driving age. On one level, it felt important that I expose them to skills they would encounter later on district-wide standardized tests. But I knew I'd only be exposing them to one more thing they were doomed to fail. Their math anxiety, can't-do attitudes and poor self-concepts hardly needed any reinforcement. Surely, attempting to teach math concepts when prerequisite skills had not been mastered would be pointless and self-defeating. I decided to start wherever was necessary for

them to achieve, catching up as best we could. I simply wanted them to be better at math at the end of each week than they had been at the beginning—regardless of where we had to start! I announced that these students needed three things to succeed in this class: They had to show up, they needed a pencil and they needed to produce daily, starting with whatever they could actually do.

There was, at first, some administrative concern that the majority of the students were still not in the district-assigned books after the first few weeks of school. But the pressure was not as strong as it could have been because I had a number of things working in my behalf. First of all, I had the diagnostic scores to back up my placements and records to document their progress. And while it was likely that a number of these students might never catch on to the most complex concepts, every child in the room had made tremendous progress in a very short period of time.

Further, the students' success was engaging: overall attitudes improved and off-task behavior was at a minimum. Students were taking risks, trying new things and beginning to believe that they could actually succeed in this class. I was even getting notes from parents, pleased and surprised to see their children bringing their books home and enthusiastic about math for the first time ever! And since my approach—and my grading system—were somewhat nontraditional, I made sure I covered my bases by including a list of math skills in each student's permanent record folder, checking off the skills each child had mastered in my class.

I learned something important in my work with these students: that our greatest strides in developing win-win relationships, self-managing student behavior and a positive classroom climate can be sadly undermined by teaching content that is poorly matched to student abilities. If it sounds like the alternative makes it too easy, keep in mind that the challenge was continual. Even though we started with something the kids could do, we did not linger there. From the first, the lessons demanded stretching beyond the comfort of previous achievement. Aside from a few practice laps, each successful trip around the track meant a higher hurdle to clear next time around.

Without the belief that success is within reach and the willingness to go after it, the kind of learning most teachers truly desire will not take place. The notion of "toughening them up" by letting them fail is a rather sadistic holdover from power-oriented, win-lose relationships. Students will have plenty of opportunities to mess up. Deliberately setting them up to fail is far more likely to slow them down, if not stop them cold. If we really want our students to make it in a tough world, they'll be far better served by practicing success than failure.

And what about the next year? Some of those eighth graders would be hitting ninth grade math classes without some of the skills of the eighth grade curriculum. But they did have the advantage of the progress they made—at least they would not be starting without the skills from elementary math as well. They knew a whole lot more than they would have learned if I had insisted on teaching over their heads all year. One more year of failure and frustration at the eighth grade level would hardly have made them more successful the following year.

We need to be careful that our concern for next year does not imbalance our intentions. We prepare kids to succeed with success, building the confidence and flexibility that will help them handle future difficulties more effectively, including the very real possibility that some future teacher may not share our concern for individual differences nor the ability or willingness to teach to a variety of student needs.

The goal of success orientation, whether in giving directions, feedback or instruction, is to remove obstacles for success for all students. It is no longer acceptable to settle for adequate performance from the kids in the middle of the curve. High- and low-achieving students need and deserve to be challenged at levels at which they can learn and achieve as well.

Even if the content is the same for everyone, there are things we can do to invite everyone to succeed. For example, when I taught spelling at the elementary level, I invariably had a handful of students who either flunked the test every Friday, or barely passed. By simply following the same routine that had not worked yet for these students week after week, what was the likelihood that their confidence or performance in this subject would spontaneously transform? Monday would come and they'd face 20 new words, Friday would come and they would fail the test. A new Monday only meant 20 more words they wouldn't learn. Something had to change and chances were, their spelling performance was not likely to be any different until I changed my approach.

I remember sitting down with five or six fifth graders to look at our options. They got so busy trying to convince me that "I don't do spelling" or "I can't spell," that the possibility of success never occurred to them. Trying to convince them that they could indeed spell, or at least do quite a bit better than they had was meaningless in the absence of hard evidence. In desperation, I asked, "How many words do you think you can learn in a week?"

The group stared at me. A few shrugged or intoned an exchange I took to mean "I don't know."

"How about five? Can you learn five?"

"I don't know."

"Let's give it a try. Get any five words right on the test and you get an A." For the moment, I also reduced the requirements of my minimally-achieving "middle" group to 10 words and asked my competent spellers to agree on three words from the science unit to add to their list.

When I relate this story to other teachers, I often get a somewhat shocked reaction. Even teachers who are comfortable with reading or math groups have more trouble with this strategy than my own students did: "Well what if the students in the top group want to know why the other kids only have to learn 5 words?" they ask. Simple! We tell them, "It's because everyone is

If we really want our students to make it in a tough world, they'll be far better served by practicing success than failure.

One more year of failure and frustration at the eighth grade level would hardly have made them more successful the following year.

It is no longer acceptable to settle for adequate performance from the kids in the middle of the curve.

different, and everyone in this class gets to succeed." In win-lose classrooms, where kids are routinely pushed into the deep end of the academic pool whether they can swim or not, it makes sense to assign 20 words to each child. Fear of protest by some students (or their parents) makes this practice easy to justify. But there's rarely a protest in a win-win classroom, because kids see, on a regular basis, the teacher's commitment to everyone's success. They quickly learn that fairness is not about uniformity, it's about uniformly accommodating, as much as possible, individual needs, abilities and preferences. (And parents who are kept current on policies and progress, particularly when contact focuses on positive aspects of their children's growth and behavior, tend to be far less adversarial than many teachers fear. See Section Four [page 166] for more information.)

The bottom line was that until I was willing to back up and give each student a way to succeed in this subject, there would always be a small group who learned nothing each week beyond "I can't spell." (I did have one or two students over the years who asked to be moved, in the beginning, to a lower group. Although I believed they could do fine at a higher level, they lacked the confidence or safety to succeed, at least at first; it cost me nothing to consent. In nearly every instance, after a few days—if that—they each asked to return to their original placement.) Some kids took a while to trust the possibility of success, but eventually each one stepped up to the plate. After a few weeks I pulled the group back together: "You guys are doing great in spelling. Do you think you can learn 7 words this week?"

"I don't know . . ."

"Let's give it a try!"

Eventually everybody got up to 20 words. No, they didn't all become star spellers, but the improvement in skill and confidence sold me on the value of a teaching approach that accepts

and begins with wherever students are in the moment and continually challenges them at a point at which they can each succeed. Sure it's easier and more convenient for the teacher to have everybody on page 70 whether they belong there or not, but if students don't belong on page 70, what we're doing is not teaching, at least not as far as those students are concerned.

Success-oriented planning leads to success-oriented instruction. In addition to thinking through the details and logistics of specific activities, planning also addresses what the kids can do, where their interests lie, and how to best reinforce the students' commitment, risk taking, perseverance and belief in their own potential for achievement.

Perhaps the greatest benefit of success-orientation in a classroom is its ability to sharply reduce instances of disruption, confusion, frustration, conflict, off-task behavior and wasted time that often occur when kids figure that as long as they're going to fail anyhow, they may as well have a good time. My willingness to back up to work with students from where they actually were (as opposed to where the curriculum mandated they should be) was, in part, self-serving. Of course I wanted to increase skills and learning, but I also wanted to stop the kinds of behavior problems I kept running into when students could not perform.

Success-orientation won't eliminate every classroom problem we might encounter, but it will certainly help prevent the majority of discipline issues that arise when kids do not understand directions or content, or when they see no possibility for school success regardless of how they behave. We will still be faced with the task of motivating a non-disruptive student, recognizing cooperation or inter-vening when a misbehavior occurs—and we'll need different tools for each. These situations will be discussed in greater detail in the following section.

"Everyone is different and everyone in this class gets to succeed."

Fairness is not about uniformity, it's about uniformly accommodating, as much as possible, individual needs, abilities and preferences.

Activity

Date_____

Here is success-oriented planning sheet to help you evaluate activities and lessons before you implement them:

What materials do I need?

Do I have enough materials?

What do I still need to buy, assemble, make or get?

How will I distribute the materials?

Will students have to move?

What changes in furniture or room arrangement will I need to make?

How can I make this transition as smooth as possible?

What will I be doing during this activity?

How free will I be to help answer questions or monitor behavior?

What resources, materials and arrangements will help students solve problems without bothering me?

When is this activity supposed to take place?

Is that the best time for this lesson?

Do they need time to settle down from their last class?

Is it too close to the weekend or holiday to introduce something new?

What else might I need to contend with or compensate for?

What alternatives are available?

What are they most likely to misunderstand?

What else do I need to go over?

Do the students need to practice anything first?

What do they need to do, have, or get before they can begin?

What can go wrong?

What do I do if any of these things actually happens?

What is Plan B if this flops altogether? (Repeat all of the above for Plan B)

Activity

Date_____

Use the chart on the next page or create a similar chart on a separate piece of paper.

In *column one*, describe the emergency or back-up materials and plans you have for those occasions on which a particular lesson doesn't work, the materials you ordered don't come in on time, or the kids finish in half the time you anticipated.

In *column two*, tell where the materials are located.

In *column three*, tell if the materials are ready for use (if not, note what needs to be done).

In *column four*, describe any special instructions, materials or preparation the students will need in order to do these back-up activities. If the students can get started as soon as they receive the materials, simply mark this column "independent."

Back-up Materials and Activities	Location of Materials	Readiness for Use	Special Instructions, Preparations or Materials Needed

Note: These types of materials and activities can be especially valuable when they're available for a substitute who may have difficulty following your plans, pulling everything together for a more complex lesson, coming in the middle of a unit or getting the kids' cooperation. Make it easy for your substitutes to succeed, too! If you feel that these particular activities may not be appropriate for a substitute, you may want to pull together a separate set of emergency plans and materials to leave in a "Substitute's Survival Folder." It's a safe bet your efforts will be appreciated and lead to a better experience for the sub, the kids, and you when you return.

Building Cooperation and Self-Management

13

Motivating and Cooperation

One year, a new student named Billy came to my fourth-grade class during the second week of school. He was shy and polite and could entertain himself for hours without bothering a soul. Billy also refused to do any work; he neither participated in discussions nor touched any of the assigned paper-and-pencil activities. He was a very pleasant kid to have around, but I was not willing to accept his presence as merely ornamental.

Reminders, threats and negative consequences were unproductive, and the call home did not generate the sort of support that might have shaken Billy loose from his resistance to school work. Talking to Billy revealed that he was quite content to while away the year counting the holes in the ceiling tile, even though he was aware that he could not be promoted from a class in which he didn't do anything.

I told him that I would continue to give him the day's assignments and be available for help. I would not, however, continue to nag, threaten or force—these efforts had not only been exhausting and ineffective, they were taking away time I could spend with other students. I was not happy with the choice Billy had made, nor with my inability to turn him around. His success in fourth grade was far more important to me than it seemed to be to him. But for the moment, I could only offer him chances to change his mind.

About two days later, the office called my room, asking me to please send certain forms down by lunchtime. I had just finished collecting the materials they wanted and looked around for a messenger. Everyone seemed to be busy with something—everyone of course, except Billy, who was at that moment, having a staring contest with a box of chalk. He was certainly available. Still, privilege had its price: I invited Billy to take the papers to the office if he'd like, as soon as his work was finished.

To my amazement, Billy ran up to me 15 minutes later, work in hand. Everything looked fine. It was the first time I had ever seen his writing. Without even thinking about it, I had stumbled upon magic: Billy would do anything to get out of my room!

Understanding the concept of motivation means recognizing that all behaviors are chosen, and that even if the choice is made unconsciously or automatically, people behave in ways that are most need-fulfilling to them. Let's look at this question from an adult perspective. Think of a household or classroom chore that you really detest doing, but do anyhow. Now explain why you perform such a distasteful task. Think of as many reasons as you can. (If one of your reasons is "because I should do it," specify the reason you feel you should.) It might help if you write your reasons down.

Chore:

I do it because:

These reasons illustrate what's in it for you to do something you really dislike. These are the options that are more need-fulfilling—that is, they pay off better for you—than avoiding the task you specified, and they only motivate you when they are indeed more need-fulfilling or more important than putting off doing the chore.

For example, let's say you chose "cleaning the bathroom" as something you hate to do. And let's say that, on occasion, you do clean the bathroom for the following reasons:

Because your roommate nags you if you don't.

Because you're afraid of the stuff that grows on the shower tile.

Because company is coming.

And let's imagine that your roommate is out of town for a week, that the shower tile still looks clean enough and your company cancels at the last minute. Are the motivators you listed (avoiding the nagging, the "stuff" or your company's shock and discomfort) as compelling as they might ordinarily be? Chances are, you're likely to put off this chore until one of those options or another becomes more pressing.

There is no such thing as unmotivated behavior. There has to be something in it for us—whether the outcome is personal satis-faction, the desire to please, a commitment to certain values or priorities, the pursuit of a larger goal, the satisfaction of our curiosity, the desire for fun or pleasure, the avoidance of punishment or deprivation, the ability to gain access to a more desirable outcome when we've finished, or some other type of fulfillment—otherwise we simply do not choose to do it.

In any situation we always have choices. The choices we make are based upon which of the available options will produce the most satisfying or need-fulfilling result. (Undesirable, unacceptable or even dangerous options are still options!) The belief or perception that we do not have a choice satisfies our desire to avoid questioning our habits,

evaluating our options or tempting conflict or criticism by doing something other than what is expected or demanded. Whether we eat the brownies or pass them up, for example, will depend on whether it's more important to us, at that moment, to stick to our diet, indulge our sweet tooth, please the person who made them, satisfy our hunger or avoid feeling over-stuffed. Even the specter of guilt, remorse or yet another beach-free summer will, for some of us, all but disappear in the presence of warm, chocolate temptation.

What appears to be the best choice for one person or one situation may not be the best choice for others. Clearly many of the choices students make will hardly appear need-fulfilling or beneficial from a teacher's perspective. For example, it's hard to imagine that most students aren't aware of the risks and dangers of smoking, using drugs or engaging in unprotected sex, or at least that these activities can hurt them. However, if, at the moment they have to decide, the students' priority is to escape, to experience pleasure, or to avoid rejection, ridicule or abandonment, they will make whatever choice will work best to accommodate that particular need.

When people cooperate with us, they do what we want because doing so serves their purposes in some way. Perhaps they are trying to make us happy, gain our approval, get us off their backs or obligate us for some later time. Or perhaps the motivation has nothing to do with us. They may cooperate because they like doing what we're asking them to do, they wish to make themselves feel worthwhile or validate their suffering, or simply because cooperating feels good to them. There is always some payoff, some need-fulfilling positive con-sequence, behind their cooperation. Being skilled at motivating others means paying close attention to that very issue: What can they gain by cooperating? What's in it for them to do what we want?

The principles and dynamics of motivation are the same in the classroom and out. Motivating students means first looking for

All behaviors are chosen; people behave in ways that are most need-fulfilling to them.

There is no such thing as unmotivated behavior.

What can they gain by cooperating? What's in it for them to do what we want?

positive consequences that are more attractive than avoiding or resisting what we're asking them to do. Second, it means using this information to create a boundary that offers them access to what they want when they do what we want. We have a number of options available, as anything that is meaningful to our students can be used as a motivator. The choices we make about which types of motivators to use reflects and, at the same time, establishes our orientation to power dynamics—win-win or win-lose. Our motivational strategies strongly influence the quality and type of relationships we establish with our students and the degree of emotional safety that exists in our classrooms as well. These factors are critical to the processes our students use in making choices about their own behavior.

When students' emotional safety is at risk, their ability to achieve higher levels of functioning (such as satisfying a desire to learn something new or working to fulfill their potential) will always be undermined by the need to adapt in order to feel safe. Throughout the years, I've seen kids of all ages make some pretty dumb decisions. True, their choices were sometimes motivated by curiosity or lack of foresight, but all too often their decisions were swayed by the anticipated reaction of someone they valued or feared. They could justify breaking rules, stealing, getting high, skipping school, being mean to someone, resisting authority, accepting a dare or even becoming sexually active with explanations like: "I didn't want her to be mad at me," "I didn't want them to make fun of me," or "I didn't want him to leave me." Nowhere was there consideration for other more serious personal consequences. In these cases, the fear of someone's negative reaction—particularly the possibility of rejection, humiliation or abandonment—always took precedence; these children always looked outside themselves before they made their choices.

If we truly want our students to be able to stand up for themselves, to refuse to self-sacrifice for the sake of peer approval, then it's essential that we do not use motivation techniques that suggest: "You are safe and

Look for positive consequences that are more attractive than avoiding or resisting what we're asking them to do.

Anything that is meaningful to our students can be used as a motivator.

Keep the focus on positive outcomes, not negative reactions.

loveable only when you are doing what I want (or when I don't catch you)." Although a teacher's approval or disapproval can be very effective with some students, using teacher responses as a primary motivator takes us back to building obedience and teacher dependence. Yes, some kids know you really mean it when the veins stick out in your neck, and the thought of you being hurt or disappointed will keep others on track. But for how long? And at what cost?

In a win-win classroom, where students can feel accepted, welcome and worthwhile even on less-productive days, motivators will more likely take the form of some pleasurable activity instead. This means that we don't need to rely on our reactions to get what we want. Teachers who use boundaries to connect the things they want with something other than their feelings or power tend to avoid the kind of stress and conditionality that compromises emotional safety. They can keep the focus on positive outcomes, not negative reactions. Their students get quiet so that the teacher will read the story, not because the teacher will get angry if they don't. They finish assignments and turn in work to get credit or a chance to go on to a new unit, not to avoid a lecture, detention or being held back. They return their library books so they can take new ones home, not because the teacher feels hurt or disappointed when they forget.

Such contingencies have been around for a long time. Grandma had this one down when she said we could have our dessert after we finished our vegetables. Either way, it was our choice. If we really hated the vegetable, it didn't matter what the dessert was. And if we really loved dessert, we probably would have eaten anything to get it. Regardless of the choice we made, the only thing at stake was dessert—not Grandma's love, approval or temper.

Is this a bribe? Absolutely! That's how motivation operates. The payoff for getting to class on time, settling down immediately and getting through the work is the privilege of having the last ten minutes of class free for a game or enrichment activities. It may seem strange that many teachers strongly opposed to the idea of positive bribes are much less uncomfortable with the idea of negative bribes (threats). Perhaps it's the familiarity of punitive strategies, but make no mistake about it: A statement that expresses "When you finish your outline you can do the coloring puzzle" is no more a bribe than "If you don't do your work, I'm calling your mother!" Both offer a payoff to the students for doing what you want, but in the case of the threat, the payoff is always about avoiding a negative response, or staying safe in some way. You'll get the same message across with a positively-stated boundary—the desirable outcome is contingent upon cooperation or work completion—but with much less stress and much less chance of engaging rebellious, resentful or passive-aggressive behavior.

The echo from the industrial-era authority relationships will question why we need to offer a pleasurable outcome to students for doing what they simply should do. We need to for one reason: it works, and it works better and with much less risk than using the threat of negative outcomes.

Further, seeing the positive results of their cooperative behavior helps reinforce the students' responsibility for their choices and increases accountability for their behavior. Experiencing a connection between positive choices and outcomes strengthens the students' recognition of the cause-and-effect relationship between the behaviors they choose and what happens to them as a result of their choices. The positive outcomes are neither the random winds of fate nor someone else's fault. Rewarding consequences also reinforce the students' belief in their ability to positively affect their own lives.

It's usually at this point in my workshops, that someone challenges, "What about 'learning for learning's sake'?" Don't we all want students to work for the love of learning? Of course we do. Is there anyone easier to motivate than the student who comes to our classroom with a burning desire for knowledge? But surely our aspirations are not simply for our own benefits. Such students are also functioning at the highest levels of need-fulfillment.

Here again we see the important of creating an emotionally safe classroom environment. If we look at the range of needs that motivate people, we find a hierarchy in which the more basic needs must be satisfied before higher-level needs. A hungry student, for example, may not be too concerned with whether or not her handwriting is improving until she gets some food in her stomach. Once the basic physiological needs are satisfied, students are free to seek fulfillment of higher-level needs.

In a win-lose classroom, the frequent existence of arbitrary power and absence of trust are likely to keep kids striving to meet lower-level needs for safety. These students rarely take risks or go beyond the bare minimum in order to avoid confrontation or to keep from drawing attention to themselves. Even those vying for positions of power and acceptance among their peers, or the ones trying to be teacher's pet, place these goals above learning simply to assure their safety in some way. Satisfying higher-level needs, including the desire for knowledge, learning and personal growth, requires an environment in which students feel safe enough to pursue these objectives. (Self-actualization is a long way off for students focused on self-protection.) A success-oriented classroom not only allows safety needs to be met, but also acknowledges the students' higher-level needs for acceptance and belonging, success and achievement, and input and control. The possibility of learning for learning's sake stands a much better chance of transpiring in a win-win classroom than in any other environment.

And yet, doing anything for its own sake must be perceived as pleasurable and rewarding in some way. Even in the ideal environment, many students have a long way to go before they can love learning or a particular subject area if the possibility of success seems to be beyond their immediate reach. Therefore, an

Seeing the positive results of their cooperation helps reinforce responsibility and accountability.

In a win-lose classroom, the frequent existence of arbitrary power and absence of trust are likely to keep kids striving to meet lower-level needs for safety.

The possibility of learning for learning's sake stands a much better chance of transpiring in a win-win classroom than in any other environment.

Even in the ideal environment, many students have a long way to go before they can love learning or a particular subject area if the possibility of success seems to be beyond their immediate reach.

activity that is perceived as unfulfilling may, at least at first, have to be connected to something meaningful and immediate to build positive behavior patterns or internalized commitment, let alone a passion for the task or subject itself. The simple promise of long-term results or possible satisfaction might not do it.

Billy's love of running errands and visiting other classrooms (what he wanted) gave him a reason for doing his classwork (what I wanted). For this student, who was initially unwilling to take even the slightest risk, the availability of something more need-fulfilling than avoiding the task was absolutely essential. Access to a positive outcome—something that Billy perceived as valuable—gave him the drive that all the threats, lectures and nagging were unable to elicit. It was a start, and one that created a positive association with the entire experience of being—and working—in fourth grade. As that connection became more firmly established, the need for the continual, unrelated reward diminished. After a couple of weeks, Billy had become self-managing and confident enough to do his work without needing to run errands after he was finished (although I still looked for opportunities to send him out of the room once in a while because I knew he enjoyed this privilege, handled it responsibly and maintained a high level of commitment in class).

Likewise, simply hearing that they would need basic math skills to balance a checkbook and plan a budget had little motivational value to those eighth graders who had neither checkbook nor budget. The only way to break the inertia was to connect their initial attempts to some immediate, positive outcomes. That might mean working a math puzzle for reinforcement, creating a new bulletin board, grading one's own assignment, getting to help another student, choosing an enrichment activity, working with a partner or moving on to the next skill at the completion of a task. Each time students experienced the positive outcomes of their own cooperative choosing, the connection was reinforced. As this association grew stronger, the behavior became

increasingly internalized and habitual.

This strategy can work in even the most seemingly hopeless situations. A high school teacher was assigned late in the year to a large group of high-risk and extremely hostile seniors after the original teacher and numerous replacements had quit. The new teacher could barely get their attention, and when she handed out an assignment, every student in the room tore it up. "We never pass anything, anyhow," one declared.

Only somewhat discouraged, she returned the next day with the same assignment and announced, "If you turn it in with your name on it, you get a C." Most of the students simply shook their heads and tore the papers up again, although six or seven defiantly scrawled their names across the paper and turned them in. The next day she came back with their papers graded, as promised, with a C for having turned something in, and another stack of work. Although the students were still suspicious, she suddenly had their attention: "If you can get a C for writing your name, imagine what you can get for doing some work!"

Again, it was a start. And eventually—between making success possible and providing other need-fulfilling options for cooperation—she hooked every kid in the class. As the trust relationship grew, students were willing to take greater risks. The hurdles also got higher and after a very short time, it took far more than writing one's name on the paper to get a passing grade.

As with Billy and the kids in my math class, staying on task, attempting new content and progressing through the curriculum eventually became their own rewards. Sure, there were students who gained competence and still didn't loved the subject area. Let's face it—there are certain activities and chores that may never be rewarding in their own right, no matter how well we can do them! (How many adults whose math skills are adequate to function responsibly in society do not actually love math?) But as achievement eroded resistance, students were becoming learners. If they didn't all find a love of learning in that class, at least it was an invitation to finding it elsewhere.

I've met too many teachers who were nearly crippled by frustration, guilt or inadequacy when they bought into the idea that any positive motivation is harmful and that truly effective teachers have students for whom simply being in their teacher's classroom is reward enough. This is a set-up of the worst and most destructive kind. Yes, ideally we'd like kids to do their math assignments for the joy and privilege of working with fractions, and certainly some will. But what about the students who find fractions somewhat less enticing, not to mention too difficult for them to do with the skills they currently have developed. (Even if you absolutely love math, would you clean your bathroom for a chance to do some long division problems in your free time afterward?) Is the point of our interaction and instruction improving our students' understanding and ability, or is it to guarantee that they never need a push, inspiration, motivation or outside incentive to learn the skill or do the work? If we get too attached to our kids falling in love with our subject area, we may be doomed to a great deal of frustration and disappointment.

There is no such thing as unmotivated behavior. Even the most dedicated among us expect something for the work we do, whether it be our enjoyment of teaching, the satisfaction of knowing we're shaping young lives, the paycheck we get at the end of the month or the fact that our job gets us out of the house once in a while. Why shouldn't kids want some meaningful payoff for the things they choose to do? We can save ourselves a great deal of heartache when we quit analyzing and making judgments about the reasons our kids are doing what we assign. So long as we aren't motivating with conditional safety or approval, whatever individual or personal forces compel cooperative and on-task behavior are none of our business.

We can certainly improve the odds of getting what we want when we ask students to do something they can do successfully, when the task has some personal relevance to them, or when doing the task gives them access to something they like doing even more. It is possible to establish a foundation in which learning, success, safety and achievement can develop into a passion or a much greater commitment than some of our students initially display. However, it's equally true that few people are likely to fall in love with something that represents failure, poor progress, criticism, impatience or other negative feedback for them.

The point is, a big part of our job as educators involves encouraging—that is, motivating—kids to do certain things, whether they like the tasks or not. If our students learn how to construct an outline, write a cohesive paragraph or determine the area of a rectangle, does it matter that some never look forward to the opportunity to do these tasks? The real test of responsibility is the willingness to do the things we need to do, not just the things we like to do.

We promise students an A if they do their work, but there are always a few students who are not motivated by grades. We allow students who finish their work to go out to recess, but there are always a few who would just as soon stay inside. On the other hand, there is always someone who would do anything for the privilege of straightening the teacher's desk, grading the spelling tests, or—as in Billy's case—running a stack of papers downstairs. But what about those students who don't seem to be motivated by anything?

Moving away from factory-era thinking means we try to become more aware and appreciative of individual student's preferences and increasingly creative about the types of incentives we offer. Because many rewards and outcomes that are valuable to students would probably not be terribly attractive to us, it's easy to overlook some great motivators. For example, few teachers would go out of their way to grade papers for someone else. Offer that privilege to students though, and watch eyes light up. The same goes for a chance to wash the blackboard, use carbon paper or ball-point pens, run the VCR, work at the computer,

If we get too attached to our kids falling in love with our subject area, we may be doomed to a great deal of frustration and disappointment.

Few people are likely to love something that represents failure, poor progress, criticism, impatience or other negative feedback for them.

The real test of responsibility is the willingness to do the things we need to do, not just the things we like to do.

change the bulletin board, listen to music or engage in any number of clean-up chores.

Other options may not be so obvious. I once asked a fifth grader to get a box of science equipment out of my car. When she returned, she put the box on my desk and shook her head. "Your car's a mess," she said.

She was right; it was rare that my car was not littered by papers, plans, materials, text books and at least a few fast food wrappers. "Would you like to clean it out when you finish your work?" I asked.

"Ooo! Can I?"

("Hmm," I wondered. "Do you clean bathrooms?")

Now, I doubt I would have thought of car-cleaning as a reward, but the task was obviously more attractive to her than it was to me. It's also hard to see "more work" as motivating, yet enrichment and content-related activities can be very appealing to students, especially if there are choices available or if "more work" clearly indicates advancement. (Ever notice how students in basal readers tend to really perk up through the last unit so they can get into the next, more difficult book?)

Learning about our students, through simple conversation or formal assessment instruments, can lead to significant insights. For example, a student in a class I was observing refused to do his work and was being referred for a variety of testing procedures. One of the supervisors happened to strike up a conversation with the student during which time the student revealed that his favorite thing about school was the janitor. The supervisor approached the custodian and was able to set up a contingency by which the student could help out after his work was done.

At one point early in my teaching career, I gave my students a learning styles survey* to find out more about how they learned best. The results indicated that the majority of my students preferred working with a partner, with greater mobility and with sound in the environment. To accommodate their learning style needs, I offered one or more of those options during certain activities as long as the students stayed on task and didn't create problems for anyone else. This survey also revealed that my most difficult reading group was made up of students who preferred afternoons and evenings to mornings. Our reading periods were scheduled early in the day when these students were not at their best. It took some juggling, but switching that group to the afternoon made a tremendous difference in the students' attention, participation, retention, performance and achievement levels. In each case, attempting to meet students' learning style preferences paid off for me as well. Win-win!

Sometimes a positive consequence can itself be as valuable a learning experience as any classroom activity. One year, our kindergarten teacher was feeling a bit overwhelmed by some of the management and housekeeping responsibilities involved in managing a large, full-day group. I offered to ask some of my upper-grade students to help. My kids required little coaxing and began helping out—as always—when their seatwork was done.

At first, the tasks were fairly mechanical or routine—mixing paint or covering tables for art activities; helping the younger students open their milk cartons, zip their jackets or get in line; or helping the teacher with organization and clean up chores. However, these students quickly began offering to help out in centers, play games, put on puppet shows or review colors, numbers, letters and various other concepts. Some of my weakest and most resistant readers volunteered to read stories to the kindergarten children. This was a real "I can" experience that was ultimately reflected in their performance in their own classroom.

We were able to get every upper grade student involved as a helper. Students who had never done homework before were asking to do their independent work at home so they could go down and help. Amazingly, some even asked to give up recess to work in the kindergarten!

Because many rewards and outcomes that are valuable to students would probably not be terribly attractive to us, it's easy to overlook some great motivators.

A positive consequence can itself be as valuable a learning experience as any classroom activity.

---

*Dunn, K. and Dunn, R. *Educator's Self-Teaching Guide to Individualized Instruction.* NJ: Parker Publishing Co., Inc., 1975.

My students were suddenly doing larger amounts of increasingly difficult work. Because the privilege demanded that the helpers stay caught up and out of trouble in all of their classes, overall discipline was greatly improved. At the same time, their successes in the kindergarten and opportunities to model were beginning to show in their interactions and behaviors with their peers and other teachers, and even at home. Self-concepts and general attitudes improved; attendance was up, detentions were down. Students who had rarely, if ever, demonstrated anything in the way of self-management, were beginning to behave more responsibly and with greater self-control. One student even walked away from a fight, took the hall pass, and stood outside the door until he had a chance to cool down. This was unheard of. I didn't even have to open my mouth! School had become more enjoyable and rewarding for everyone, and I was amazed at the amount of time I had for instruction when I wasn't distracted by student misbehavior.*

One caution in looking for meaningful motivators: When we attempt to determine "what's in it for them," we need to differentiate between the assumed or projected benefits (which usually reflects our value system) and the actual benefits (what the students perceive as a positive outcome). If Grandma said, "Eat your vegetables, and you can have some liver!" how many children would this promise motivate, regardless of liver's nutritional value? In Billy's case, graduation from fourth grade was meaningful and important to me; but it was not meaningful enough to Billy to motivate him to participate in class. Adults can often appreciate the long-range benefits of the things we ask our students to do far better than they can (although some of our more mature students may have also made that connection). Still, many of these students have the rhetoric down, particularly if they are good at teacher-pleasing, but they probably won't actually be motivated by positive consequences beyond

their immediate experiences. For the most part, the more immediate and personally meaningful the positive outcome, the more likely the cooperation.

For example, a student is more likely to be motivated to write a coherent paragraph in order to print it out on the computer this afternoon than to make himself more attractive in the job market ten years from now. In most cases, we are justified in our commitment to the importance of whatever it is we want our students to do. But unless there is also an immediate—or foreseeable—positive consequence for the students, in most cases our commitment will do us little good. Even adults find immediate and personal consequences more compelling than long-range possibilities. (Would our efforts at dieting, for example, be more successful if we could actually see a difference each time we turned down a doughnut?) People who write their term papers the day they're assigned find it motivating to get the tasks out of the way. The rest of us put things off until our grades, raises or jobs depend on it— and then may still let it go if those payoffs aren't as important as the other things that kept us from writing in the first place.

When I first started thinking about motivation, I had a great deal of factory-era conditioning to overcome. Although I knew that I wanted to experience meaningful payoff for the work I did, there were times I resented having to motivate kids. This double standard did not serve me, nor did my belief that I shouldn't have to motivate them to help me build the relationships—or cooperation—I really wanted.

I was worried that motivating kids with positive outcomes would teach them to expect a reward every time they did something, a concern I've heard echoed time and again by educators and parents in my training sessions. Over the years, it's become quite clear to me that no one, grownup or child, does something unless he sees some immediate or long-term benefit. It's basic human nature to expect a

*I was amazed at the amount of time I had for instruction when I wasn't distracted by student misbehavior.**

For the most part, the more immediate and personally meaningful the positive outcome, the more likely the cooperation.

*From *Building Responsible Learning Behaviors through Peer Interaction*. Unpublished doctoral dissertation by Jane Bluestein, University of Pittsburgh, 1980.

positive outcome for the choices we make. (Why are you reading this book? Whether it's to fulfill a requirement for a class you're taking, an interest in the topic, a need for information or a desire to please the author, you anticipate some payoff or you would certainly be doing something else with your time.) Motivation doesn't teach kids to expect a payoff, it simply accommodates their need for one.

Motivation doesn't teach kids to expect a payoff, it simply accommodates their need for one.

I also feared that motivating students would encourage selfishness and manipulation until I understood that it's not the desire for the payoff that is selfish or manipulative but the behaviors that follow when we don't have healthier ways of getting what we want! Good motivation skill actually discourages selfishness and manipulation. Accommodating kids who like to negotiate and make counter-proposals also builds valuable life-skills and, in the long run, can create incredible levels of commitment and cooperation.

It's not the desire for the payoff that is selfish or manipulative but the behaviors that follow when we don't have healthier ways of getting what we want!

Industrial-era thinking brings up another concern: "If you let Billy take a message to the office, don't you have to let everybody take stuff down when they finish their work?" Of course not. In that particular class, some kids would work for the grades, some would work to get on to the next assignment, others would work for some structured free time, and a few did the assignment because they really liked that particular subject and usually did well in it. Sending them on an errand as motivation would have been silly and redundant. Likewise, I had students who found no fascination with running around the school on missions for me. Attempting to motivate them with messenger privileges would have been pointless. Students do not have similar personalities, tastes and work habits, and most genuinely appreciate having their individuality recognized.

Let's go back to the chore you were thinking about earlier in this chapter. Suppose that for some reason, I feel that it's important for you to practice this chore in some different

setting—say, at my house (or classroom). Hypothetically speaking, what would it take to motivate you now? Try to think of at least five outcomes (rewards) that would work for you. Be specific: if you say "money," for example, what's your bottom line?

In workshops, I offer the example of coming to clean my bathroom (usually because there are numerous participants who find the chore as distasteful as I do). The range of responses from any group of teachers gives strong support for the differences in personal tastes, preferences and priorities and the need for using different motivators with different people. Some attendees offer to come and clean my bathroom for nothing—evidence of either their (admitted) need to please or the fact that some chores are simply less obnoxious in someone else's home. Others ask for unspecified amounts of money, but, when I offer a nice, shiny dime, most of the hands go down. Some will do it for ten dollars; other won't budge for less than a few hundred.

Still others wouldn't clean my bathroom for a thousand dollars, although they might agree when I offer to write their lesson plans for the rest of the year in exchange. Various others, originally resistant, have relented for a great home-cooked meal, a weekend without their kids, an offer for me to do their ironing or dishes for a week, a chance to get out of grading papers for a month or five pounds of chocolate. One teacher said she'd do my bathroom and more if I'd just take the time to write her a note telling her that I appreciated what she had done!

See, we all have our price and we always have choices, and so do the kids we're trying to motivate. In motivating cooperation—with kids or adults—it's well worth our while to offer them something they can't refuse. And as long as everyone's dignity and safety are protected, that doesn't have to cost us a thing.

Guidelines for Motivating Cooperative Behavior

- Offer outcomes that are meaningful and important to students to elicit otherwise non-existent behaviors you desire (that is, to motivate them to perform a particular behavior they are not currently demonstrating).

- Keep in mind that the process of motivating is different from strategies used for reinforcing existing cooperation or intervening when a misbehavior occurs, although boundaries used to motivate also reinforce (when the positive outcome becomes available) and are useful for intervention (the positive outcome becomes unavailable until the child has a chance to demonstrate more cooperative behavior). Details will be provided in chapters which follow.

- Remember that offering a variety of acceptable choices can successfully accommodate students' desire for autonomy and control. Very often, simply having a choice of desirable options will be motivation enough.

- Offer positive outcomes for completion of specific, limited tasks. For example, "If you finish this worksheet by the time the show starts . . ." or "If you stay in your seat until this page is completed . . ." is preferable to offering a reward for "being good." Be clear about what you want the student to do as well as what the student will get to do in return.

- Reward accomplishment and cooperation— not obedience or people-pleasing.

- State boundaries in a positive manner: "If you do . . ." "When you finish . . ." or "As soon as . . .," for example. Avoid using threats and negative consequences, or communicating the boundary as a threat of punishment or deprivation: "If you don't . . ." Typically, the implicit conditionality of the availability of the positive outcome is the only hint of negative consequence necessary.

- Keep initial demands small, short and simple, and keep rewards small, frequent and immediate. Raise the hurdles gradually and decrease the reward over time. (For a student like Billy, you might start with an errand after each assignment he completes, working toward finishing the morning's work, and then the full day. Eventually, verbal reinforcement with sporadic opportunities to run an errand will probably be sufficient to maintain the desired behavior.)

- Identify student preferences and what your students perceive as meaningful through dialogue, observation or assessments (such as interest inventories, learning style surveys, sociometric questionnaires or time-on-task assessments). Use this information to plan and select positive outcomes.

- Select only win-win outcomes (those that will not hurt, deprive, or inconvenience someone else).

- Make rewards available on a non-competitive basis. For example, rather than offering copies of the dinosaur word-search puzzle to the first row that's finished, make the puzzle available to every student as soon as he or she is done. (Students who do not finish in class can take the puzzle home to complete.)

- If the positive outcome can only be available to one or two students at a time (such as washing the board or emptying the trash), make sure the other students have access to those privileges at some other times—and that they have other incentives available to them in the meantime.

- Although it would be silly, if not impossible, to hide the fact that we're pleased when our students do what we ask, try to avoid using conditional approval or acceptance as a motivator (for example, routinely asking students to do something because it would make you happy or because you "really like students who . . .").

- Tokens and stickers can be effective, even with older students, if limited to very specific tasks. Avoid offering tokens more than once or twice a day—if that. The management alone can drive you crazy. Think about activities you can offer instead.

- Use rewards that help build responsible behavior and, if possible, reinforce content. Examples might include enrichment activities, structured free time, grading one's own papers, peer helping or tutoring, access to a video, an extra trip to the library, filing or housekeeping chores.

- Activities that involve cooking or food preparation can be valuable motivators and great learning experiences, but avoid offering food—especially sweets—to counter resistance, to reward cooperation or to cheer or pacify a student who is upset.

- If possible, state the boundary once. Avoid nagging and reminding. If the student fails to cooperate, lack of access to the positive outcome is a far more effective consequence than a lecture.

- If a student does not complete the task or does not seem to be motivated by the reward you've offered, consider the following:

  - Can the student do what I've asked him or her to do?

  - Is the student overwhelmed by the amount of work required in the time I've allowed? Do I need to back up a bit?

  - Is the outcome meaningful to the student? What else might work?

  - If the student does not complete the task because she's just having an off day, hold the incentive, if possible, for another time: "Let's try again this afternoon (or tomorrow)." Accept the student, even if her behavior is not acceptable.

Activity

Date_____

Use the chart below or create a similar chart on a separate piece of paper.

In *column one,* list some of the behaviors you ask of your students.

In *column two,* tell what's in it for you for the students to perform each behavior you have listed in column one.

In *column three,* identify the long-term objectives for the students (what you feel the students will get out of performing each behavior in the long run).

In *column four,* identify the immediate payoffs for them (what the students get or perceive as a meaningful outcome when they perform each behavior).

Desirable student behaviors	What's in it for you	Long-term objectives	Immediate payoffs

Now go back and look at column 4. Of the responses you marked, which (or how many):

• were related to teacher approval or avoidance of punishment?

• offered tokens, tickets, stickers or food?

• offered higher-interest activities upon completion of the task?

• offered choices related to the task itself?

• were left blank?

In what ways are your motivational strategies successful:

• in getting your students to do what you want?

• in building responsibility, initiative, and self-management?

• in protecting the emotional climate in your classroom

Activity

Date_____

In what ways have you investigated your students' needs and preferences? If you feel you need more information, take some time out to collect some data before going on with this exercise. You may find some of the following strategies helpful:

- Develop a "fill-in" type inventory, with questions such as "After school I like to _____" "The best thing about school is _____" or "I wish I could take a class in _____" Students can write in answers, dictate answers or interview one another.

- Develop a "check list" type inventory, with a number of hobbies, sports, types of music or TV shows, types of stories, after-school activities and so on. Ask students to check activities they have tried or use the inventory to evaluate their interest in each item, say, on a scale of 1 to 5.

- Administer a commercial interest inventory or learning styles inventory.

- Discuss the students' interests in a formal discussion or values activity.

- Discuss the students' interests informally, as a matter of conversation.

- Discuss the students' interests as perceived by their parents or other teachers.

- Ask your colleagues what has worked for them in motivating particular students.

Activity

Date_____

Design a chart similar to the one below. Plan enough space to devote one line to each student. If you are working with several classes, you may wish to select one class (or group of students) that has been the most difficult to motivate.

Write the students' names in the left-hand column and in the space to the right of their names, jot down topics or activities of interest to each individual. Examples might include: horses, cooking, comic books, Sesame Street, mysteries, drawing, working with Melissa, grading papers, reading to younger students, swimming, airplanes, dancing, playing soccer, watching the Steelers, making jewelry, and so on. Add to this list as you learn more about each student.

Student	Motivators

From this information, what other kinds of activity-type motivators might work in your classroom (which you are willing and able to provide and that your students might find need-fulfilling)?

What changes would you propose in your motivational strategies?

Before completing this exercise, try implementing some of the changes you proposed above for at least three or four weeks.

Describe the impact of the contingencies you implemented on:

- Student cooperation

- Student self-management, responsible behavior:

- Student attitude, self-concept, initiative:

14

Choices and Empowerment

Ms. Cahill, a first-year teacher, was trying to get her seventh-grade math students to warm up with ten subtraction review problems in the first few minutes of class. After three days, the students had used up most of the class period not doing the review work! Ms. Cahill collected barely-completed assignments from only a handful of students and never did manage to get to the new material she intended to teach after the planned 10-minute review activity. Clearly, something was not working. Rather than persist with the aggravating and unproductive pattern that was starting to establish itself, Ms. Cahill decided on a different approach!

The next day, instead of ten problems, the students walked in to find fifteen on the board. Several students groaned at the increase in work. Ms. Cahill assured them that they would not be required to do all fifteen: "Just pick the ten you like best," she offered. Guess what? Before the class let out, every student had completed at least ten problems; amazingly, over half had done all fifteen. The difference was in the power that having a choice offered to the students. The sense of control over which problems to do made the students much less resistant to doing the assignment; simply being allowed to choose was enormously motivating. The next few days were devoted to improving their time, but most

important, a pattern of win-win, cooperation and on-task behavior was starting to emerge.

Early on, the importance of offering choices had become apparent to me, but for an entirely different reason. After the learning center fiasco (described in Chapter 8) that exposed my fifth graders' lack of independent learning skills, I decided to try something simpler. The next morning, I came in armed with two stacks of worksheets, one for math, the other for spelling. I distributed both of them and told the students that both needed to be done before recess, which was an hour away. Immediately, one of the students asked which one they had to do first.

"It doesn't matter," I answered. "Just get them both done."

The class was dumbfounded. They looked uneasily at one another and back to me. "Well, which one *should* we do first."

"I don't care as long as they both get done."

I was amazed at the difficulty the students were having—not only in deciding whether to do math or spelling first—but also in determining how to decide. Faced with a choice between math and spelling and they were lost! OK, I could understand how asking them to self-manage in small groups, do complex activities independently or design their own projects could have overwhelmed them. But how could they possibly be

I was amazed at the difficulty the students were having—not only in deciding whether to do math or spelling first—but also in determining how to decide.

stupefied by two worksheets? These kids were in fifth grade—more than a few for the second or third time. How much more could I back up?

I waited as few students began to eye their papers. One or two actually started working on one sheet or the other. A few, however, appeared stricken. One student was on the verge of tears. I couldn't stand it anymore: I asked her if she wanted me to help her choose (which, incidentally, is a choice in itself). She sniffed and nodded.

"Why don't you do the math assignment?" I suggested.

She hesitated. Almost imperceptibly she answered, "I'd rather do the spelling." (This was another one of those moments when I wondered why I had ever gone into teaching.) Later that day I realized that this trauma was part of her learning the skill of decision making. And I also thought about the number of truly consequential decisions these kids currently faced or would be facing in the not-too-distant future. How could we expect these kids to make intelligent decisions about whether they should finish school, smoke cigarettes, try alcohol, become sexually active or participate in gang-related activities if they were flabbergasted by something as simple as which worksheet to do first?

As if I didn't have enough to cover that year, now I had to teach decision-making, too! I was just beginning to appreciate the fact that learning to choose was a skill as much as any other I would have to teach, one that needed to be taught from the ground up, and practiced and refined along the way. Well, it seemed as good a place as any to begin, and I knew that unless I helped them develop and practice these skills, I'd never see the kind of independent learning behaviors my plans would eventually require.

The practice of offering choices to our students serves several purposes, including reinforcing decision-making skills, addressing the students' needs for input and control in their lives and motivating cooperation through empowerment. This process is quite different than simply telling students what to do. The one-sided power behind a command is in itself likely to provoke resistance. We defuse that power and put the responsibility back on the student when we switch from demanding to giving choices. Although choices employ the process of asking, at no point are we asking the students if they want to do the work or not. Nonetheless, the perception of this option may always exist: Even in a do-it-or-else assignment, there is an implicit occasion for students to say no. Offering choices focuses the students away from yes or no possibilities to two or more different yes options.

Choices also generate commitment from students. Had I simply handed those two papers to the students insisting that they do math first, I would have probably seen some students comply. Either way, the only person committed to the activity would have been me. In offering them a choice, the second they put their pencils to one of the two papers, they had made a commitment.

Offering choices teaches a lot about negotiation and win-win problem solving, too. For example, I had never been terribly creative about the spelling lessons I assigned, and early on had a student register a complaint about the required practice of writing each word five times: "This is stupid!" Donald announced.

OK, so it wasn't my best assignment, but the repetition did seem to help some of the kids. "Well, Donald, the whole idea here is to learn these words. If you have a better way to do it, go ahead."

The next day, Donald came in with a crossword puzzle using nearly all of the 20 words, with definitions he had made up himself. He had also written a story using the entire list and had created a word search puzzle (which I could duplicate, at his behest, for the rest of the class). Of course, he knew these words inside out.

I imagined that if this kind of freedom worked for Donald, it might just spark the rest

---

Learning to choose is a skill that needs to be taught from the ground up, and practiced and refined along the way.

As if I didn't have enough to cover that year, now I had to teach decision-making, too!

Although choices employ the process of asking, at no point are we asking the students if they want to do the work or not.

of the class. So the following week, instead of the traditional no-choice program we had been following, I came in with a list of ten possible activities, including oldies-but-goodies like "Write each word five times" and the various assignments in the book. I also included the ideas Donald had inspired and left Number 10 as "Design your own activity using at least 15 of the words."

Each student was to choose any three of the ten activities in order to receive full credit for their seatwork for the week. These choices allowed the students to accommodate their personal learning needs. Some preferred the security of the sequence we'd always used; others favored the challenge of the newer choices. Others skipped around, trying one set of activities one week, another the next. And Number 10 inspired some projects that were far more complex than anything I would have dreamed up for them to do.

Productivity was up—not just from the kids who had always done well and had become bored in spelling, but also from students who had never done much in this subject. The students were taking more responsibility and initiative for their own learning, and everyone was practicing decision-making. The simple addition of choice accommodated power needs and made the tasks more attractive, bringing us one step closer to that precious goal of learning for learning's sake. (When my top spelling group picked words from the science unit to add to their list, I was delighted and a bit surprised when they selected—and learned—words like "meteorologist" and "brontosaurus" instead of "wind" or "dirt.") Perhaps, even more important, however, was the opportunity to model flexibility and reinforce win-win priorities: "Your needs (for freedom and creativity) are important and so are mine (for your performance and learning). We can both get what we want without a power struggle."

Well-constructed choices have two components: options that satisfy the students' need for control, and limits that satisfy their need for structure. Sending my fifth graders to work independently in groups in centers around the room did not provide adequate structure. They had become used to teachers making all the decisions for them and had lost their confidence, if not their ability, to manage on their own. I've seen preschoolers far less overwhelmed by a room full of games and activities when they were asked to select something to do. Yet give high school students a choice of two novels to read and some of them will stare at you like deer caught in your headlights, paralyzed at the prospect of having to decide.

Even by second or third grade, many kids who, in kindergarten, would automatically go for a mop or a rag to clean up a spill, will freeze after knocking something over and simply wait to get yelled at! It doesn't take long for some children to learn that they are not well served by thinking, deciding or initiating in a school setting. Lack of practice or safety create significant obstacles to the development of these important skills.

One of my teaching interns and I were watching in amazement as a number of her 7-year-olds evaluated one paper after another, over and over again, trying to determine which two (of three) activities they wanted to do. She finally realized that even this simple choice lacked the structure her students needed at that point. She gave them "until the big hand is on the three" to decide; after that it was her choice. (If they didn't get what they wanted today, "We'll try again tomorrow," she'd tell them.)

Many new teachers in particular, are so excited about teaching that we want to try out every exciting plan and idea we've devised, seen or read about the moment we're in front of a group of children. This was certainly true in my case, where I was also hoping to eliminate resistance, indifference and a variety of disruptive student behaviors with activities creative and interesting enough to hold their attention. Experienced or intuitive teachers know the value of starting small in a highly

Well-constructed choices have two components: options that satisfy the students' need for control, and limits that satisfy their need for structure.

It doesn't take long for some children to learn that they are not well served by thinking, deciding or initiating in a school setting.

structured environment and then relaxing the structure gradually as students develop and demonstrate learning and decision-making skills. A little initial restraint can go a long way; we'll have plenty of chances to offer greater challenges to their self-management as they build up to them.

In the example, "Decide which of two worksheets to do first," the students control the sequence, while the teacher controls the tasks. True, there isn't much flexibility here, but this type of choice is a perfect starting point for students who have not had much of a chance to develop decision-making skills. Other simple choices might propose that the students decide which two worksheets out of three to do, what color paper to use for an art project or whether they want to display their projects or take them home.

Within the limits of what we determine to be negotiable, we can usually find all sorts of opportunities to offer choices to our students.

As students build confidence in their decision-making capabilities, we can ease up on the limits, offer more and increasingly complex options. We might ask them to decide whether they'd prefer practicing a math skill by doing a page in the book, a cross-number puzzle or a skill card in a commercial kit. They might choose how to arrange certain materials in a display, select a topic and design for a new bulletin board or visit a learning center during independent work time. As they progress, they might decide whether to present a report in written, drawn, constructed, performed or video format.

Offering choices in no way undermines the authority relationship, in fact if anything, it enhances the kind of cooperation that can occur in a win-win power dynamic.

Eventually, we can begin giving students options that demand even higher levels of self-management and responsibility: asking them to select a work space for a given period of time, decide when they're ready to rejoin a group, or determine whether they need more practice on a particular skill. One teacher offered a restless bunch of second graders a choice between a one-minute break immediately or a five-minute break when they finished the lesson in ten minutes.

Only in a win-lose classroom does empowering students mean disempowering teachers.

Within the limits of what we determine to be negotiable, we can usually find all sorts of

opportunities to offer choices to our students. And as the limits expand and options increase in number and complexity, students gain a stake, not only in the overall climate of the classroom, but in their own learning and personal growth as well.

But even Ms. Cahill had some concerns about this strategy, successful as it was. "Does the practice of offering choices cause children to expect a choice about everything?" she wondered. "By concentrating on what's in it for them am I teaching them to be selfish? Am I putting them in charge?"

In a way, we are putting children in charge—autonomy encourages commitment and the greater the buy-in, the more cooperation we can typically anticipate. But of what are the students actually in charge? They're not controlling the classroom, and they're certainly not in charge of us. They're simply in charge of which ten problems they're going to do on a particular page or how they're going to demonstrate their understanding of a particular concept. Offering choices in no way undermines the authority relationship, in fact if anything, it enhances the kind of cooperation that can occur in a win-win power dynamic. Only in a win-lose classroom does empowering students mean disempowering teachers. The adult still decides what is and is not negotiable. Remember, Ms. Cahill did not ask the students to choose whether they wanted to do math or not; she simply found a way to offer the students some input in the situation. There will always be a number of non-negotiable factors in our classrooms, as in life. Our jobs in creating win-win interactions, involve determining what, indeed, is negotiable and offering choices whenever possible in those situations and within limits that work on behalf of everyone concerned.

As to the issue of selfishness: the win-win classroom certainly fosters self-care—meeting one's own needs without hurting, disturbing or depriving anyone else. This is very different from a self-centered (or selfish) attitude which either ignores or disregards the needs of others. Perhaps the potential to enhance our students' self-caring capabilities is the best reason for offering choices and building decision-making mastery in the first place. For self-care is a bottom-line character skill that enables children to act in their own best interests, with consideration and concern for others, when there isn't an adult around to tell them what to do.

Guidelines for Offering Choices

- Choices build responsibility and commitment, and communicate the teacher's respect for students' needs and preferences.

- Choices, like boundaries, are motivational tools that encourage cooperation through input and empowerment. Offer choices in the absence of desirable student behavior, to *encourage* the student to perform a particular behavior he is not currently demonstrating.

- Choices can also help prevent disruptive behaviors, however other strategies will be suggested for intervening negative behavior or reinforcing performance, growth and existing positive behavior.

- Present available options in a positive manner. Be careful that the choice doesn't end up spoken as "do it or else."

- Be honest. Make sure that all options you offer are acceptable. Avoid setting the students up to people-please by choosing the right option or reading your mind. Make sure there are no wrong choices: If you don't want the student to choose something, don't make it an option. (For example, if you want them to do the outline first, offer sequence options about the other activities—after the outline is finished.)

- Make sure the choices you offer are clear and specific. Asking a child to "Select a meaningful learning activity," leaves you open for some pretty broad interpretations. Instead, define choices with clearly-stated limits. "Select one meaningful learning activity from the five on the board" is much easier for the student to understand—and perform successfully.

- Start simple. If a student is having difficulty making decisions, it may be that there are too many options or that the limits are too broad or unclear.

- If a student is having difficulty with even a simple choice, add another limit if necessary, by asking him to choose within a certain amount of time (after which you get to help him choose). Be patient. Some young students and well-conditioned order-takers need time and practice to develop confidence in their ability to choose.

- Increase options as the students can handle them, either by widening the range of choices you offer or by making the options more complex.

- Depending on your goals, schedule and resources, you might leave room for students to change their minds if they are disappointed with a choice they've made. If time and management require the student to make a choice and stick with it, make that clear when you present the available options. Reassure the students that they can "try again later (or tomorrow or next week)."

- As they become more capable, encourage the students to participate in setting up choices (or negotiate an alternative assignment, for example) whenever possible. Clear limits are especially important in such cases; you might also want to suggest that they present their ideas to you for a final OK before they act.

- If students suggest a choice that you think is inappropriate, tell them your concerns and ask if they can come up with another idea. (Stating "That won't work for me," is a terrific way to get this message across without attacking the student.) Reiterate your criteria if necessary. If something is just plain non-negotiable, say so, but help the student look for acceptable options available within those limits.

Activity

Date_____

Use the chart below or create a similar chart on a separate piece of paper to list the kinds of choices that are available to students in your classroom. Clarify the options you offer by describing the choices in the left-hand column and the limits on the right. (If you aren't offering many choices in your learning environment, use this space to describe some choices you could offer. Take a few weeks to try out some of the choices before coming back to complete the other questions.)

Choices	Limits

How many of the choices you offer relate to:

____ time or sequence (order of activities, when the students can do the work)?

____ location (where in the school or classroom the student can work on the activity)?

____ social preferences (choosing to work with someone, selecting a partner, working alone)?

____ content (choosing their own topics, selecting activities or topics from a given list, designing own projects)?

____ medium of presentation (oral, written, drawn, using computers, audio or video equipment)?

____ other?

In what ways have your students had difficulty making decisions?

What have you done or what are you doing to remedy those difficulties?

In what ways are the choices helping:

- to establish a win-win classroom environment (and teacher-student relationship?)

- to generate cooperation and productivity?

- to build responsibility, self-management, empowerment and independence?

- to develop decision-making and problem-solving skills?

- to encourage win-win behaviors such as flexibility and negotiation?

- to encourage learning for learning's sake?

What other choices could you offer your students?

15

Maintaining Positive Behaviors

My first year of teaching seemed, at times, to be more of a laboratory to discover what *doesn't* work in a classroom than anything else. Over one weekend early in the year, I channeled my creativity and frustration into developing a system of giving out tokens for what I considered good behavior. I collected all sorts of "prizes" to give out as awards—colored pencils, erasers, keychains, inexpensive games or toys, even candy. I put a price tag on each one and made up about a million little construction-paper "tickets," which I planned to distribute throughout the week and then have a "shopping" period during which the kids could exchange their tickets for prizes. In my desperation, it seemed like a good idea at the time.

I'd give an assignment and walk around the classroom dispensing tickets to kids who were on task, kids who finished their work, kids who weren't disrupting. They got tickets for turning in homework, for getting quiet, for being prepared, for being on time. Want to guess how much teaching I did that week?

Not only that, but this system seemed to create its own set of disruptions: tears over lost tickets, accusations and fights about stolen tickets and lessons interrupted with questions about prizes, purchasing or earning extra tickets. The clincher came a few days later when I asked them, at the end of the day, to settle down for dismissal and someone queried: "Are we gonna get a ticket?"

"Enough!" I thought—and into the trash went all the tickets and, for the moment, any shred of hope or optimism I might have had left.

Token reinforcement has its place and I've seen teachers use tokens successfully, particularly when used infrequently, when it was conceivable that any student in the class could earn the token (and not just the first or the best) and when the criteria for receiving these tokens were very specific. Giving stickers, stars or points, for example, for a special project or completion of a particular assignment, for progress on a checklist or even just for fun can be quite useful at times, as long as it doesn't drive you—or your students—to distraction. However management of token systems can be a real nightmare and most often verbal or activity reinforcement are far more effective.

There has been a great deal of misuse and misunderstanding of the concept of positive reinforcement. Throughout the past several decades, teacher education programs that addressed discipline issues at all have usually focused on using praise, either to motivate or reinforce cooperative behavior. This emphasis probably grew out of the intention to discourage negative teacher behaviors, such as yelling and criticizing. Unfortunately, the times that teachers are inspired to yell and criticize generally are not conducive to using positive reinforcement effectively. Furthermore, the processes of motivation and reinforcement are

The processes of motivation and reinforcement are not interchangeable.

Positive feedback can come in the form of a high grade, a sticker on a paper, a positive comment written in a margin, an earned activity or privilege, or a nod, smile, wink or touch from the teacher. As long as it follows the cooperative behavior and is meaningful to the student, it works as a reinforcer.

not interchangeable: Teachers who attempt to use reinforcing techniques to motivate cooperation will often run into (or create) other problems in their relationships with students.

I became aware of the frequent misapplication and misunderstanding of this technique when I began observing beginning teachers in their classrooms. During the first week of school, I walked into a classroom to see Ms. Harding standing in front of the room, trying to get her 25 first-graders settled down so she could continue with her lesson. Despite her firm and patient requests, the students were out of their seats, wrestling on the rug, fighting over toys, throwing game pieces and books across the room or running through the language center. Ms. Harding began to feel the panic of being out of control, and frantically thought over the tricks she'd learned in student teaching. She managed to focus on the one student who was still, thankfully, in his seat.

"I *like* the way Bobby is sitting," she announced.

With that, Bobby perked up and sat at attention, beaming. Although one or two other students stopped to look at Bobby, the chaos continued.

Ms. Harding tried again. "I *really* like the way Bobby is sitting."

Bobby sat up even straighter, folded his hands and smiled proudly. Again, the rest of the class was barely distracted from their fun. And as Ms. Harding continued, louder and more intense in her praise for Bobby, his behavior got better and better while the rest of the class continued to fall apart. Ms. Harding was literally saved by the lunch bell, which got the students' attention long enough for her to furiously proclaim that unless they all took their seats that instant, they would never leave that room again!

So much for positive reinforcement, she thought.

Too bad. Because positive reinforcement does work (remember the dancing chickens of Ed Psych 101?). The technique is logical and well-founded. Why, then, does it seem to lose

so much in its translation to the human classroom?

Part of the problem seems to be in the use of the reinforcer, which, in broad terms, can be described as a device—whether word, object or deed—that will increase the likelihood of the student repeating or continuing a particular behavior. In order for a reinforcer to work, it must *follow* the desired behavior, which means that the student has to somehow initiate the behavior. In other words, we can't reinforce a student's handwriting if she hasn't written anything, and we can't reinforce her quiet behavior if she won't clam up.

Positive reinforcement encourages the student to continue or repeat a particular existing behavior. Frustration and disillusionment with the technique can occur when teachers attempt to use reinforcement to evoke (or motivate) a desired behavior that does not yet exist. Ms. Harding discovered this problem when she found that the reinforcer (her praise) had a positive effect only on the student she reinforced. Praising Bobby did not inspire the other students to settle down and imitate him.

When I share this story, many teachers, especially those working with younger children, argue that very often, praising Bobby is quite effective in getting Susie to sit down. True. In those instances, this strategy might satisfy the teacher's immediate objectives, but let's take a look at how this process works—and what it can cost.

Positive feedback can come in the form of a high grade, a sticker on a paper, a positive comment written in a margin, an earned activity or privilege, or a nod, smile, wink or touch from the teacher. As long as it *follows* the cooperative behavior and is meaningful to the student, it works as a reinforcer. Now certain reinforcers, such as praise, are more likely than others to communicate conditional teacher approval. When these reinforcers work, they do so because they appeal to a basic human need to feel valued and worthwhile. Since many of our students value our approval, and since praise is such a familiar factory-era motivator, we are often tempted to use praise, as both a motivator and reinforcer. Although usually delivered with sincere intentions, praise does have its price.

When Ms. Harding said, "I like the way Bobby is sitting," she was broadcasting a judgment: Bobby's sitting was good and teacher-pleasing; the behavior of the rest of the class, clearly, was not. By praising Bobby, she communicated to the others, "If you act like him, you too will be good and please the teacher, too." This is not to advise against acknowledging our preferences to our students—in fact, it would be pretty hard to mask what pleases us and what doesn't. But such deliberate praise tends to overemphasize the pleasure we take in our students' cooperation. Using "I like . . ." as a positive judgment of a student's behavior, encourages the student to be good simply to make us happy and implies a lack of worth and acceptance when he or she does not.

Sound familiar? Welcome back to building obedience and teacher-pleasing. Sure, Susie will sit down when I praise Bobby: she wants me to like her too. It sounds efficient, and with some young or teacher-dependent children it can be. But such judgments can build dependence on external approval for self-esteem, and can actually interfere with the development of responsibility and self-management. Had Ms. Harding simply wanted to reinforce Bobby's behavior—for Bobby's sake—she could have simply recognized how quickly he got quiet or even the fact that he was ready. And she could have done it very quietly. The fact that she announced her approval of one student to the rest of the class is a good indication of her desire to manipulate the behavior of the other students with her praise.

Praise has other drawbacks. When we praise one student to try to evoke performance or cooperation from others, the negative implications are obvious—especially to the others. In this case, praise of Bobby is criticism of anyone who isn't acting (sitting) like Bobby.

This implicit criticism also occurs when an unrelated event or situation is praised: "Your brother was such a good student" or "But your other papers were so neat." Announcing to the class that "José wrote the best story in the class" simply informs everyone that they aren't quite up to José's talents. (Do we really want everybody to write like José, even if he is great?) This tendency to reinforce and promote uniformity is another holdover from industrial-age thinking. Such attempts at shame and manipulation promote win-lose competitiveness, discouragement and "I can't" attitudes.

Even among the students receiving praise, the technique can create problems. For one thing, praise reinforces an externally-referenced student self-concept and a dependence on someone else for one's feelings of self-worth. After a while, even the absence of praise can be perceived as a criticism.

Second, not all students are comfortable being singled out. Our approval is only effective as long as it's important to our students. However, with dependent students, the need for teacher approval often competes with their need for peer approval. Sometimes even typically cooperative students, feeling pressured or embarrassed, respond to praise with disruption or withdrawal. (How long before Bobby realized that the other kids were having a whole lot more fun than he was?) And praise can seem redundant to non-dependent students who did what was asked because they simply wanted to do the task or because resistance never existed in the first place.

Often implicit in praise is the expectation that once demonstrated, there is no reason for the behavior to diminish or discontinue. We might communicate this expectation subtly ("See, I knew you could do it!"), directly ("Why can't all your papers look this good?") or even sarcastically ("Well, it's about time!"). If our praise even remotely suggests "and you'd better keep it up," it may actually have the opposite effect.

Children can be extremely sensitive to our motives, whether or not we're clear on them

Although usually delivered with sincere intentions, praise does have its price.

Using "I like . . ." as a positive judgment of a student's behavior, encourages the student to be good simply to make us happy.

Praise reinforces an externally-referenced student self-concept and a dependence on someone else for one's feelings of self-worth.

ourselves. Even very young children can detect insincerity and manipulation. One kindergarten teacher reported having a student ball up a paper she had just gushed over. "She just says that to get you to be good," she heard him tell his friend.

If we tell our students that they're smart, for example, in order to get them to act smart, they'll see right through our maneuvers. Such flattery does not build self-esteem or commitment, regardless of the sincerity of our intentions. A student who doesn't feel smart will certainly hear our praise with suspicion, believing either that we just don't understand or that we must not be so smart ourselves. That student might even attempt to prove that we don't know what we're talking about. Either way, our endeavors will probably be more successful at eroding trust than anything else.

The fact that praise sounds so positive has led many a teacher to believe that these kinds of statements held the key to a students' self-concept. True, hearing nice things and being appreciated does feel good if the person communicating those feelings means anything at all to us. And while appreciation and recognition can support a well-grounded, highly-internalized sense of self-worth, they do not create self-worth. Self-esteem does not mean "I am great because my teacher thinks I'm great." If we can only feel adequate and worthwhile when we're receiving praise, what happens when the person upon whose praise we depend forgets to appreciate us? And what, heaven forbid, if we make a mistake or have a bad day?

Self-esteem is an inside job, but we, as educators, can certainly contribute to its development. Self-esteem requires the satisfaction of lower-level needs, such as belonging, success and, very importantly, empowerment. If we respect the students' need for control and offer them opportunities to make decisions and experience the outcomes of their choosing, we are building self-esteem. If we hold students accountable for their behavior without compromising their safety, we are

building self-esteem. If we provide a success-oriented structure in which students are challenged at a level at which they can achieve, we are building self-esteem.

In other words, if we are committed to the principles of a win-win classroom, we create an environment in which self-esteem can emerge and develop. However, the operant word is *self*. If a genuine sense of worth does not come from the student's self, positive external messages will be superficial and fragile at best.

Despite all these cautions, positive verbal reinforcement can be a legitimate and highly effective tool in a 21st century classroom. In addition to strengthening desirable student behavior, well-constructed reinforcing statements allow us to focus on the positive, communicate respect for the child's efforts and personal needs, help the child develop internalized management and motivational capabilities and encourage an "I can" attitude. And this can all happen without building a dependence on outside approval or reinforcing people-pleasing.

To reach this goal, we switch to recognition statements, which offer a healthy alternative to praise or "I like the way . . . ." Recognition statements use a two-step process to strengthen existing positive behavior. For the first step, we describe the behavior. For the second, we tell the students how their cooperation pays off for them.

Consider the following examples: "I see you got all the materials in this center put away. Now you can go to lunch." "Super! You're all caught up now. Looks like you'll be eligible to play this Saturday!" Statements like these allow us to see how recognition differs from praise in several ways that are significant to the goals and objectives of a win-win authority relationship. For example, praise typically connects the worth of the student to the student's behavior, or the value of the student's behavior to the teacher: "You're so good! You remembered your library book," or "I'm so happy when you come prepared." Recognition statements, on the other hand, connect the student's behavior to positive outcomes that benefit the student:

Self-esteem does not mean "I am great because my teacher thinks I'm great."

If we respect the students' need for control and offer them opportunities to make decisions and experience the outcomes of their choosing, we are building self-esteem.

If we are committed to the principles of a win-win classroom, we create an environment in which self-esteem can emerge and develop.

"You remembered your library book! Now you can take another one home." Neither the worth of the student nor the teacher's reactions are a factor here.

In addition, praise tends to be stated in general terms: "You were good today." Recognition tends to be more specific: "You put all the art materials away before you left the center." Recognition is also more descriptive and less judgmental than praise. For example, instead of stating "I like the way you remembered your library book," we can say, "I see you remembered your library book." Even "Look at how neat your handwriting has gotten!" is preferable to "I like the way your handwriting has improved," if your goals include reducing students' dependence on teacher approval. Recognition can be expressed with fervor and excitement and still not emphasize the teacher's needs, values or judgments.

When recognition uses valuing words, the value is connected to the performance or achievement, not the person: "The ending to the story was really exciting," or "You're making great progress in spelling." Recognition can also express appreciation: "You really added a lot to our discussion," "Nice try," or "My, you really worked hard today!" Even short, non-descriptive comments like "Great!" or "I agree," communicate appreciation for the value of the child's contribution without emphasizing the benefit to the teacher.

These examples may sound far more impersonal or detached than they actually are. (I once had a graduate student seriously misinterpret my cautions against using conditional approval. The day after our class, she ran up to me saying, "Boy, am I glad I'm in this class. I almost gave someone a compliment yesterday!") Recognition has its own power without connecting the student's worth or ability to please to the student's behavior. Recognition validates behavior without judging worth or expressing conditional approval. In a win-win environment, we can get away with an occasional outburst of praise

and we are certainly free to be generous with compliments, provided that our sentiments are genuine, spontaneous and not designed to influence or manipulate behavior. It's entirely reasonable and legitimate to tell a student he looks great in a certain outfit, that we missed her when she was absent or that we're just glad that they are in our class. In a non-conflict setting, when we have no attachment to particular outcomes and no agenda other than the desire to share a particular sentiment, such feelings can communicate a great deal of respect and appreciation for a student and his or her achievements.

The second part of the recognition statement, connecting the performance or cooperation to the positive outcome, will challenge us to differentiate between our needs and those of our students. Our own needs are almost always tied to the requests we make. We all want our students to write neatly so that we'll be able to read their work. We want them to put the materials away so that we won't be stuck with a mess. But if students cooperate simply because of what's in it for us, they're being teacher-pleasers. When we reinforce their cooperation by linking it to how it pays off for us—even if their cooperation is self-motivated—we reinforce obedience and devalue their internal motivation.

What we really want to reinforce is the connection between the students' behavior and what's in it for them: "You put all your materials away. Now you can go to lunch." This second sentence, "Now you can go to lunch," goes beyond simply acknowledging the behavior. Adding this step verbally reinforces the personal empowerment of being able to positively impact one's own life. In other words, having access to something the student wants is the result of something the student did. Restating what's in it for them after they have completed a behavior, connecting the benefits of their cooperation specifically to the choices they have made, strengthens personal responsibility and win-win interaction patterns.

Recognition statements, on the other hand, connect the student's behavior to positive outcomes that benefit the student.

When we reinforce cooperation by linking it to how it pays off for us—even if a student's cooperation is self-motivated—we reinforce obedience and devalue their internal motivation.

Once we've used a boundary to establish the connection between what we want and what the students want, we can simply revert to the language we used to motivate when we wish to reinforce their cooperation.

In order for our statements to actually reinforce, they must have value and make sense to our students.

This is where we begin to appreciate the value of using boundaries instead of rules. When we promise positive outcomes that are meaningful to the student, we motivate the behavior we want: "As soon as you finish the assignments in your folder (meaning that the work is complete and legible, or however else you choose to define "finished"), you can work at one of the enrichment centers." Once we've used a boundary to establish the connection between what we want and what the students want, we can simply revert to the language we used to motivate when we wish to reinforce their cooperation: "Way to go! You finished all your assignments. Now you can work at an enrichment center."

As with motivators and rewards, it's easy to trip over personal values and preferences, projecting what's important to us and assuming that the same things have similar meaning to the students. As innocent as they may seem, statements such as "You must be proud" or "I'll bet you're happy now," presume that a student feels a certain way, even though the experience may hold an entirely different meaning or value to her. Instead of suggesting how a student should or must feel, we can acknowledge our observations ("You're obviously excited about this" or "You seem pleased."), ask students how they feel or simply recognize the accomplishment ("You worked very hard on this!"). And we can support their accomplishment by tying it in with something concrete and beneficial: "Now you can go on to the next level" or "Now you can type it up on the computer."

We also need to be careful that we don't connect the students' positive behavior to something they perceive as negative. (How would you feel if I recognized the great job you did cleaning my bathroom by saying, "Now that you're finished, you can iron!"?) In order for our statements to actually reinforce, they must have value and make sense to our students. Connections that promise "Now people will think you're neat" or "Now you can help grade papers" may not be exactly punitive, but a child who doesn't need to be perceived as

neat or one who has no interest in grading papers will probably shrug in response. "That will help you get into the college of your choice" will only be meaningful to a kid who is striving for that goal, perceives it as accessible in some way and, in many instances, is close enough to achieve it.

The best verbal reinforcers are those tied into the actual (or realistically possible) experiences of our students. For example, consider the following statement: "You remembered to put the caps back on the markers. Now they won't be dried out when you go to use them tomorrow." These comments will have a greater impact on a child who has actually tried to write with a dried-out marker than one who never has. Still, the reinforcer maintains its validity in the fact that it is directly connected to the benefits to the student; even if the student can't imagine the negative consequences, we're still reinforcing the cause-and-effect nature of his or her behavior.

If the positive outcome of a student's behavior is too remote or abstract, we can still reinforce the behavior by connecting it, as we did in setting up our boundaries, to something more immediate and concrete. For example, learning to regroup in addition problems has a number of positive outcomes, but most of them are related to being able to do something more complex in math at some point in the future. When a child experiences a breakthrough in this process, it may be quite reassuring to tell him that now he'll have an easier time with the next lesson, but we will probably see an even more powerful effect by stating, "Now that you understand this skill, you can work with these new math puzzles and games (which will allow him to practice his recent accomplishment)."

Regardless of the values of verbal reinforcement, there is probably no reinforcement for cooperation stronger than experiencing the positive outcomes our boundaries promise. The privilege of helping in the kindergarten, going on to the next lesson, getting to work on an enrichment puzzle, playing a game or going out for recess when students finish their work builds commitment and good work habits. So does being able to continue to listen to music, hear the story, sit on the floor or work with a friend as long as their behavior reflects the requirements previously established. The actual positive experience increases the likelihood that their cooperation will continue and, over time, become habituated and internalized. It strengthens the students' sense of personal power and their ability to make their lives "work." Verbal reinforcement can provide additional support even in cases in which the student has access to a tangible reward or privilege. At the completion of the task or even along the way, verbal reinforcement can emphasize the value of the positive behavior as well as the connection between cooperation and payoff, but it is usually the actual experience of an earned privilege or reward that carries the most weight.

And yet, despite the efficacy of correctly used positive reinforcement, our factory-era training can get in the way. Much as there is some resistance to motivating children, there is often a similar reluctance to reinforce with rewarding activities or privileges. We're concerned that children will expect something for everything they do. Well, of course they will! Just like adults! The desire for a payoff is built into the experience of being human, not something we "teach" with reinforcers. Remember that there is no such thing as unmotivated behavior. Experiencing a rewarding outcome does not teach kids to expect rewards any more than eating teaches them to be hungry.

The use of reinforcers and recognition statements can present a challenge to teachers at all grade levels. Elementary or preschool teachers typically face a struggle with changing praising patterns and the habit of relying on "I like the way . . ." And the need for recognition and reinforcement seems to be harder to sell to some secondary teachers who may equate reinforcement with gushy praise. But this need applies to students of all ages and may be even more effective in the upper grades, where some students are so starved for any type of positive exchange with meaningful adults in their lives that even the simplest recognition can go a long, long way.

The last two chapters talked about setting boundaries and offering choices to elicit or motivate desired behaviors that did not yet exist. Positive reinforcement is what we rely on once those behaviors occur. The boundaries that motivated the cooperative behavior provide the reinforcers (positive outcomes) once the cooperative behavior occurs. In other words, the possibility to run an errand may have motivated Billy to do his work; once the work was done, experiencing the actual privilege reinforced his cooperation. This reinforcement increases the probability that the behavior will recur, so long as it the reinforcer is need-fulfilling and available within a reasonable amount of time after the performance of the desirable behavior.

The purpose of reinforcement is maintaining the desired behavior. Even when we occasionally need to tie the behavior to an outcome that is not inherent in the task itself ("Since you finished and corrected your work early today, you can take this note around to the other teachers if you'd like."), we are still increasing the likelihood that the desired behavior will recur. Perhaps along the way the desired behavior will become more automatic. Perhaps the students will even learn to love what we're asking them to do. But either way, we are strengthening our relationships with our students, wearing down the need for resistance or defiance and building the kind of classroom environment in which learning can occur and one that everyone can truly enjoy.

At the completion of the task or even along the way, verbal reinforcement can emphasize the value of the positive behavior as well as the connection between cooperation and payoff, but it is usually the actual experience of an earned privilege or reward that carries the most weight.

Experiencing a rewarding outcome does not teach kids to expect rewards any more than eating teaches them to be hungry.

Guidelines for Reinforcing Positive Behavior

- Use positive reinforcement—verbal or non-verbal (interactive, token or activity)—to acknowledge and strengthen already-existing behaviors. Avoid attempting to use reinforcement before the desired behavior has occurred. (Strategies to encourage the student to initiate a desired behavior or to intervene a disruptive behavior are presented in other chapters.)

- Watch for a tendency to use praise to help a student solve a problem or feel good about himself. Flattery can appear manipulative even to a young or needy student. Such messages are superficial at best and will not contribute to the student's genuine sense of self-worth.

- Avoid using teacher approval as a means of reinforcing desired behavior. Learn to distinguish between reinforcers intended to maintain a particular student behavior and genuine expressions of appreciation, affection or enjoyment of your students. In a win-win classroom, behaviors such as a smile, touch, nod or wink—which obviously communicate the fact that the teacher is pleased—are not used as expressions of conditional approval or caring. Although they may sometimes be used as reinforcers, such behaviors may also appear randomly, regardless of the student's performance or behavior, as expressions of appreciation or affection.

- Phrase reinforcements as an affirmation or acknowledgement of a behavior the student has demonstrated and the positive consequences now available (not as "if . . . then" statements, which are more useful for *motivating* behavior that has not yet been demonstrated). Reinforcements may be effectively communicated in either oral or written form.

- To reinforce a desirable behavior, *first describe the behavior that took place.* Be specific and concrete and avoid making judgments about the behavior or the worth of the student.

- Whenever possible, *attach a comment that connects the immediate benefits of the student's behavior to the student.* (Occasionally, it may be appropriate to state the positive outcomes in terms of their benefits to the group.) Focus on the payoff for the student, making sure the outcome is positive and meaningful. Avoid projecting your own feelings and values, which may or may not be relevant to those of the student, or suggesting how the student should feel.

- Look for the positive. You can almost always find something to recognize in any performance. Reinforce what was done right and work to correct or improve the rest.

- Perhaps because of the rigidity of roles during the factory-era, there was a tendency for teachers to recognize certain behaviors in boys (such as strength, mechanical skill, and ability in math and the sciences) more frequently than girls (who are more often reinforced for neatness, creativity, attractiveness, and writing and artistic abilities). In recognizing students, be aware of any tendencies to promote stereotypes.

Activity

Date_____

Use the chart below or create a similar chart on a separate piece of paper.

In *column one,* identify five specific "desired behaviors"—that is, behaviors you want your students to exhibit.

In *column two,* imagine that the student has just demonstrated the desired behaviors you identified in column one. Write a recognition statement you might use to acknowledge the student's cooperation, one that describes what the student has done (without judging the value of the behavior or the student).

In *column three,* write a statement that connects the student's cooperation to a positive outcome (what's in it for the student).

Desired Behavior	Recognition Statement	
	Description of Behavior	Payoff for Student (Positive Outcome)

Activity

Date_____

Identify several positive student behaviors you acknowledged (after the behaviors were demonstrated) during the past two or three days:* How specific were your recognition statements in describing the desired behavior?

How successful were you in avoiding communicating personal judgments and teacher approval?

How successful were you in avoiding attempts to use praise of one student to elicit a cooperative behavior from another?

How successful were you in avoiding attempts to use praise to dismiss a student's problem or make him feel better?

Describe some of the instances in which you were able to connect the student's behavior to the positive outcomes of his behavior:

How well were you able to focus on (and communicate) the immediate benefits to the student?

In what ways are you satisfied with the reinforcement strategies you currently use?

In what ways would you like to change or expand these strategies?

---

*You may want to tape record a lesson or ask a colleague to observe. In either case, the object of this activity is to identify specific language: what you say to recognize positive behavior and also how you connect it to the positive consequences to the student.

16

Encouraging Independence and Problem Solving

How many times, in the course of your day, do you find a student at your elbow with some problem or another: "What are we supposed to do?" "My dog ate my homework." "Alex is bothering me." "I can't find the scissors."

Our students' lives can seem pretty cluttered at times with problems that may or may not require our help. These interactions can be rather distracting: they eat up a lot of valuable instructional time even though they can usually be resolved without our intervention. Yet students have a number of reasons for wanting to share their problems with us.

Sometimes students share just for the sake of sharing and the social contact and conversation the interaction can offer. The student may not be seeking solutions as much as acknowledgement and validation. But sharing problems, especially when it involves whining or complaining, can also be a means of getting attention, killing time or dumping responsibility for something students don't want to resolve. In many cases, kids of all ages—especially good "order takers"—come to us because they honestly feel incapable or powerless in facing even the simplest dilemma.

A student experiencing a crisis does need our help. Certain traumas, such as abuse,

neglect, divorce or death, probably require more support than most classroom teachers are able to provide. Clearly, these instances should be referred for outside intervention, although our support and understanding can be very reassuring in the meantime.*

Fortunately, however, most of the crises affecting our students on a day-to-day basis are more likely to involve complaints like, "She looked at me!" or "Somebody stole my pencil." When students bring problems to the classroom and are unable or unwilling to solve them on their own, their problems can very quickly become our problem. For our mental health and the needs of the other students, we need to try to prevent student problems from interfering with teaching, learning and the overall operations of the classroom. How do we put the responsibility for students' problems back on their shoulders—without ignoring or abandoning them—when these problems do come up?

Teacher dependence and a student's need for attention can become a never-ending distraction. Even our deepest desire to be needed can be sapped by the constancy of a train of students pulling on our sleeves. As a teacher in a multi-age (grades 1–3) classroom, Mr. Marshall was plagued by one student he

How do we put the responsibility for students' problems back on their shoulders— without ignoring or abandoning them—when problems do come up?

Even our deepest desire to be needed can be sapped by the constancy of a train of students pulling on our sleeves.

---

*Kendall Johnson's book *Trauma in the Lives of Children* (Alameda, CA: Hunter House Publishing, 1989) and *Helping Children Cope with the Loss of a Loved One* by William Kroen (Minneapolis: Free Spirit Publishing, 1996) provide some outstanding guidelines for helping students deal with crisis and traumatic events in their lives.

Now, while the student's need for attention is certainly the student's problem, his inability to meet that need without continually disrupting his teacher invites joint ownership.

Mr. Marshall came up with a win-win solution—a boundary that not only acknowledged the student's need for his time, help and attention, but also set limits that would protect the teacher's own needs as well.

privately dubbed his "shadow." No matter where Mr. Marshall went—in or out of the classroom—it seemed that Shadow was never far behind. Shadow didn't need much time; he was just always there. One day, his teacher decided to keep a tab on the number of times Shadow "needed" him; by lunchtime the number of interruptions was nearly four dozen!

Now, while the student's need for attention is certainly the student's problem, his inability to meet that need without continually disrupting his teacher invites joint ownership. Had Mr. Marshall been exclusively concerned with his own needs, he might have been able to "win" by isolating the student in some way. Had his concerns been only for the student's needs, Mr. Marshall could have completely relinquished his own requirements for privacy and time with other students to devote his attention to Shadow. But Mr. Marshall came up with a win-win solution—a boundary that not only acknowledged the student's need for his time, help and attention, but also set limits that would protect the teacher's own needs as well. (He also contacted Shadow's parents to discuss his intentions.)

He approached Shadow with five paper clips and a plan: "I understand that you need to talk to me during the day and I really enjoy visiting with you. And you know, sometimes I spend so much time with you that I don't get to talk to the other students and I don't get my work done. What I'd like to do is to give you these five paper clips. Put them on your belt, OK?

"Now whenever you want to talk to me, it'll cost you one paper clip. These need to last until recess; I'll give you five more afterwards to last until lunch and more for the afternoon. As long as you have a paper clip, I'll be happy to take the time out to talk to you. Once the clips are gone, you'll have to wait until after recess to get some more."

Of course, on the first go-round, it didn't take too long for the paper clips to disappear; Mr. Marshall knew it would be a very long time until recess came, and that his follow-through

during that stretch would be essential. Being out of paper clips didn't slow Shadow down a bit, but Mr. Marshall's reaction did.

On the first five visits, Mr. Marshall excused himself from the group he was teaching, held out his hand for a paper clip and then gave his full attention to Shadow. On the sixth visit, Mr. Marshall simply said, "Recess." He then turned around and continued with what he had been doing. He did not say another word. If Shadow persisted, so did his teacher. Firmly. Politely. Never once giving Shadow the impression that he was angry or didn't care—this was not a moral victory, but simply a matter of everyone's rights being protected.

In a traditional, win-lose classroom, most of us deal with attention-getting behavior somewhat reactively. (How many teachers, unwilling to set a boundary for fear of hurting a child's feelings, blow up at the child after three or four interruptions?) Mr. Marshall's request had all of the characteristics of a well-stated boundary. It was proactive, communicating the limits and payoffs before Shadow had a chance to take up all of his time again. It was stated positively, promising five opportunities for Shadow to get the attention he wanted. It was clear, having a tangible and finite number of paper clips on his belt and a specific time limit (until recess). It was win-win, allowing both student and teacher to get what they wanted. And because Mr. Marshall had the courage to kindly and firmly follow through, it worked! The teacher did not need to yell or punish— which, incidentally would have fed Shadow's desire for attention, negative though it would have been; he simply needed to hold to his boundary.

Suddenly Shadow had to determine the importance of his questions and decide if Mr. Marshall was the only person who could help him. He was somewhat more selective with his use of the five late-morning paper clips, even more so by the end of the day. By the third day, he was down from 20 to 10 clips a day; by the third week, he had been weaned from the paper clips—and his need for Mr. Marshall's constant attention—completely. By that point, he had learned to work with other students and was much more capable of solving real problems on his own. He became more sensitive to Mr. Marshall's needs, as well as the other students' needs for the teacher's attention, and made genuine attempts to avoid interrupting. Not bad for a six-year-old!

A rule of thumb for problem solving in the classroom (or anywhere): the person with the problem is responsible for the solution of the problem without making it anyone else's problem. Yet, regardless of our commitment to these goals, it's still easy to get hooked by our students' needs, even when we're not really needed.

Behind this temptation is a belief rooted in factory-era authority relationships that suggests that the leader should be aware of and involved in every aspect of the groups' functioning in order to maintain control. In a 21st century classroom, which emphasizes student self-control, students are encouraged to take the initiative for solving their problems within limits that allow teaching and learning to continue. Sure, there are times we need to jump in, but in many instances, we don't need to know that the problem exists!

Another temptation comes from the fact that it's usually very easy for us to see how the problem could be resolved or avoided. Sometimes this feeling comes from the frustration of being interrupted (if we just solve this problem for them, maybe it will go away), sometimes it comes from a lack of trust in our students' problem-solving capabilities (which may be a product of win-lose traditions as well as prior experience).

If we view our role as that of "rescuer," we're also likely to see solving other people's problems as part of the job. Many of our students have sold us on their helplessness, and assuming responsibility for their problems can be especially tempting if we're inclined to want to protect them. Add to that our need to be needed, important, wise,

influential and powerful, and it's easy to see the difficulty in separating ourselves from our students' problems.

Falling into this trap, however, does no one any favors in the long run. To begin with, every time we solve a problem that our students can solve themselves, we end up robbing them of a chance to practice taking—and demonstrating—responsibility. We actually interfere with the students' learning and growth. It may appear that we are saving time, but by reinforcing helplessness and teacher dependence, we are instead creating opportunities for future interruptions to occur. Additionally, it won't take long before we start feeling resentful and reacting negatively ourselves.

Much of the time, our students' problems compete with our own needs for privacy, concentration and our ability to stay on task. After a while, the interruptions and lack of self-management are bound to get on our nerves. Whether it's the nature of the problem or the teacher dependence itself, when our patience wears thin, our reaction is not likely to be very helpful or supportive.

Let's face it—some of their problems can seem pretty strange or even silly to us. I once had a student approach me on the verge of hysteria, claiming that one of the other students had called her a camel. Sometimes trying to take these incidents seriously can be a challenge, but it's important to remember that the pain and stress the student is experiencing is very real to her. Often our automatic reactions and responses to these or more serious events can create other problems, block further communications and erode safety. Responding in a supportive and accepting way often requires a great deal of awareness on our part, as well as some new skills. For example, it may help to pause to regain our patience and perspective before we say something that would dismiss or trivialize their feelings: "Don't be ridiculous. You can't possibly be upset about that!" Sarcasm and distractions are no more effective: "Why aren't you this worried about your math grades?" These kinds of comments

A rule of thumb for problem solving in the classroom (or anywhere): the person with the problem is responsible for the solution of the problem without making it anyone else's problem.

Every time we solve a problem that our students can solve themselves, we end up robbing them of a chance to practice taking—and demonstrating—responsibility.

are problematic, and certainly non-supportive, because they tell students how they should feel and judge what they actually do feel as wrong and unimportant. The message will either result in frustration and resentment on the part of the student (which can erode trust in teacher-student relationships) or self-doubt and eventual repression (which can have serious, long-term negative effects for the student). Denying the problem, ignoring the student or refusing to listen can be just as invalidating and non-productive.

Other responses like overreacting, or reacting with anger, can be just as damaging: "I guess I'm just going to have to move you if you can't get along with anyone," "If you weren't so irresponsible, you wouldn't be having these problems," "What did you do to her?" or "That does it! I'm calling your parents." Now the student has two problems: not only is the original issue unresolved, but somehow she's being scolded, punished, blamed or attacked for having the problem in the first place! As familiar and automatic as many of these responses may be, it's easy to see that they don't do much for the emotional climate of the classroom or the student's ability to feel safe in sharing with us when something is wrong!

Also popular and, in its own way equally destructive, is a tendency to ask a student "Why does that bother you?" For one thing, it assumes that the child knows why something is troublesome or, at the very least, requires the student to shift from an affective process (experiencing feelings) to a cognitive one (explaining them). Second, asking why something is bothersome requests the child to explain or defend her feelings, with the implicit message that our acceptance of the feelings and the child's right to them is conditional, requiring that she have a good enough reason for being upset. In a supportive, emotionally safe classroom, it doesn't matter whether the child is upset because she has an inexplicable fear of camels or because her best friend called her a name. She doesn't need an excuse for her feelings, nor does she need to name or

describe them; she just needs to know it's OK to feel them.

Another ineffective way of handling student problems is by giving advice (telling the student how to solve the problem). Even teachers skilled in avoiding other destructive reactions have a hard time with this one! It's nearly impossible to resist stating what seems like an obvious solution to us: "Just ignore her." "Well, go play with someone else." "Have you told her how you feel?" But a child in crisis isn't always looking for a solution—sometimes she just needs a safe space to feel, which is often a critical step in getting to a place where she can find a solution on her own!

As innocent and effective as it may seem, there are major drawbacks to giving advice. For one thing, advising immediately draws us into the problem, making us responsible for it and its solution. For another, our advice can sometimes create new or additional problems and also makes us vulnerable to blame if things don't work out. Further, children need confidence and skill in their ability to take care of problems on their own. After all, there won't always be an adult around to tell them what to do. Giving advice not only deprives the student of the opportunity to learn responsibility and problem-solving techniques, it also suggests that she's incapable of doing so (often heard as "too dumb").

So many of our responses can be non-supportive, inappropriate for a win-win environment and sometimes downright harmful. Yet there are alternatives, skills for listening and helping children find solutions constructively, ways to care without becoming enmeshed in feelings and problems that our students are experiencing. Success-oriented problem solving requires some groundwork. To begin, we need to let the students know—from the start—that there will be times we will not be able to help them with their problems, and that our insistence on their finding their own solutions does not mean that we don't care. To maintain a win-win atmosphere, we also need to remind them that solving their

In a supportive emotionally safe classroom, it doesn't matter why the student is upset about something.

She doesn't need an excuse for her feelings, nor does she need to name or describe them; she just needs to know it's OK to feel them.

A child in crisis isn't always looking for a solution—sometimes she just needs a safe space to feel.

problems cannot create problems for anyone else. Additionally, we need to teach them to work independently and help one another in non-disruptive ways if they haven't already demonstrated these skills.

In addition, we need to be sure that there are options available within these limits by which the students can indeed resolve their conflicts on their own. For example, if a student is upset that another student is bothering her or interfering with her ability to do her work, is she allowed to move her desk or find another place to work? If a student does not have necessary materials, does he have the option of asking around before class starts to borrow a pencil or share a book? Without positive ways to generate solutions to their problems, students will surely find negative routes.

Additionally, the better we communicate our boundaries before we're invited to help out, the more consistently we can enforce them. For example, take a simple statement such as "Open your books to page 35." Regardless of the age of the students, the size of the group, the subject area or the location of the school, there seems to be a universal and immediate student response: "What page?" Most teachers become more than a little exasperated having to explain everything more than once. (And every time we do, no matter how angry and frustrated we are, we tell the students that it's OK for them not to listen the first time).

There are success-oriented ways to discourage this type of teacher dependence. For one thing, make sure you have everyone's attention before you start. (One second-grade teacher asks her students to "Look at me" whenever she has anything important for the group to hear. More important, she waits until all activity and talking ceases and all eyes are on her.) Next, tell the students before you give your directions: "I will only say this once." Finally, provide positive options for students who may be tired or inattentive, or those who have difficulty remembering or understanding oral directions. Writing the directions on the board or allowing students to go to one another

for help (without disturbing anyone) make it much easier for students to become independent and self-managing.

Similarly, good boundaries will help minimize the number of interruptions you experience when students feel compelled to report on the behavior of their peers. Tattling can drive anyone to distraction, and I don't mean reports of a fire in the library or a stranger in the bathroom. (You can be sure that no matter how strict your no-tattling boundaries are, you will hear about the serious stuff.) I'm talking about the annoying attempts to drag us into non-life-threatening conflicts with peers: "Maya was looking at me," "Garry said a bad word," or "A.J. kicked my chair." What do we do when we've set everything up to encourage student self-management only to find a child tapping on our shoulder because somebody "stealed my pencil"? What happens if we refuse to allow these problems to become our own?

One third-grade teacher told her students that she had simply gotten too busy to listen to them tattling. "I know you want to tell me these things and I don't want you to think I'm not interested. I'm sorry that happened, and I can't help right now!" She also presented them with the option of putting it in writing, supplying a "tattling form" that asked the following: Your name, the name of the person who is bothering you, something nice about that person, a description of the problem and finally, the most important question, "What are you going to do about the problem?"

She also made herself available at a later time to talk over the problem and discuss the solutions the student had proposed or attempted. She assured the students that she was truly concerned despite her unwillingness to become directly involved in their conflicts. She put the responsibility back on the kids, communicated her faith in their ability to resolve their conflicts and was able to maintain the role of facilitator, not rescuer! In addition, by saying, "I want to hear about this in a little bit. In the meantime, fill out this form so I'll

Make sure that students have options for resolving conflicts non-disruptively on their own.

Without positive ways to generate solutions to their problems, students will surely find negative routes.

have more information," she removed herself from the temptation of immediately reacting with habitual, non-supportive responses before she had a minute to collect her thoughts and respond in a more positive way. Further, by providing a constructive outlet with the tattling form, she made it possible for students to work through their feelings on paper, evaluate their options and choose positive alternatives to negative situations. Finally, she not only avoided attempts to draw her into problems she did not own, but she also reinforced the students' sense of their own ability to resolve conflicts and get their needs met without creating problems for anyone else!

Another teacher, totally frustrated with an endless stream of tattling sixth graders, finally exploded: "That does it! From here on in, no more tattling unless somebody dies!" The students got the point, had a laugh and still, on occasion, forgot the rule. However, from then on, any time a student came up to complain about another student, all the teacher had to do was remind the complainer that since the other student was still alive, they'd have to work the problem out peacefully among themselves.

Another way to avoid owning the students' problem is by removing the power and morality from conflicts. For example, many teachers, especially those working with upper-grade students or in departmentalized settings, frequently complain about the times their kids show up unprepared. If a student shows up in our classroom without a pencil or a book, obviously he or she has a problem. But the student's lack of preparation does not auto-matically have to become our problem as well.

Something as simple as lack of a pencil can become a moral issue: "But they *need* a pencil. They *know* they need a pencil. They *should* have a pencil. And yet here they are empty-handed. What's wrong with them?"

In a win-lose classroom, teachers typically blow up, criticize and deliver a lecture about responsibility and self-sufficiency, after which they either give out a pencil or they don't. But in the meantime, they've gotten upset, they've

wasted valuable instructional time and their students are no more self-managing or respon-sible as a result. Even if the kids come prepared tomorrow to keep their teachers from getting upset with them, their cooperation is still not self-motivated, and it's come at the cost of unnecessary stress to the emotional environment and relationship.

It is possible to deal with a forgotten pencil in a non-emotional, disengaged and non-judgmental frame of mind. We handle similar situations with adults that way. (Have you ever forgotten your pen as you went to write a check in the supermarket? How did you solve the problem? How would you have felt if the cashier had yelled at you about being irresponsible? After all, you knew you were going shopping. You knew you would have to pay for those groceries. Didn't you? See? Imagine how you'd feel if you were treated this way. Probably the only thing you'd learn from the encounter was that you didn't want to shop there anymore!)

We do not need to adopt the students' lack of preparedness as our own problem nor take it as a personal assault. What are your boundaries? What are your resources? Do you have enough pencils to keep a few on hand? Are you willing to loan them out without making a big deal out of it? If so, when, how and under what conditions? Can they borrow a pencil from a friend? Make sure the kids know ahead of time which options are available to them so they have the information they need to succeed.

The real issue is that the student needs something to write with in order to do her work, right? Sure it would be nice if she remembered, but for the moment, she didn't. It usually doesn't cost us much to loan a child a pencil or keep a few in a can for emergencies. It certainly costs us nothing to give a student a minute to find a pencil while we get the class ready or after the other students begin their seatwork. This is the heart of success-orientation and win-win interactions. (I always found that the less fuss I made over pencils, the fewer problems my kids had remembering. If

We do not need to adopt the students' lack of preparedness as our own problem nor take it as a personal assault.

If teachers have gotten upset, they've wasted valuable instructional time and their students are no more self-managing or responsible as a result.

my extras disappeared, they borrowed from one another, and eventually even started restocking the can on their own.) Although the habits from a win-lose perspective would have us believe otherwise, a forgotten pencil does not devalue a student or make him bad. Allowing him to borrow or buy a pencil no more "teaches" a child to be irresponsible than your needing to borrow one at the check-out counter will insure future forgetfulness.

When a student has a problem, we can provide support without actually becoming involved with the problem or its solution. Sometimes listening alone is enough, especially when our attention and concern are demonstrated by validating behaviors, such as eye contact, nodding and encouraging comments ("Uh-huh," "I see," or "Tell me more"). Very often, just having the chance to unload can help the student process the various dimensions of the problem well enough to see a solution for himself. If you're not available at the moment the student needs you, as will often be the case, set a boundary that acknowledges the child's desire for your attention and let him know when you'll be available: "This is important. I need to explain this assignment to this group. I'll be free to talk to you in about ten minutes" (or "when the big hand is on the three," "when the bell rings," "at lunchtime" or even "after school"). Rarely will a child thus acknowledged not be willing to wait. Your commitment to a win-win solution—and your desire to take care of yourself and still accommodate the child—can go a long way toward building a child's patience and respect for your time and priorities.

Often, the less we say, the more helpful we can be. When we are able to listen—without jumping in to advise, analyze or share our own experiences—we show appreciation for the student's concerns and still leave full responsibility with him. By not telling the student what to do, we are also demonstrating our trust in him.

More elaborate responses are also appropriate. You can check or communicate your understanding of the student's message by restating what he has said in your own words, without evaluating, judging, interpreting or commiserating: "You're saying that her teasing bothers you." "You weren't expecting him to do that." "You asked her to stop and she ignored you." This strategy can help the student feel validated and understood, gain understanding of the problem and find his own way out. And as we develop our ability to objectively reflect what we are hearing, we can also avoid the more familiar negative responses.

So, when one of your students complains that somebody called her a camel, instead of questioning ("What does that mean?"), minimizing ("That's nothing to be upset about."), excusing ("Oh, she didn't mean it."), challenging ("Why does that bother you?"), advising ("Just ignore him."), threatening ("If you don't stop coming up here . . ."), blaming ("What did you do to him?"), distracting ("Just get busy.") or attacking ("You're just too sensitive!"), you can simply restate the heart of what the student is telling you: "It upsets you when someone calls you a name."

Sometimes this response is enough: you have acknowledged the student's concern, validated her feelings and let her know you understood what she was saying to you. Your lack of criticism, disappointment, judgment or impatience have made clear your unconditional acceptance—both of the student and her right to have her feelings (even if they seem silly, frivolous or incomprehensible to you). You have also left the responsibility for the solution of the problem with the student because your response did not involve you in the cause or solution of the problem. This is support in the truest, kindest and most helpful sense of the word.

Regardless of your response to a student's complaint, if he is new to solving his own problems (or insecure about his ability to do so), it's likely that he came to you in the first place in the hopes of having you fix the situation. Even when you have set the stage for personal responsibility ahead of time, your refusal to get involved can sometimes add to

I always found that the less fuss I made over forgotten pencils, the fewer problems my kids had remembering.

Set a boundary that acknowledges the child's desire for your attention and let him know when you'll be available.

Your lack of criticism, disappointment, judgment or impatience have made clear your unconditional acceptance—both of the student and her right to have her feelings.

132

Many problems, conflicts and outbursts that occur in the classroom can be averted by providing constructive, non-hurtful outlets for feelings.

Feelings and problems are a part of life and no amount of devotion to content-curriculum will keep feelings out of your classroom.

When our classrooms support children's affective development, we create space for far greater cognitive strides to occur.

the student's frustration. Some students need a little time to get used to the idea of being responsible for solving their own problems, or to realizing that you really are there for them even if you aren't doing the work for them.

The greater challenge for most teachers is resisting the seduction of being needed. Often, disengaging will require reframing your role in the lives of your students. If you believe that part of your job is to protect your students from problems and conflicts, it'll be hard to resist the temptation to say, "Well, I'll go have a talk with her," when one student has a problem with another. You'll find yourself in the middle of endless conflicts, wasting time and energy trying to fix blame or determine "Who started it?" If, on the other hand, you see your role as helping your students learn how to take care of themselves in conflicts with others, you will, so long as their immediate safety is not at stake, take a much different role. (Remember, you won't always be there when problems come up in their lives.)

At times, you may need to work with individuals or groups of students—preferably at a non-conflict time—to build positive social and interactive skills, such as sharing, courtesy and taking turns, build conflict resolution skills and impulse control or teach alternatives to blaming and excusing. Helping children learn to set boundaries, ask for what they need or take care of themselves in other positive ways can help you maintain a supportive role while preventing or minimizing many conflicts that would otherwise end up in your lap.

Many problems, conflicts and outbursts that occur in the classroom can be averted by providing constructive, non-hurtful outlets for feelings, particularly anger or frustration. Historically, schools have typically operated with a "leave-your-feelings-at-the-door" kind of attitude; rarely do they provide the physical space, let alone emotional support, for processing feelings that can interfere with learning. Perhaps if students could indeed leave their feelings outside our classrooms, this would make sense. If you can involve parents

or the school counselor (should your site be fortunate enough to have one), so much the better. Don't imagine that the students' needs or demands on your instructional time will be limited to their cognitive development. Feelings and problems are a part of life and no amount of devotion to content curriculum will keep feelings out of your classroom. Instructional activities, such as roundtable discussions, brainstorming sessions, values clarification or role-playing, along with dialogue addressed to resolving specific problems can help build social and emotional development in such a way that, in the long run, you'll have much more time to devote to academics. Remember, we are not just teaching math, history or music—we are teaching children; when our classrooms support their affective development, we create space for far greater cognitive strides to occur.

Still, this commitment may be hard to maintain. Most people who grew up with industrial-era dynamics learn right off the bat that feelings aren't OK. In order to self-protect, they learned to "stuff" their feelings, pretending that they were *fine* rather than risk an adult's ridicule, criticism, impatience or some other negative reaction. These children typically grow up to become adults who are uncomfortable with children's feelings. Their discomfort can manifest in responses that, regardless of their intentions, ultimately make it unsafe for children to express feelings, which perpetuates this cycle of non-support.

When children lack the skills, outlets or sense of safety necessary for expressing feelings in non-hurtful ways, they end up repressing feelings, or holding them in. In the short run, this may serve the teacher and the class, but the long-term effects can be very destructive to everyone involved. "Stuffed" or repressed feelings often end up exploding, sometimes at the slightest provocation, or come out in hurtful, destructive or self-destructive behaviors. (This is often the case when we see kids exhibit "$5.00 reactions" to "10¢ events.") Further, despite every admonition to "just say no," to a child invested in not experiencing painful feelings, any mood-altering substance or behavior that appears to offer relief can become quite attractive. If nothing else, imagine trying to teach the student whose girl friend just broke up with him last period, the child who just found out that her parents are getting a divorce or the youngster who was teased relentlessly by a group of his classmates at recess. Your most creative lessons and enthusiastic presentations are likely to be lost on these individuals until they've had a chance to deal with what they're feeling.

Certainly some children will need significant amounts of help at times, but many teachers have quickly defused conflicts, averted problems and redirected destructive energy by giving kids a means of getting the feelings out in non-hurtful ways. Is there someplace in your classroom (or school) where students (or teachers, for that matter) can go when they feel a need to cry? What can angry students do to get rid of their anger without harming property, other children or themselves? Sometimes a few minutes out of the classroom, with a chance to go get a drink or wash his face, can provide some relief, safely get the student out of the immediate affective crisis and help him regain his focus and concentration. Likewise a few laps around the playground or a chance to pound clay, punch a pillow, draw a picture or write a letter (especially if the student has a chance to tear the paper up into tiny pieces when he's done).

One kindergarten teacher posted a large picture of a story-book character on the bulletin board and invited the students to "Tell Mrs. Murphy" if they had a problem and the teacher was too busy to talk. If she saw a student spending an unusual amount of time whispering to the picture on the board, she would make a point to check in with the child later to see if everything was OK. More often than not, the student would assure her that, "Mrs. Murphy took care of it."

A counselor used a stuffed bunny with great big ears for kids who needed a friend who would listen. And a mid-school teacher accomplished the same objective by drawing a picture of a big ear and taping it to the bottom of a door in the back of the room. The fact that there always seemed to be a student back in that corner made it clear that the need to deal with feelings is critical at any age.

Regardless of the outlet you provide, your willingness to acknowledge the student's feelings and help him channel them nondestructively can significantly reduce disruptions and arguments in the class and can ultimately contribute to the child's ability to self-manage both feelings and actions. Additionally, any outlet that does not create problems for others is far more consistent with the values and objectives of a 21st century classroom than an insensitive, invalidating or repressive reaction.

We can also prevent many classroom conflicts when we model and teach good boundary-setting skills. Even preschoolers can learn to say "stop," and walk away from someone who is being mean and refuse to participate until their classmates play nice. Unfortunately, many of the techniques taught to children have side-effects we may not realize. For example, teaching students to ask a classmate, "Why did you take my crayons?" invites excuses, blame and arbitrary acceptance or judgment. If kids want to protect their stuff, teaching them to say "Please ask first" or "I'll be happy to share if you ask me" is far more honest and direct.

Likewise "I-messages," which attempt to use one's feelings to change how others act. Now I'll admit to using and promoting this technique at one time. After all, "When you . . ., I feel . . ." certainly sounded a lot more positive than attacking and name calling. But it didn't take me long to realize that children who say, for example, "When you call me names, I feel hurt and angry," not only communicates that they are the emotional victims of the name-caller, but also reinforce what was obviously intended as hurtful behavior in the first place! And despite the argument that "I-messages" are meant as positive exchanges, I fail to see anything

The need to deal with feelings is critical at any age.

We can prevent many classroom conflicts when we model and teach good boundary-setting skills.

positive in the accusation and disempowerment inherent in telling someone "you caused my feelings."

In a win-win environment, individuals take responsibility for their own feelings. "I'm really angry" is quite different from "You make me angry" or "When you (do this), I feel angry." "I'm really angry" expresses a feeling without blaming, projecting or self-victimizing. It may indicate a need (or request) to talk, to get the feelings out or even be left alone. If the anger is connected to (or was triggered by) someone else's words or actions, the focus is on the angry person's reaction and interpretation, not the behavior that triggered it. In fact, the reaction often has little to do with the other person's behavior.* In this environment, if one person wants another to change his or her behavior, that person simply asks: "Please stop calling me names" or "Let's talk (or play) when you're not calling me names." If we can teach children to say "When you . . ., I feel . . .," we can certainly teach them to use boundaries to ask for what they want instead.

The pressure most teachers feel when students have problems is often related to finding a solution. Sometimes just knowing it's OK to be upset, just having the space to feel, is all that's necessary. The student whose friend called her a camel happened to come to me a few days after I had attended a conference workshop that dealt with accepting and validating feelings. Lucky for her, because my typical, automatic reactions were anything but! I remember fighting my natural inclination toward impatience—especially with this particular student, who had done her share of name-calling—biting my lip so I wouldn't say anything while she was talking and thinking very hard about how I wanted to respond. When she said she was upset, I simply agreed: "Sometimes it hurts when people call us names."

She stared at me for a second and then assented: "Yeah." That was it! She walked back to her desk and sat down and got back to work. For that moment, she didn't need a solution. Simply being heard and having permission to feel bad was all she apparently needed, after which she had no need to hang onto her hurt feelings (or use them to justify hurting back).

Immediate intervention is necessary to protect property or a student's physical safety or to keep a situation from getting out of hand but this is not the time to be looking for solutions. The time for resolving a problem is generally not when a child is in crisis. A child in crisis needs support for his feelings. Once the feelings have been acknowledged, felt and worked through and the student has shifted out of the immediate affective experience, then it may be time to explore options and find solutions. We can play a valuable role in this process, even when we aren't telling students what to do. As our role shifts from problem solver and rescuer to encourager and facilitator, we start doing much more listening than talking. Instead of blaming, giving advice or getting in the middle of their problems, we help them find answers by asking them questions. Certain questions, posed in a warm and receptive tone, turn the responsibility for problem solving back to the students, help them process, explore and resolve their conflicts, and demonstrate our belief that they are indeed capable of working things out.

Rather than automatically telling the student who complains about the teacher who constantly picks on her to "just behave better in his class," we ask questions: "What's going on?" "How would you like him to treat you?" "What have you tried so far?" "What's worked for you in the past?" "What else are you willing to try?" "What might happen if you do that?" "How badly do you need to pass this class?" "What other options do you have?" "What if that doesn't work?" "Will doing that hurt you later?" "Can you live with that?"

In a win-win environment, individuals take responsibility for their own feelings.

Sometimes, just knowing it's OK to be upset is all that's necessary.

The time for resolving a problem is generally not when a child is in crisis.

---

*For example, a teacher who feels hurt, defensive or invalidated because a student says a lesson is stupid is very likely to be up against much larger issues such as the need for approval (the student's and other's) or a fear of failure or inadequacy, or the feelings wouldn't have come up. This isn't about the student.

Even very young children can respond—or learn to respond—to questions aimed at helping them solve their problems. True, it's expedient to say "just ignore her," but if you've gotten this far in this book, you probably want to accomplish more than reinforcing order-taking or just getting this child out of your hair.

Each question you ask puts the responsibility back in the child's hands. Many students will be disappointed, shocked or even angry when this happens: They are so accustomed to getting advice or being told what to do, they often have no idea how to respond on their own. As the one doing the asking, you may, from time to time find that getting constructive responses from children can be quite a challenge. There are few things more aggravating than setting time aside to talk to a child who responds to every question with a shrug. At this point, it's entirely appropriate to say, "I understand. Why don't you think about it for a bit. We can try again when the bell rings.") In this way you make it clear that you are willing to help the child solve this problem, although you have no intention either of solving it yourself or giving attention to indifference, indecision or irresponsibility.

The process of asking questions does not need to be particularly time consuming. Many times, one or two questions are all that's necessary. In fact, many teachers eventually get to the point where they simply say "What do you need to do about that?" or "How are you going to solve that problem?" to get the students focused on taking constructive action. Still, there will be occasions when the process requires time or attention we are unable to offer at that moment.

Even our willingness to sit and listen needs limits. Students often need to talk when it's not convenient for us. Sometimes we try to assess the urgency of the student's needs, asking, "Is it important?" Now, of course the student will think so. What we're really asking is for the student to determine, "Will I think it's more important than what I'm doing at the moment?" If it's not a good time for us—

whether it's important to the student or not— we don't need to ask. We simply let the student know when we'll be available. (The question will be equally superfluous if the student is in the obvious throes of a very serious trauma or physical distress that require immediate attention.)

Watch the tendency to dismiss the student with quick advice. Remember, when Mr. Marshall gave Shadow the paper clips, he was not telling the student how to resolve his need for the teacher's attention. He just gave the child the tools he could use to manage this need. In this way, Mr. Marshall took care of his own problem—his need to limit the number of times Shadow could ask for help.

If you're not in the mood to listen or if your patience is questionable, your tone of voice and body language will make that clear. Be honest: "I'm too busy (tired, angry) right now to give you the kind of time and attention you deserve." Then give the student a specific time to return: "I do want to talk to you. I'll be finished with this group in ten minutes. Let's talk then."

Feelings are neither right nor wrong, and whether or not we would react as our students do, their feelings are real. Acceptance doesn't require us to make the students' problems—or their feelings—our own, nor does it suggest we have to try to carry on a conversation with a student who is gasping for air between sobs. It does allow us to offer support (plus an understanding word, a reassuring touch, an invitation to go get a drink or be by himself and an unlimited supply of tissues) while we wait for the child to settle a bit. "Let's talk in a few minutes" tells the child it's OK to feel whatever he's feeling, that we will give him the time and space to feel. Upset or not, the child is acceptable and valued. There's no pressure to hide or defend his feelings, no reason to interrupt the learning process by acting them out disruptively. And in this environment, the student is safe to take the risks necessary for learning the skills of self-care, self-management and independent problem solving!

Each question you ask puts the responsibility back in the child's hands.

Show you are willing to help the child solve this problem, although you have no intention either of solving it yourself or giving attention to indifference, indecision or irresponsibility.

It's important to get the students focused on taking constructive action.

Things to Remember about Creating a Safe, Supportive Emotional Environment in the Classroom

- Students have feelings in and out of the classroom. Teachers will encounter students' feelings from time to time no matter how much curriculum we have to cover and no matter how far behind the students may be.

- Teaching children to deal with their feelings and problems independently and in healthy, constructive ways will ultimately leave more time for teaching content.

- It's OK for children to have feelings without explaining or defending them to anyone. Cheering students up may make *us* feel better, but it rarely addresses the issues kids have or teaches problem solving. (No matter what, this is *not* the best time of their lives.)

- Feelings are not behaviors. Feelings are never right or wrong, but behaviors that hurt other people are not OK. Teachers do not need to protect other people from a child's feelings, but we may need to intervene in hurtful behaviors.

- It's OK to express feelings as long as doing so does not hurt anyone or create problems for others.

- Most children (and many adults, for that matter) do not have healthy, non-hurtful outlets for expressing their feelings, especially anger or frustration. Nearly all students can benefit when we discuss and present options available to help kids externalize their feelings—or get them out—without hurting themselves or others, especially if we do this proactively, before there is a problem, and in a non-conflict time.

- Possible non-destructive outlets may include the following: Having a stuffed animal or picture they can talk to when you're not available. Being able to draw a picture or write a letter about how they're feeling—and then tearing it up! Writing in a journal, going for a run, hitting a pillow, tearing up paper, or going down the hall for a drink of water and a chance to catch their breath!

- Teachers and students are distinct, separate individuals. It is not necessary to feel someone else's feelings or own his or her problems to show that person we care.

- Teachers are not responsible for changing or controlling the child's feelings. It's more loving and supportive to communicate that a child's feelings are heard, respected and taken seriously—even when we don't understand them.

- Children learn to deal with feelings more effectively when they don't have to stuff or hide them to protect a critical, guilt-ridden or over-reacting adult.

- Teacher responses that interfere with children's ability to own, feel, express or process their feelings can block communications, teach children to mistrust their own feelings and perceptions, and interfere with the development of their problem-solving capabilities.

Guidelines for Encouraging Independence and Problem Solving

- Non-supportive responses to avoid:*

  Dismissing or Minimizing. "That's nothing to be upset about." "So she called you a camel. Big deal."

  Excusing. "She didn't mean it." "He didn't know what he was saying." "She must be having a bad day." (Suggests it OK for people to do hurtful things as long as they have an excuse.)

  Denying. "Oh, you don't really feel that way." "That doesn't really bother you." "Teachers don't hate their students."

  Distracting. "Well, at least you're passing your other classes." "You're lucky you didn't get detention." "Cheer up. You should be happy."

  Medicating. "This cookie should make you feel better." "Just get busy." (Using some form of substance—usually food—or activity to distract students from their feelings.)

  Attacking or Shaming. "I told you that would happen!" "How could you be so stupid?" "Don't be such a baby." "Nice girls don't say words like that." "You're just too sensitive." "Can't you get along with anybody?" (May also include sarcasm, disappointment, impatience, criticism or contempt.)

  Blaming. "What did you do to her?" "That's what happens when you don't put things away." "Well, if you had just put the caps back on the markers, this wouldn't have happened." "You got what you deserved."

  Challenging. "Why does that bother you?" (Requires students to defend their feelings to convince the teacher that the feelings are legitimate thus securing the teacher's conditional acceptance.)

  Enmeshing. "That wouldn't bother me." "Your problems drive me crazy." (Confuses teacher's reactions or reality with the student's.)

  Commiserating. "Well, he's just a jerk." "You don't need her." "You're so unlucky."

  (Denies student's responsibility, is dismissive and can suggest that the student is a victim or disempowered, in the situation or in general.)

  Rescuing. "I'll go talk to her about it." "I'll tell her to stop picking on you." "What's your excuse?" (Relieves student of responsibility, either by the teacher taking responsibility for the problem, or by providing a loophole in a boundary.)

  Advising. "Just ignore her." "Go tell her you're sorry." "Go play with someone else." (Relieves student of responsibility for finding a solution by telling the child how to solve the problem.)

- Get clear on your role. In the long run, it is far more helpful to teach children to protect and defend themselves and to find their own solutions to problems than it is to do these jobs for them.

- Listen. If you're not available when they need you, let them know, as specifically as possible, when you will be free. When they're talking, make eye contact and minimize the amount of talking—and interrupting—you do.

- Distinguish between feelings and behaviors. There's a difference between wanting to hurt someone and actually hurting someone. For example, it really is OK to *want* to drop out of school or strangle a classmate—although actually *doing* either one has serious consequences. Accepting a student's right to his feelings does not give him permission to exhibit hurtful or destructive behaviors.

- Accept the students, their feelings and their rights to have their feelings. Your acceptance will be conveyed by the absence of judgmental, shocked, critical or disappointed words, looks or body language. Even if you disagree with their feelings or don't understand them, resist the desire to make someone wrong for his or her feelings.

---

*Adapted from *Parents, Teens & Boundaries: How to Draw the Line* by Jane Bluestein, Ph.D. (Deerfield Beach, FL: Health Communications, Inc., 1993.)

- Validate the student's reality. Anything you say or do that gives children permission to have feelings will validate the experience. Again, the absence of disagreement or judgment will help, as do comments like, "I see," "I understand" or "Of course you're angry about that."
- Maintain your boundaries. Let your students know when you'll be available to talk or help. Watch the tendency to take responsibility for their feelings or problems by trying to fix the situation, cheer them up (fix them), or by rescuing or advising.
- Trust their ability to solve problems independently and provide instruction and support necessary to do so, preferably in a non-conflict setting. Model and teach conflict-management, demonstrating non-destructive ways to have and express feelings and building skills for setting and maintaining boundaries.

- Provide healthy, non-hurtful outlets for feelings (and meeting needs).
- Ask—don't tell. When students are ready to start looking for solutions, use questions to guide them and help them identify and evaluate options available and anticipate probable outcomes. Caution: Watch out for questions that disguise criticism or advice: "What were you thinking?" "Why don't you tell her how that hurts your feelings?"
- Respect the fact that the student may not want to talk about it right now, or may not be comfortable talking with you. Leave the door open for future discussion. Look for or suggest other resources (such as the school counselor, a student support group or an outside agency) if the student would prefer or if you are personally not comfortable discussing a particular topic.

Activity

Date_____

When a problem occurs in the classroom, it is always best if we can evaluate the situation before acting— or reacting. To practice, think of a problem one of your students recently shared with you or asked you to solve. (Keep this list of questions on hand to plan, practice and evaluate other incidents as they come up.)

Describe the problem below:

In what way could this be (or become) your problem?

What do you need to do to prevent it from becoming your problem?

What do you need to do to keep it from becoming your problem?

In what ways have you set the stage for your students to solve this problem (and others) on their own?

What else might you do to avoid similar future incidents?

What options does the student have for solving this problem on his or her own?

What other options might you make available for similar future incidents?

In what way have you acknowledged the student's needs and feelings?

How did you help the student solve this problem without making it your own?

What outlets are available for your students to express or externalize feelings (get them out of their systems) without hurting themselves or others?

What other outlets might you provide?

How successful were you at avoiding a negative response (advising, asking "why," criticizing, scolding, moralizing, trivializing, sarcasm, etc.)?

Which negative responses are most difficult for you to avoid?

In what ways have your students shown growth in independence and problem solving skills?

In what ways have you become better able to separate yourself from your students' problems (and turn the responsibility back over to them)?

What are your plans to further enhance your—and their—growth in this area?

∞

17

Consequences and Follow Through

When we encounter a great deal of resistance, rebellion or aggression, we have a choice: We can devote our energies to survival (and reacting) or to relationship building.

For many of the teachers I've encountered, this is the chapter that promises to satisfy the one real question they have about discipline: "What do I do when . . ." From a traditional, win-lose perspective, the word *discipline* rarely conjures more than a notion of reactions to misbehavior. The difficulty in overcoming this orientation is evident in the impatience I occasionally encounter: Even teachers intrigued by the idea of preventing discipline problems often can't wait to get to the part that tells them what to do "when." I once spent five intensive days teaching a graduate class that emphasized the proactive principles and strategies of 21st century discipline. On the last day, a man in the class was still not sold: "Yeah, yeah . . . Relationships. Prevention. Win-win. That sounds nice and all, but what do I do when one of my kids throws a chair at me?"

I thought for a second: "Duck?"

Now I honestly wasn't trying to be glib. I simply didn't know. The whole point of this process is to develop an environment in which it would never occur to a child to throw a chair, either because he had other, more constructive outlets for his anger and frustration or because prior needs had been adequately accommodated beforehand. Extreme outbursts can occur even in the healthiest environment, however they tend to be rare and isolated events. More typically, this kind of behavior is an indication that the relationships and power dynamics in that classroom need some work.

If things have gotten to the point where you have a student-initiated projectile sailing toward your head, you don't have time to determine the most effective win-win strategies. You have reached the point of survival and your only recourse is to take whatever action is necessary to avoid injury. Higher-level needs will always take a back seat to more basic demands and there are few things more basic than protecting one's physical safety. Unfortunately, functioning at a survival level takes a tremendous toll on relationships and emotional well-being, not to mention learning!

When we encounter a great deal of resistance, rebellion or aggression, we have a choice: We can devote our energies to survival (and reacting) or to relationship building. Now this latter option takes longer, is more work and requires a greater degree of consciousness, deliberateness, awareness and commitment on the part of the teacher than simply reacting. Restructuring relationships and reconfiguring power dynamics also requires a willingness to change—to adopt different behaviors, attitudes, even language patterns—in the way we interact with kids. Is it any wonder that so many of us are willing to neglect the work we can do toward accomplishing these goals in non-conflict times and look for a quick fix to bail us out when something disruptive occurs? I can certainly understand why so many discipline "programs" that offer formulas and magic solutions for dealing with misbehaviors are, in some settings, so attractive, popular and ultimately disappointing. Again, if you've made it this far (assuming that you didn't skip right to this chapter!), I'm guessing that you're looking for something beyond survival, that you're not just searching for reactions and strategies that allow you to win at all costs.

Unfortunately we can devote our entire teaching existence to developing positive interactions and win-win dynamics and will still, on occasion, encounter—and have to deal with—disruptions. Even with the best intentions to separate ourselves from our students' conflict, when they lack the skills for resolving their problems non-disruptively, the disturbance can quickly become problematic for us and the rest of the class (and, on occasion, even other classes). Negative behavior can occur in any classroom, however, because of the interactive footwork and relationship dynamics previously established, these incidents are handled quite differently in a win-win environment than in the autocratic classroom of past decades.

For example, imagine that Jamie and Nicholas are fighting over who gets to read a particular book first. Both are pulling on the book and shouting at one another, creating quite an uproar in the classroom. Students are being distracted from their work, the teacher is unable to continue the lesson, and who knows what's happening to the book.

Now, there are a number of possible teacher responses to this conflict behavior. For example, a teacher might get up and burst out, "What's wrong with you two? Put that book down and get to your seats! You'll both be in after school to write a few pages on how you are supposed to behave in class."

Other than possibly restoring quiet, the only real benefit of this win-lose technique is that it might protect the book. This is a punitive response that teaches more about the teacher's power than about effective ways to

share books or resolve conflicts. The teacher has taken responsibility for the misbehavior; the students have learned nothing about negotiating or problem solving. Chances are the next time they run into a similar conflict, they will attempt the same approach, perhaps a little less publicly so they don't get caught.

As an alternative, the teacher might also go over and take the book from the students, saying, "That's going to damage this book. Here, Jamie, you take it until lunchtime. Nicholas, you can have it for the rest of the afternoon." The fact that the teacher does not personally attack the students will certainly make this response seem more attractive than the previous example, but there is still no opportunity for the students to learn self-management from this conflict. Again, the book is safe and the fight has been broken up, but at what cost?

The teacher has absorbed the responsibility of solving the problem, however in this example the solution is arbitrary and seems to punish one child while rewarding the other. The conflict has not been satisfactorily resolved in the students' minds—even for the student who got the book (and has probably lost interest by this point). The teacher's intervention can actually escalate the negative feelings generated in the original argument. There has been no opportunity for negotiation and problem solving; in fact, the teacher's behavior reinforces dependence and helplessness by repeating a pattern in which conflicts are solved by someone else.

As another option, the teacher might go over, take the book away and ask, "OK, what's going on here? Who started this?" Now, in our minds, it might seem logical that if we can just determine how this problem started and why it's happening, we can make the most impartial judgment. But beware of this temptation to jump into disagreements between kids. For one thing, the involvement can be incredibly tedious, time-consuming and unproductive. For another, asking for background—especially with the intention of collecting data so that we

I can certainly understand why so many discipline "programs" that offer formulas and magic solutions for dealing with misbehaviors are, in some settings, so attractive, popular and ultimately disappointing.

If the teacher has taken responsibility for the misbehavior; the students have learned nothing about negotiating or problem solving.

Beware of the temptation to jump into disagreements between kids.

If ever our ability to withstand win-lose programming is challenged, it will be when a student misbehaves.

There are indeed certain behaviors that truly do not warrant teacher attention, and those that deserve only the most minimal regard.

can solve the problem, puts all that responsibility on our shoulders. Most of the time, these questions reflect a need to assign blame and punishment—options that only serve to reinforce teacher power.

Beyond protecting the book and getting the noise to subside, the conflict is not our problem. Therefore, a more effective approach might sound like the following: "Stop! Books are not for pulling! Please put that on my desk until you can decide how it will be shared."* For an even greater chance of success, we might also remind them that resolving the problem means talking—not yelling or hitting—and that neither the process nor the actual the solution can create problems for others.

This approach offers quite a few benefits. The teacher has attacked the problem without attacking the students, without dredging up judgments about personalities or past misdeeds, and without lecturing or arguing. In addition, the teacher left responsibility for solving the problem with the ones who had created it. True, absolute silence had not been restored, but then, interpersonal problems rarely get sorted out in silence.

This approach also does not guarantee immediate quiet and harmony: the teacher allowed the conflict to continue, but by setting limits and using a boundary to explain how the students could have what they wanted (access to the book), the kids also had a chance to engage in a process of resolving a conflict without disturbing anyone else. The only misbehavior addressed was the argument over the book, and the only consequence of the misbehavior was the removal of the object both students desired until a solution could be reached. There is no need for blaming, punishing or making anyone wrong, so the worth of the students, the value of their feelings and the importance of their needs have been protected.

If ever our ability to withstand win-lose programming is challenged, it will be when a student misbehaves, either by failing to cooperate or complete a task, or by demonstrating disruptive behavior. It can be easy to take negative behavior personally, especially if we've been committed to building a positive learning environment. And it takes a great deal of practice before we automatically respond to spilled paint, for example, by calmly directing the child to a sponge instead of barraging him about his clumsiness.

The temptation to use power, punishment and criticism** can be averted in several ways. Rather than punishing or criticizing undesirable behavior, we can: respond in a variety of nonreactive ways, give students specific information about behaviors we want, or follow through on boundaries we have previously set. In some cases we will use all three strategies at the same time. Let's look at the options we have for responding nonreactively to disruptions or misbehavior.

I remember a professor back in my preservice days talking about the value of ignoring certain student behaviors. Prone to thinking in rather black-and-white terms, I dismissed her advice, equating ignoring with condoning. I have since discovered that there are indeed certain behaviors that truly do not warrant teacher attention, and those that deserve only the most minimal regard. I believe that this professor was simply admonishing us to pick our fights carefully. She may also have been trying to let us off the hook for feeling as though we needed to control or get involved in every single behavioral exchange that occurred in our classes.

Sometimes we simply need to determine whether the child is creating actual problems for us or just getting on our nerves. Not all behaviors require intervention, or even acknowledgement. For example, one teacher

---

*For more examples of the language of acceptance and other valuable communication strategies, see *Teacher and Child* by Haim Ginott. (New York: Avon Books, 1972.)
**Also sarcasm, impatience, shaming or disappointment.

complained about a fourth grader who sucked his thumb. She wanted to know what she could do to get him to stop. She admitted that the behavior did not keep the student from doing his work and, since he always removed his thumb from his mouth before he started talking, it did not interfere with his ability to be understood. This behavior was not a problem for anyone except the teacher and it only bothered her because "it looked funny." Surely there will be other, more important matters to which we can devote our time and energy.

A school counselor recently told me about a high school girl who had been sent to her office as punishment for drawing a picture of a dragon "instead of listening" to a history teacher's lecture. The girl tearfully explained to the counselor that drawing actually helped her listen and proved this fact by pointing to various sections of her drawing and relating, nearly word for word, what the teacher had been saying as she drew this part or that. Here is a perfect example of a teacher creating a discipline problem out of a nondisruptive student behavior. In fact, because of the student's particular learning styles (low auditory, high kinesthetic), she was actually on task. The drawing was helping her absorb the information the teacher was presenting!

In a similar vein, I've seen unbelievable amounts of valuable instructional time wasted on scolding, warning, punishing, giving students detention or sending students to the office because of chewing gum! The argument always maintains the necessity of punishing this particular behavior to discourage students from putting gum where it doesn't belong. And yet, the teachers who make the least fuss over gum chewing or those who have strict conditions under which gum chewing is allowed, rarely report these kinds of problems. Win-win teachers who find the habit personally offensive can minimize problems

with a simple admission that gum chewing is distracting or bothersome to them, and providing other positive outcomes (and outlets) for their students.

I'm not a fan of gum chewing but I'm not particularly bothered by it, either. As long as I couldn't see it, hear it or smell it, my students were allowed to chew it. This was a very big deal for some of them. Do you think they would allow one another to interfere with this privilege by putting gum anywhere other than the trash can wrapped in tissue or scrap paper? Not on your life! And whenever I noticed a student absentmindedly cracking his gum or blowing bubbles, simply pointing to the trash can was the only signal necessary—for that student, the privilege was lost for the rest of the day. We'll try again tomorrow. No big deal.*

We can also avoid creating a major incident out of a small slip-up by minimizing our reaction to the student's behavior. I first encountered this possibility in my observation of Ms. Cahill, the math teacher I mentioned earlier, who increased the number of subtraction problems on the board from ten to fifteen. I learned a valuable lesson from this teacher—and not just about giving kids choices. There was one boy in the class who reacted especially negatively when he saw that the amount of work had increased: "Fifteen!" he cried. "I ain't doin' no fifteen problems. That's too many."

Now here is a perfect opportunity to get into a conflict with a student, and there probably isn't a district in the world that wouldn't back a teacher who chose to punish this kind of attitude or disrespect. The tendency to react negatively is almost instinctive for many of us. In fact, we may even feel that we're not doing our job if we don't react! (Even as an observer, I found that this student was pushing my power buttons—and he wasn't even talking to me!) But Ms. Cahill showed me an

We can avoid creating a major incident out of a small slip-up by minimizing our reaction to the student's behavior.

The tendency to react negatively is almost instinctive for many of us.

---

*Many teachers, including a large number of Special Education teachers, have since told about how gum chewing seemed to "anchor" some of their kinesthetic learners (and many students identified as attention-deficit or hyperactive). The chewing, they claim, channels some of the students' energy and actually helps them concentrate and stay on task, especially when the students had to sit or study quietly for extended periods of time.

Saying "That won't work for me," conveys your unwillingness to accept their suggestion without criticizing, shaming or making them wrong.

The "smaller" our reactions, the less energy we feed a potential conflict.

Some disruptions can be intervened quickly and quietly, with a minimum of involvement, by physical proximity.

alternative; indeed, she showed me that there *was* an alternative. She looked at the student. She looked at the board. And then she did something that never would have occurred to me: She *agreed* with him! She responded, "You know, you're right! I guess I was having so much fun putting those problems on the board this morning that I just got carried away. Tell you what, class: Why don't you pick the ten problems you like best? You don't have to do all fifteen."

This incident precipitated her first big breakthrough in getting kids to complete and turn in work. (A number of students actually did all 15 problems.) However there was more going on than just giving choices and meeting power needs. Ms. Cahill was, in the way she responded to a potential conflict, building a foundation for future cooperation. I saw this happen again a few days later when the same boy came in complaining, "I'm sick of doin' these problems on the board!" Again, an opportunity for conflict, another temptation to win at a student's expense. And again, Ms. Cahill agreed: "Hey, I don't blame you. I think I'd be pretty tired of them myself." And, at that point, she offered the class a choice between doing ten of the problems on the board, ten of the problems on page 64, or making up ten problems of their own (as long as they were similar subtraction problems that required regrouping).

My first reaction, based in my own win-lose conditioning, was that, by not producing some negative consequence or punishment for this student, she was saying that it was OK for him to be disrespectful. In fact, she was not saying it was OK; she was saying that it was unnecessary. At no point did she relinquish her authority nor compromise academic requirements (the students still had to do ten problems, it just didn't matter which ones they did). She "won," and she did not need to make anyone lose. It didn't take long for the students to realize that Ms. Cahill was on their side; to the best of my knowledge, she never had a problem with this student after that and the degree of cooperation and sense of

partnership she developed with the entire class was fairly well cemented by the second or third week of school.

The "smaller" our reactions, the less energy we feed a potential conflict. Teachers who are open to students' negotiations for alternate or self-designed activities and assignments, for example, often encounter somewhat outrageous proposals at times, either from students who are unrealistic about what could actually work or those testing the limits of acceptability. Either way, if students propose that you cancel a lesson in favor of using the period for a game or time off, it's not necessary to attack them for trying to take advantage or thinking you're a pushover. Instead of exclaiming, "What? Are you crazy?" a simple, straightforward statement like, "That won't work for me," conveys your unwillingness to accept their suggestion without criticizing, shaming or making them wrong. You might even make a counter-proposal that will work for you: "How about settling down and doing what I've got planned? We should be able to finish a few minutes early. You can earn some free time at the end of class."

If a student knocks over a stack of papers and immediately bends down to pick them up, there is absolutely no reason for us to react at all. Some disruptions can be intervened quickly and quietly, with a minimum of involvement, by physical proximity. I've seen very chatty children suddenly get down to work simply because the teacher walked over to their table. Simply getting closer to the disturbance was the only involvement necessary; the teacher didn't need to say a word about the kids being off task a few moments before. Also, non-threatening eye-contact or humor can be extremely effective in redirecting children's attention and getting them back to doing what we want. If these behaviors elicit the cooperation we're after, there's no need to involve ourselves further.

Often, additional information or instruction will be all that is necessary. If a child creates a mess she doesn't know how (or is afraid) to clean up on her own, simple directions or an offer to help go much farther than criticism, a lecture or an impatient look. Many teachers quickly eliminate occasional outbursts of offensive language, for example, simply by responding with a raised eyebrow or a simple, nonreactive comment: "Uh-uh," or "Let's not say that word in here."

Certainly, any attempts to set up no-fail situations in the first place will help. Success orientation techniques such as expressing our boundaries before there is a problem ("I will read each spelling word only once"), giving special directions ("Here's how you can pour the juice without spilling it") or writing instructions on a task card or on the board will certainly avert a myriad of misunderstandings.

And simple courtesy and respect can work wonders. Students are much more likely to respond cooperatively to "Please put that toy away until lunchtime" than "Put that thing away now!" ("Please" and "Thank You" are not just magic words for children to use with adults.) On occasion, however, a student will resist even the most positively-stated request. There are a few tricks to avoiding a situation in which we back students into a corner. For example, switching from telling to asking can help: "You need to clear your desk. Where would you like to put that toy until lunchtime?" may be more effective than even "Please put it away" because the former statement offers a greater number of positive choices. Telling or ordering may appear non-negotiable, but every do-it-or-else statement still offers a yes or no option. In the above example, putting the toy away was not negotiable, but the location was. Much resistance can be avoided when we respect a child's need for power within non-negotiable limits.

Offering two or more specific positive choices can also help prevent resistance and refusal: "Would you like to put that toy in my desk drawer or in your locker?" Adding a reason can also help: "Please put that toy away so that it can remain in this center (so that no one trips over it, or so that you can get back to work now)." Likewise, the word "until" offers

hope and a promise of getting one's needs met at a later, specific time: "Please put that toy in your locker until your work is done (or until the dismissal bell rings)."

Finally, any time we can validate a student's desire to do something we're not willing to allow we can also promote cooperation: "This is a really nice toy. I know you wish you could play with it now. We need to get ready for the test and I think it might get in your way. Why not put it on my desk for now? You'll have some time to play with it when we're finished." All of these techniques leave the student with a forward focus and an understanding that his or her needs are being considered and respected.

Our old win-lose patterns can be instantly engaged when we confront an obstinate student. Unfortunately, if the child refuses to give up the toy despite all of our positive efforts, our first instinct is to immediately back up into power: "Give it to me now or I'll take it and you'll never see it again." Giving in to the urge to overpower a student can undo a great deal of the positive results gained by working towards a win-win environment.

A point-blank refusal can quickly turn into a no-win situation. The first casualty is often our perspective on the real issue, which, in this case, is that the student do the work—not that he obey the teacher. Backing off may mean sacrificing a short-term objective (getting him to give up the toy) to a long-term process (becoming responsible for doing his work regardless of temptations and distractions). But only in a win-lose classroom will your unwillingness to overpower or hurt a student make you come out a loser. Is it worth a power struggle that may or may not work?

Ideally, it's best to avoid power confrontations, but if one does come up, it's best to disengage quickly, if at all possible. We can always refuse to argue or try to coerce the student to cooperate: "I'm not about to try to force you to give up this toy. If you can work without being distracted by it, there's no problem. If not, I'll be happy to help you put

Simple directions or an offer to help go much farther than criticism, a lecture or an impatient look.

Students are much more likely to respond cooperatively to "Please put that toy away until lunchtime": than "Put that thing away now!"

Much resistance can be avoided when we respect a child's need for power within non-negotiable limits.

Once the students recognize the teacher's investment in their getting their needs met, disruptive or obnoxious behaviors become rather pointless.

We don't need to cause someone to lose in order for us to win.

it away. Keep in mind that your work must be finished in order for you to participate in this afternoon's activities (go out for recess, get credit for the assignments or merit whatever meaningful outcome is dependent on the work's completion)." Then walk away.

If the student's behavior is only causing problems for herself, the eventual unavailability of the meaningful consequences will teach her far more than your power or anger. (If her behavior is not causing a problem for anyone including herself, there may not have been a need for your involvement in the first place.) Think of ways you can avoid similar incidents from occurring in the future. When cool heads once again prevail, announce: "You know, we've never needed limits about toys before so it's not fair for me to take them from you without notice. But keeping toys at your desk is interfering with your learning. I know these things are important to you. At the same time, your attention is important to me. If you want to bring your toys to school, you'll have to keep them in your locker or in my desk during class time. You can play with them during recess."

No blaming, scolding, disappointment or moralizing. We've gotten around the "I'll show you" mentality of a punitive, win-lose relationship because we don't need to cause someone to lose in order for us to win. We now have tighter limits and more specific boundaries. If the problem persists, further action may be necessary, from a letter home requesting support for your limits to a total ban on toys.

Often teachers will stop me and ask, "But what if they still refuse?" (We can be relentlessly attached to that reactive context!) No matter how many proactive strategies we discuss, the dialogue always seems to return to "but what if . . .?" These teachers are usually terribly disappointed—and sometimes actually feel betrayed—when I tell them, "I don't know." But the point is that I *don't* know, nor am I any better equipped for handling win-lose (or no-win) confrontations than anyone else. I will, however, assure these teachers—just as

relentlessly—that as a win-win classroom climate evolves, the occurrence of this type of resistance and rebelliousness becomes increasingly rare. Once the students recognize the teacher's investment in their getting their needs met, disruptive or obnoxious behaviors become rather pointless.

When a student behaves destructively, hurting or endangering another student, property or himself, our immediate goal is to intervene before further damage can occur. Very often, one word firmly spoken is enough. One upper-grade elementary teacher used to ask her students to "freeze" when she wanted their attention. They always enjoyed stopping in what ever position they were in—the sillier the better—until she would release them with "Unfreeze." The same technique was also effective in preventing various students from dropping crayons in the fish tank, following through on a punch or continuing to absent-mindedly carve gouges into the top of a desk. The word "Stop!" can also work, giving the student a chance to stop before any damage is done, rethink before he gets in any deeper, and back up and whenever possible, correct mistakes. The break can also give us the chance to get the student's attention for further information, suspend a privilege or even momentarily remove a student from the situation, if necessary.

When a student's behavior becomes extremely distracting or disturbing to others (without posing any actual danger to life or limb), our attention shifts closer to survival—and preventing things from getting worse. These are the instances in which we'll see the greatest value in providing an outlet to reduce emotional stress or hard feelings. It's difficult to have a constructive dialogue or make a positive decision if one is near hysterics (this goes for both teacher and students). Frequently a soft word of understanding or a gentle touch on the shoulder can prevent an incident from escalating—but this is only possible for us to do if we stay calm. We can also help the child by validating his feelings and offering an alternative to taking it out on the class—or on us: "I can see that you're upset. Why don't you get a drink of water and we can talk when you get back?" Asking the child to leave the environment is not a punishment for the angry student. It is a technique to help us stay calm, to protect the rest of the class, to give the student a chance to disengage and catch his breath and to defuse the negative energy that's built up. Although it's extremely unlikely to happen in a truly win-win classroom, if the student becomes too violent or dangerous to approach, send someone for help.

Very often, a student's outbursts are indications of a lack of effective alternatives to handling anger or frustration. Negative behaviors such as stealing, lying or bullying can be signs that the student's control needs are not being met in more positive ways. Students who refuse to do assignments may be prompted by previous school failures, a genuine sense of "I can't," a desire to self-protect (staying safe by minimizing the teacher's expectations or demands) or a need for attention, albeit negative. Weak social skills can also account for a number of problems that arise.

Students who have consistently been on the losing end of win-lose authority relationships and those who have built a habit of solving conflicts by hurting other people, need some concrete alternatives to lashing out. They also need time to develop trust in you and the system. A win-win classroom, with a measure of time and faith, can provide the options, acceptance and acknowledgement that will enable even the most severely damaged children opportunities to find more constructive means of fulfilling their needs.

Further, the more positive choices and consequences available, the more the students have to lose when they do not cooperate. This is why teachers who use boundaries in a reward-oriented environment, typically confront far fewer problems and see less resistance, negativity or irresponsibility than teachers who rely on more traditional win-lose approaches. When conflicts, disruptions or off-task behaviors occur,

boundaries offer a powerful tool for intervening without creating additional stress.

My appreciation for the value of this approach evolved from earlier efforts to shift from punishment to (negative) consequences as a response to a student's misbehavior or uncooperative attitude. The attempt to focus on the more predictable, more related, and less hurtful or arbitrary qualities of consequences was admirable. I valued the intention to get away from criticism, derision, humiliation, deprivation, isolation or physical pain. I also appreciated the fact that the child's feelings, self-concept and self-motivation were finally being considered. I applauded the dedication to finding strategies that were less judgmental, less concerned with the morality of an act and less likely to dramatize the "wrongness" of a student.

But I still found too many similarities between the way most teachers, myself included, applied consequences and the way they used punishment: In most cases, the only real reframing in shifting from "punishment" to "consequences" was linguistic. Both options relied on negative reactions to negative behavior and most of the so-called consequences I saw teachers use had all the characteristics of the punitive behaviors we were supposedly trying to avoid.

The next step for me was the shift that allowed me to think in terms of reward orientation, where consequences are now the *good* things that happen as a result of cooperation. In using boundaries, as in real life, consequences can certainly be positive or negative. However in this context, a negative consequence typically refers to the lack or removal of a positive consequence. Throughout this chapter, when I talk about negative consequences with regard to boundaries and follow-through, I am referring to instances in which a privilege or positive consequence either is removed or remains inaccessible until more cooperative behavior appears. Examples may include: asking students to split up and sit elsewhere when

Frequently a soft word of understanding or a gentle touch on the shoulder can prevent an incident from escalating.

Very often, a student's outbursts are indications of a lack of effective alternatives to handling anger or frustration.

The more positive consequences available, the more the students have to lose when they do not cooperate.

their talking becomes disruptive, not giving credit for work that isn't completed or turned in on time, or turning off the movie when students start talking when the previously-announced condition for showing the movie required quiet. Obviously, this strategy requires a reward-oriented environment in which the emphasis is on the availability of a variety of positive consequences.

Using boundaries as a tool for expressing the connection between positive outcomes and cooperative behavior puts even more responsibility on the student and relies even less on the teacher's power. The positive focus is far more win-win and the effectiveness—for generating cooperation, building responsibility and encouraging strong, solid relationships between teachers and kids—is far greater than anything I'd observed that used negative consequences as deterrents.

For example, boundaries can help with one of the most basic, if not most difficult, task teachers face—learning to separate the students from their behavior. While we may recognize on an intellectual level that a student is indeed more than simply a-person-who-forgets-library-books, it's easy for the forgetfulness to overwhelm our attention, especially if it's something that's happened before. Likewise, we can intervene far more positively when we see a "poor choice" instead of a "possessed child."

Punishments and many negative consequences make little distinction between the student and his behavior, tending instead to rivet the worth of the child on one particular act. In such instances, not only is the behavior bad, so is the student. Boundaries focus exclusively on the behavior, not the worth of the student. Neither previous behavior nor personality traits are factors, nor are the teacher's feelings about a student. Boundaries allow a misbehaving student to still be acceptable, valued and welcome in class, even if her behavior is not. While the positive consequences promised by a boundary are conditional, the teacher's acceptance is not.

Punishment may satisfy the teacher's need for control and power, but its use can create resentment, hostility and resistance, fueling negative teacher-student relationships, power struggles and further disruptions. Teachers using punishment also model a way of dealing with conflicts by hurting or using force, especially when physical consequences are involved. This behavior implies that "you can get what you want as long as you are bigger, stronger or meaner."

Punishment is also outcome-oriented, devoted primarily to immediate compliance and short-term results. Punishment burdens the teacher with the primary responsibility for the solution of the problem and rarely goes beyond the immediate objective of getting the undesirable behavior to stop. Since many, if not most, negative consequences operate the same way as punishments, many of the problems associated with punishments exist here, too.

On the other hand, boundaries (and conditional availability of positive consequences) do not attack or undermine the student's sense of worth. Boundaries actually work to meet the child's needs for power and control within limits that protect others. Since boundaries convey the conditions under which a positive consequence is available to a student, the lack of this desirable outcome is directly related to the student's misbehavior, lack of cooperation or failure to meet the conditions specified. Boundaries are not structured either to hurt the student or bring pleasure, satisfaction or revenge to the teacher. They can minimize power struggles because they emerge from the desire to protect everyone's needs and safety—not from the teacher's power. Additionally, their emphasis on positive outcomes which benefit the student communicate the teacher's commitment to win-win.

Boundaries allow the teacher to achieve the same immediate objective as the threat of a punitive outcome, but they also provide students access to processing steps not otherwise

Using boundaries to express the connection between positive outcomes and cooperative behavior puts even more responsibility on the student.

Boundaries focus exclusively on the behavior, not the worth of the student.

available. Thus boundaries, which connect the student's behavior to some outcome other than the teacher's reaction, reinforce for the student the relationship between her behavior choices and their consequences—good and bad. Punishments or penalties, on the other hand, teach the student only to beware of the teacher's power. In addition, punishment relieves the student of responsibility for changing her behavior by suggesting that once the punishment has been served, the student is free to continue misbehaving until she is caught again. In this way, punishment actually reinforces dependence on teacher control and interferes with opportunities for the student to develop self-control.

Boundaries allow us to respond constructively to student misconduct and still maintain our win-win intentions. But there's more to boundary setting than simply communicating the connection between what the teacher wants and what the student wants. The key to making boundaries work—indeed the *only* way they will work—is with follow-through. Follow-through is the part of the process that puts the authority in win-win authority relationships, establishes our credibility, creates the sense of safety and predictability students need and most effectively gets us the commitment and cooperation we want.

To illustrate the way boundaries work, consider how a retail store operates. Let's say that this particular store opens at 8:00 a.m. and it closes at midnight. Now these hours act as a boundary: Get to the store between these hours and you can shop; get there after midnight and you'll find that the store is closed—not to teach you a lesson, not to punish you for being late, but simply because it's after midnight. There's nothing personal, punitive or vindictive going on here. The store is simply closed. Period. Hopefully, the experience will give you the information you need to make more constructive choices the next time you want to go there.

The dynamics of expressing boundaries and following through are the same in school

settings as elsewhere. And they can be equally effective in any setting when follow-through indeed occurs. For example, I taught a class of fifth graders right before lunch one year. This group seemed to take forever to clear their desks and get quiet—my two criteria for dismissal. I found myself giving these students more and more time to get ready to leave until I realized that five minutes into the lesson, I was starting to feel the pressure to clean up for a lunch period that was still 35 minutes away. Giving the students additional time had obviously not resolved the problem.

I decided to go back to announcing a brief clean-up period a minute or two before the lunch bell rang. And I also made sure they were aware of what would be happening ahead of time. At the beginning of the next class, I announced, "Listen, we've got a lot to cover today. Getting ready for lunch has been a problem for us, and today we'll have less time than normal. When we finish the lesson, I'll let you know that it's time to clean up. I'll say it once. After that, it's up to you. As soon as you clear your desks and get quiet, you can go down to eat." I proceeded with the lesson as always, stopping at 11:58 to announce cleanup. At that point, I got busy with some papers on my desk.

Now I had thought that this clear, non-powering announcement along with the potential for missing out on high-priority lunch and playground time, would clear up this silliness once and for all. I was wrong. For some reason, it almost seemed to have invited the kids to test how serious I was. (This may tell you something about the previous consistency of my follow-through.) Students who hadn't been doing much of anything earlier in the period suddenly decided to get busy. Quiet kids started talking.

There was a part of me that wanted to scream. It took every ounce of self-restraint to stay calm and write a note to send down to the lunch service staff to mention that my class might be late: " . . . however, please put their lunches out as usual." To the students, I did not say a word. I didn't even glance at the clock. Every student had heard my announcement; every student had heard the lunch bell. After that, it was up to them.

Around 12:22, I noticed that it had gotten pretty quiet and when I looked up, the last student was clearing his desk and getting ready to go. Evidently someone had noticed some friends out on the playground and more than a few had started getting hungry. We got down to the lunchroom two minutes later where the students were shocked to find their lunches had gotten cold. Many students had not finished eating and only a few had barely gotten out the door to the playground before the bell rang to return to class.

Of course, the students were upset. I wasn't too thrilled myself about not getting a lunch break that day.* But the sacrifice was worth it: The next day, I had finished the lesson early to let them get started on their homework when I noticed, at 11:56, that each student was ready to be dismissed. (I'm still amazed that they had all learned to tell time so quickly.) Now that they had initiated the cooperative behavior, I switched to reinforcement: "Looks like you're ready for dismissal (describing the behavior). Now we can get down there a little early today (what's in it for you)." For the most part, that was the end of the lunchtime blues. Their cooperation became increasingly habitual and internalized. My willingness to follow-through taught the students that their cooperation was simply what was necessary to get to lunch on time, not to make the teacher happy or avoid the teacher's punitive or angry reaction.

I will admit to being rather unnerved by taking what seemed to be fairly drastic measures. But then any form of follow-through will seem drastic or even frightening for teachers who have a tendency to back down on their boundaries, as many of us often do. Follow-through requires a tremendous courage, commitment and con-

The rule of thumb for setting boundaries is this: If we aren't willing to follow through, we don't bother setting the boundary in the first place.

sistency. Some of us invent all sorts of techniques, tricks and rationalizations for interfering with our follow-through.

The rule of thumb for setting boundaries is this: If we aren't willing to follow through, we don't bother setting the boundary in the first place. Obviously, we want to avoid putting our students in the position of having to miss out on desirable outcomes or take responsibility for errors, mistakes in judgment and accidents. But we can wait for their attention, give clear directions, assign reasonable amounts of work and provide every opportunity for each student to make cooperative choices and there will still be incidents these measures fail to prevent. Then it's time for follow-through.

If we state that a privilege is only available under certain conditions, once a student has violated these conditions, the situation must change until the behavior stops (or for a more positive behavior appears). Unfortunately, there is often a great deal of time between the misconduct and the removal of a privilege or positive consequence: we tend, instead, to fill the gap with inconsequential responses, such as warnings and reminders. A warning may appear to have an immediate positive effect, however the impact of warnings tend to be quite temporary and come at a high cost. However, even if the only drawback to this habit was the amount of time it wastes, it would still warrant some serious reconsideration.

For one thing, warnings undermine a teacher's credibility. (Why respect a boundary if you can get away with ignoring it several times?) Warnings also communicate a great deal of inconsistency: We tend to be fairly arbitrary in our use of warnings as well as the number of warnings we're willing to give students before we really let them have it. This response may come at any time (after maybe three or four reminders on a good day, after one or two if we're not in a very good mood) and is nearly always critical and threatening. When

*I also suspected that the parents would be upset, so I drafted a letter explaining what had happened to send home with the students in that class at the end of the day. And I made sure to call the parents who might not get my note before they heard a slightly different version of what had happened.

we get in the habit of giving reminders after or during a misbehavior, we are, in essence, devaluing the limits we place on the privileges we offer, inviting the students not to take them seriously. (How respectful would you be of a store's closing time if the store stayed open, or reopened, to let you in whenever you showed up?) Worse yet, by giving warnings, we're also removing the power from the boundary itself and putting it back in our laps. Additionally, we compromise emotional safety, partly because of the absence of predictability and partly because, when the warnings don't work, we usually blow up, reacting out of anger and frustration. When the loss of privilege occurs immediately, the first time the misbehavior occurs, it is a function of the student's uncooperative choosing; delayed by warnings, it becomes a function of the teacher's power.

Not all warnings are verbal. Frowning, finger-wagging, or writing a student's name on the board simply delay a meaningful consequence from occurring. As with verbal warnings, these teacher behaviors do little beside drawing attention to the misbehavior—which may actually end up reinforcing what we're trying to stop. In addition, they rarely work because they don't prevent or interrupt access to a positive consequence—the students can continue to sit together, watch the movie or take home another library book. In nearly all instances (except, perhaps, for the most diligent teacher-pleasers), continuing the negative behavior will always be more need-fulfilling than avoiding teacher's dirty looks.

Warnings seem convenient to us because it's actually easier to tell someone not to do something again and again than it is to actually intervene. Warnings may seem generous and kind, and for a while they do protect children from experiencing the negative outcomes of their own behaviors. But this is exactly the long-range result we're trying to avoid: Each time warnings delay—or replace—consequences, they deny the student the opportunity to become more personally responsible for his behavior and less teacher dependent as well.

This interference is called "enabling;" by protecting students from negative outcomes, we fail in our obligation to hold them accountable for their behavior. Giving warnings or reminders by restating a boundary *before* there is a problem is completely legitimate and will help prevent many problems. However, once a disruption, violation or episode of "forgetfulness" occurs, the immediate and unequivocal removal of a privilege makes quite clear our willingness to insist that the terms of our boundaries be respected in the future.

We may also delay follow through by using a child's misbehavior as an opportunity for discussing previous failures or bringing in our own feelings of disappointment or frustration. Other time-wasters include lecturing about the importance of cooperation, asking the student to repeat the rules, and engaging in discussions or arguments about the fairness of a consequence. Closely related is the tendency to ask the student why she doesn't have her homework, why she forgot her pencil or why Lamont was bothering her.

Asking why is a common response that seems harmless, even constructive, but it also engages us in the students' problems. The question invites excuses, implying that if the student is creative—or pathetic—enough, he's off the hook. Excuses invite the arbitrary use of teacher power and acceptance ("Impress me and maybe I'll let you out of your responsibility.") and more often than not will evoke negative reactions, because the students' answers provide ammunition for criticisms, lectures or attacks. Excuses also invite us to solve the problem for the student.

Does it really matter if Alfred doesn't have his homework because "a tornado took it out of my lunch box" or because he felt like watching TV instead? Does he no longer need to turn it in? Asking why suggests that your limits are only limits if students can't find a loophole. There's no reason to respect a boundary you can talk your way out of. Plus, asking "why" puts us in a position of having to judge the

We tend to be fairly arbitrary in our use of warnings as well as the number of warnings we're willing to give students before we really let them have it.

When we get in the habit of giving reminders after or during a misbehavior, we are, in essence, devaluing the limits we place on the privileges we offer, inviting the students not to take them seriously.

Giving warnings or reminders by restating a boundary before there is a problem is completely legitimate and will help prevent many problems.

validity of an excuse, which can be very arbitrary. I've also seen teachers become rather resentful when a student comes up with an extremely compelling story, which puts the teacher in the position of having to relax boundaries in order to not seem like a completely unreasonable human being. However, when we intend to follow through on our boundaries, "why" doesn't matter, even in the most extreme cases.

A high school teacher once told me a rather dramatic story about one of her 3rd-period English students. A typically reliable senior, he came in early and told her that he didn't have his assignment ready to turn in that period. Instead of asking why, the teacher simply repeated her boundary, in this case a homework policy that stated, "If it's on my desk by the time the 3:00 o'clock dismissal bells rings, you can still get full credit for it."

The student countered, "No! You don't understand! I did my homework last night. I did all my assignments. I put everything out in the car before I went to bed so I'd be organized when I got up. Well, my father got drunk again last night and took my car after I went to bed. I don't have any of my stuff with me today."

The teacher listened and then she said, "I have three things I want to tell you. First, I want to assure you that you are in no way responsible for your father's drinking. Second, I want to tell you that you are in no way responsible for what your father does when he drinks. And third, I want to tell you that you are responsible for the assignments you get in this class. If you want credit for this one, it needs to be on my desk by the time the 3:00 o'clock bell rings."

The student was stunned. "That's not fair," he protested. "I'm not doing it again."

The teacher agreed! "I understand. I'd probably feel the same way. I want you to know that I respect whatever you decide to do about this assignment."

This is a superb example of how possible it is to be completely supportive, loving and unconditionally accepting even while maintaining our boundaries. I applaud the courage this teacher exhibited in not succumbing to a very convincing, reasonable and, by all accounts, true story. Don't imagine that this experience didn't cause her many hours of soul-searching. But by the end of the day, she was convinced that she had done the right thing; at about five minutes to three, the boy came in with his paper done over.

"It's not as good as the first one," he confessed.

"That doesn't matter," the teacher responded. "A hundred years from now, nobody's going to remember this paper. But for the moment, there are bigger things at stake here, not the least of which is the fact that you're living with someone who can make your life pretty complicated, even if it's not on purpose. Have you given any thought to how you can take care of yourself in the future?"

"Yeah," he answered. "I'm gonna keep all my stuff in my room from now on. He won't mess with it in there."

"Sounds like a plan," she concurred.

There are many times in life where "why" won't matter: The IRS doesn't care why your income taxes are late. And the store won't reopen, the movie won't start over and the restaurant won't serve you a meal after closing time—no matter how good your excuses are for not getting there on time. Compare the message this student would have received had this teacher arbitrarily decided that her policies didn't apply in this case, to the learning that occurred when she held fast. Here was a wonderful opportunity to see the extent of his accountability and to learn to fulfill his responsibilities rather than fix blame, an opportunity that would have been lost had this teacher not followed through.

When we have done as much as we reasonably can to make success possible and the student still makes a non-cooperative choice, a great deal of courage, commitment and consistency is necessary to allow students to encounter the consequences of their behaviors. If a child forgets his permission slip, he misses the outing. If she breaks or spills something in the classroom, she fixes, replaces, cleans up or works off the damages—whether the damage was done accidentally or in anger. If he can't control his urge to splash in the paint center, he has to play somewhere else for that period (or day).

It may seem cruel to refuse to buy a student a meal the fourth time he forgets to bring in his lunch money (even if you told him last time that he'd reached his credit limit), but for the sake of the child's growth toward responsible adulthood, there is no more loving response. Unless a student's life, health or safety are threatened, being regularly allowed to experience the connection between his behavior and the outcomes of his behavior encourages alternatives to blaming, helplessness and irresponsibility. It also assists the student in making more positive choices down the road. At no point is the child bad, stupid or wrong—it's only the choice that could have been better.

Now before you accuse me of being completely heartless, let me suggest that there are ways to build flexibility into your boundaries *proactively* without arbitrarily relaxing limits when your students have a convincing story or happen to catch you on a particularly compassionate day. Setting a blanket "grace period" or offering almost-full credit for work handed in a day late can accommodate students with more serious excuses as well as those who simply forget or use their time unwisely. Some teachers count only a percentage of the work due, say 32 out of 35 assignments, giving students three assignments they can ignore for whatever reasons or, perhaps, do for additional credit. Some teachers let students earn a "night off" when they've turned in homework complete and on time, ten or fifteen times in a row. One teacher gave each student a "Get Out of Jail Free" card, to be used, if desired, to get out of anything except a test. If the child didn't do his homework and turned in the card, he got full credit; if the card had already been used, no credit was available, regardless of the excuse.

Following through on a previously-announced boundary is a pretty straight-forward affair. As always, actions speak louder than words, so keep words to a minimum and let the actions speak for themselves. Announce, "I will continue reading this story as soon as it gets quiet. That offer is good for ten seconds." Then we act—waiting, sitting quietly, with a neutral (not angry) facial expression. Fight the urge to repeat the announcement or embellish it with any further discussion; either one will sound as though you're trying to talk the kids into doing what you want. Your silent and explicit refusal to read over their conversation is far more powerful—and convincing—than anything you might say.

And even that may not get them quiet: Students will always choose the more need-fulfilling option and, in this instance, will only cooperate if their need to hear the story overrides their need to chatter. If the uncooperative behavior persists, it's time to close the book and get on with the day: "Please take your seats and get your math folders out. Let's finish this story tomorrow (or later)," using the same neutral tone as that used for expressing the boundary in the first place.

Now look at what you've accomplished. You've asserted your need for quiet attention when you read. You've connected their choices (talking) to a consequence (not getting to hear the rest of the story), one that has nothing to do with your approval. You still accept the students, although you did not accept their behavior. You have not expressed anger, nor have you attacked the students and made them wrong. You've kept your blood pressure down. You've reinforced the limits that go along with the privilege without using power or force. And you've also left the door open to try again at another time.

But what about those situations in which only one or two students are disrupting the reading? We can prevent many disruptions before we start reading if we can anticipate students' needs ahead of time. For example, many low-auditory students can listen far less disruptively when they can do something else while they are listening. Much of what is often labeled hyperactive behavior or low impulse control can often be successfully channeled into tactile or kinesthetic activities, such as playing with some clay, a rubber band, a string of beads or even a piece of string while listening. Likewise, asking students to choose a place to sit (at a desk, on the rug or floor, for example), where they won't be tempted to talk, allowing them to read along if they have their own copies of the book (or from an overhead or filmstrip), or even allowing them to draw or work on another activity while you're reading can minimize opportunities for disruptions.

That being said, you can take every precaution and still have children talking or acting up. If we've said that we'll only read while there's no talking, it doesn't matter whether there's only one student talking or thirty. We close the book and move on to something else. ("We'll try again after this activity is finished.") Teachers who are consistent in following through report that even very young students will exert pressure on one another—for the benefit of the group—for everyone to settle down quickly. Once the boundary is expressed, the responsibility for hearing the story in these classrooms is completely out of the teacher's hands.

And what about those situations in which we can't really abandon what we're doing to move onto something else. Stopping in the middle of a special, high-interest activity is one thing, but we certainly wouldn't want to have to drop every plan that doesn't sustain our students' attention. One first-grade teacher made a habit of stopping mid-sentence as soon as she noticed that the kids had gotten distracted. Most of the time, her silence brought them back immediately. However, when the talking continued, she started looking at her watch. In the beginning, this

Following through on a previously-announced boundary is a pretty straightforward affair. As always, actions speak louder than words, so keep words to a minimum and let the actions speak for themselves.

Many low-auditory students can listen far less disruptively when they can do something else while they are listening.

behavior, by itself, had little meaning to the students, so she announced, "You know, we really need to finish this lesson. Your talking is taking up some of our work time. We've wasted one minute so far. Since I haven't told you about this, I won't hold you responsible for that minute. However, from here on in, any wasted time will cut into our self-selection period (a collection of high-interest activities scheduled for later in the day) so we can get everything done." From that point on, she would simply sit and wait. Saving the valuable, fun enrichment activities for the end of the day gave her kids the incentive to stay on task, especially as they came to realize that and the amount of time available for the activities depended on their cooperation throughout the day. After the first few days, she rarely had to do more than look at her watch to get her students' attention.

This strategy is not meant to suggest that we spend the entire year sitting and waiting for our kids to clam up. However, we may need to let them really mess up and miss out on some really great positive consequences before we can honestly expect them to gain enough awareness of their own misbehavior to eventually stop it from recurring. This is especially true about noise level. It's easy for students to lose sense of how loud they're getting, and it's impossible for us to give any specific limits (in terms of decibels) that will have meaning to them. However kids can have a remarkably intuitive sense of what "too loud" sounds like in any particular classroom. It's only the teacher's consistent follow-through that allows this awareness to develop.

It is fair and helpful to let them know ahead of time, "I'm going to need for you to keep the noise down while I work on these papers (or with this small group). You are welcome to work with a partner during this time (or choose your own seats, for example). If I need to stop because of noise or misbehavior, I will ask you all to return to your assigned seats." The process of becoming self-monitoring is gradual and it often takes time. However, if the positive consequence is meaningful and significant, and we have the courage to follow through when there is a problem, the process usually doesn't take too long.

One teacher told me about a time her limits—and her patience—were tested by a group of middle school kids who were allowed to work together "as long as the noise doesn't interrupt my group," she'd told them. As will often happen, the noise level quickly escalated to the point at which she could barely hear the student sitting next to her.

She excused herself from her group and went over to the noisy center. "This isn't working," she told them. "You guys need to find someplace else to sit this period. We can try again tomorrow." (Listen to how neutral and non-accusing this sentence is. No attacks, no criticism, no lectures about their rudeness or lack of consideration. "This isn't working. You need to move." Magic, no?)

Except, as respectful as she was, every student in this group started to protest, "That's not fair. It wasn't me. We weren't talking." She told me that it took more restrain than she ever imagined she had to keep herself from completely losing control. Instead of challenging or backing into what was quickly beginning to look like a no-win situation, she calmly announced, "I know that you like working with your friends. And I know that you can appreciate that this can only happen when working together doesn't create a problem for anyone else. Well, it's creating a problem for us. I'm going to give you another minute to decide how you're going to handle this situation. I'm sure you can work this out because we all want this privilege to continue." And then she walked away.

The students grumbled for a few seconds and then they all got up and found someplace else to work. At worst, the teacher was willing to back up the next day and return to solo assignments, giving the class a chance to try group work again after a few days. Fortunately, her willingness to back off (which is not the same as backing down) and her commitment to the students "winning" under cooperative circumstances helped avert what could have become a rather nasty incident.

In factory-era authority relationships, misconduct is an invitation for the teacher to exercise power and control. Our immediate response, in this situation is "What can I do to the student who has misbehaved? How can I teach him a lesson?" In a 21st century classroom, the lessons to be learned from one's misconduct come from the consequences of the misconduct, from missing out on privileges and positive occurrences—not from the power of the teacher. This also gives us the freedom to allow students to regain access to positive consequences once they have stopped misbehaving and, if necessary, repair any damage the misbehavior has caused. Students miss lunch, recess, free time, self-selection or the rest of the story because they failed to behave within the terms or limits that would allow those privileges to continue. They did not miss the activities as a punishment for misbehaving.

With a punitive or reactive response we're tempted to remove a privilege forever: "You'll never be able to sit together again." What do students have to gain by cooperating under these conditions? Follow-through (the immediate interruption of the privilege) allows for the possibility of greater success at another time: "You each need to return to your seats. You can try working together again this afternoon," or "Please leave this center now. You're welcome back here when you feel you can play without hitting."

Boundaries allow you to leave the door open for the students to change their behavior and "get it right." This means that Andy can return to the group as soon as he feels—and demonstrates—that he can control his urge to hit. Keisha can have another crack at the paint center tomorrow as long as she is willing to confine the paint to the paper. Donia can take a new library book home as soon as she brings back the pile she has at home. Even a student who has refused to do his work—a behavior

Backing off is not the same as backing down.

In a 21st century classroom, the lessons to be learned from one's misconduct come from the consequences of the misconduct, from missing out on privileges and positive occurrences—not from the power of the teacher.

Allow students to regain access to positive consequences once they have stopped misbehaving and, if necessary, repair any damage the misbehavior has caused.

particularly hard for most teachers to deal with—is more likely to rethink his refusal if we can leave him a way out: "You will need to decide if not doing the work is worth missing out on credit (a grade, recess, graduation or whatever positive outcome will be available as a result). In the meantime, I will leave your work on your desk in case you change your mind."

When a misbehavior occurs because no previous limits had been set, it is certainly appropriate to back up and insert additional limits or instruction: "Move those cassettes please. I forgot to tell you to be careful not to put them on the heater," or "And by the way, you have one minute to find a place to work and get busy." From that point on, student violations require us to act. Once the announcement has been made, we are well within our rights to remove the audio tapes "for today" or assign the indecisive student to a seat of our choosing. These are the consequences of the students' inability to function within the previously announced limits. The tapes are removed so they don't melt; the student is assigned a seat so that the class can go on with its work.

Sounds great, but how can a busy and distracted teacher think so fast? Like all of the other skills discussed in this book, learning to respond constructively in a negative situation is a process. These behaviors are difficult to plan, but as you move from blaming and punishing, and as you realign your interactions with win-win values, the rest follows. Start noticing what you say. When you can, take a second to think about *what* you want to say. (One teacher told me that she would often respond to unexpected questions or requests with, "Wait! I need to think about how I want to answer you.")

Clearly, the more positive choices and outcomes are available, the more a student has to lose when she does not cooperate. In some settings choices and incentives are easy to structure and provide; others require a bit of creativity. For example, teachers working in a departmentalized system feel a greater degree of time pressure, as they are literally working from one bell to the next. Only having students for 45 minutes presents a number of problems one doesn't encounter in a self-contained classroom, such as having to go through the "settling down and getting started" phase with six or seven groups of students. But in these settings, it is just as important to have choices and positive consequences available as motivators.

One mid-school teacher complained, "I'm barely getting 20 minutes of instruction into a 40-minute class. How can I take the time to provide options and rewards?" Yet her efforts at creating a win-win classroom, and her attention to her students' needs and interests, paid off. She found that by building in time for need-fulfilling options, she actually increased instructional time by approximately ten minutes a day! (Some of the options she offered included allowing choices about in-class projects and assignments, offering a variety of enrichment puzzles and activities or free time at the end of the lesson, or allowing the students to listen to music while they were doing seatwork.) Another teacher gave an otherwise recalcitrant group of 10th graders the incentive to get to her chemistry class by serializing a story and reading for the first five minutes of class to anyone who arrived on time (as long as it was quiet). She offered to read at the end of class, too, if they got through their work ahead of schedule—which they often did—and was delighted when the majority of her students went out and got their own copies of the book to read along.

Although it requires a sharp change in focus from industrial values, increasing options for choices, negotiating and rewards will surely improve motivation and cooperation, decrease negative behaviors and give us built-in leverage when necessary. And as we become more skilled at win-win teaching, we will find ourselves with fewer conflicts and less resistance, and a chance for better relationships with our students, more time for instruction and far less stress in the workplace.

Rules and Punishment

(Application or Imposition of Negative Consequences)

- Win-lose

- Power-oriented

- Goal: Punishing negative behavior; applying negative consequences in order to shame, teaching student a lesson, making student lose.

- Operates by exacting payment or penalty which, once served, does not obligate student to change behavior (instead, encourages to avoid further punishment).

- Result of teacher's power, getting caught

- Rarely related to the problem behavior

- Equates student with behavior; attacks person

- Related to worth of student; both behavior and student are wrong or unacceptable.

- Judgmental, focus on morality of behavior

- Arbitrary, often comes as a surprise; often no limits (or unclear or ambiguous limits) are set beforehand

- Teacher is responsible for correcting negative behavior

- Teacher role: Setting and expressing rules; policing, catching, blaming, disempowering; exacting penalties for misbehavior (application of negative consequences)

- Lesson: Avoid power; invites students to get sneakier

- Conflict Resolution Model: Force, hurt, deprive, threaten

- Outcome oriented

- High cost to students' feelings, self-esteem, sense of control

- High cost to teacher-student relationship

- Students may respond with hostility, aggressiveness, rebelliousness; can create additional conflict

Boundaries and Follow-through

(Contingent Availability of Positive Consequences)

- Win-win

- Interaction-oriented

- Goal: Encourage positive behavior; give incentives for cooperation. Also to stop destructive or disruptive behavior and reestablish positive behavior, encourage student self-correction. Build commitment to cooperation.

- Operates by allowing positive consequences (meaningful outcomes) for cooperation, work completion.

- Result of students' choices and uncooperative behavior

- Directly, specifically related to negative behavior (and loss of privilege previously established)

- Separates student from behavior; attacks behavior

- Unrelated to student's worth; only behavior is a problem (student is still acceptable)

- Objective focus on outcome or effect of behavior

- Logical, predictable; limits and consequences established beforehand

- Student is responsible for correcting negative behavior

- Teacher role: Setting and communicating limits, intervention, facilitating student processing; removing or withholding positive consequences until desired behavior appears

- Lesson: Personal responsibility; invites students to change behavior

- Conflict Resolution Model: Negotiation, compromise

- Process oriented

- Protects students' feelings, self-esteem, sense of control

- Teacher may experience anger, disappointment, resentment, vengeance
- Need-fulfilling to teacher; focus on teacher's need
- Message to student: "How can you avoid what you don't want?"
- Focus: "What do I do when a student misbehaves?"
- Punishment often maintained even after negative behavior stops

- Does not violate teacher-student relationship
- Students more likely to respond with cooperation; can avoid additional conflict
- Teacher can remain neutral, calm, and accepting of student; may get angry but generally the experience is less stressful to all involved
- Need-fulfilling to student *and* teacher
- Message to student: "How can we both get what we want?"
- Focus: "What do I do to encourage cooperation and commitment?"
- Negative consequences (absence of positive consequences) usually discontinues once student chooses more positive behavior

Teacher Behaviors to Avoid

- Hurtful or punitive responses:
  - Yelling, blaming
  - Criticism, name-calling, put-downs, shaming (violation of worth)
  - Humiliation, derision
  - Deprivation of unrelated objects or privileges
  - Isolation, abandonment; conditional acceptance
  - Hitting, physical consequences
  - Sarcasm
  - Any task, look, word or behavior intended to hurt or get back at a student
- Praising unrelated or previous behaviors to try to get the student to cooperate (or stop misbehaving)
- Ignoring misconduct that violates your safety, rights or needs or those of any of your students (includes the right to teach and learn)

- Lecturing, moralizing or attempting to talk the student into cooperating.
- Regularly calling on another teacher, administrator or parents to handle behavior problems that occur with your students in your class.
- Delaying a meaningful consequence (such as interrupting or removing a privilege or positive consequence) with non-meaningful consequences such as warnings, threats, a dirty look or writing a student's name.
- Asking for excuses instead of immediately withdrawing positive consequences; asking "why." Making excuses for the student or allowing others to do so.
- Reacting or getting involved in situations which the students are resolving non-disruptively on their own.
- No-win, power struggles; disempowering; backing a student into a corner.

Guidelines for Handling Negative Behavior

- Think prevention. Although no one can predict every possible opportunity for disaster, a large number of problems can be avoided by taking the time to anticipate what you and your students will need, considering any possibility for misunderstandings or difficulties, and setting very specific limits ahead of time.

- When something comes up, try to isolate what's bothering you. Are you reacting to a personality trait or value conflict, or is the student's behavior actually interfering with the teaching or learning process?

- Attack the problem, not the person. Mentally separate the student from the behavior. It's the interruption that's annoying—not the student.

- Minimize your reaction. Count to ten, or at least to five. Use this time to remind yourself that you don't have to get angry, lecture, criticize, interrogate or punish. (Often, you don't even have to get involved!) Staying calm can help you avoid compounding the problem at hand. A brief pause can also allow the student to resolve or correct the problem behavior on his own.

- Deal specifically with the behavior—not the morality of the behavior, previous incidents or the personality behind the misconduct.

- If your reaction starts to create a win-lose (or no-win) situation, stop and back off: "Wait. This isn't the way I want to handle this." If necessary—and possible—withdraw for a few seconds to regain your perspective.

- At all times, stay responsible for your actions and words. We are most vulnerable to negative adult behavior patterns in the presence of negative or disruptive student behaviors. Regardless of our commitment to maintaining a positive, win-win environment, there will be times we will most likely slip up and say or do something hurtful or destructive. At those times, be careful to model responsible language and *not blame the student*. For example, avoid statements like, "You make me so angry," or "If you hadn't done that I wouldn't have said that to you." If you act or speak in a hurtful way, apologize and switch to more a constructive approach—just like you would want the student to do!

- Look for ways to offer many choices and positive outcomes for cooperation, building in incentives and motivators. Examples may include additional work, puzzles, fun enrichment exercises or cooking activities; free time to start on homework, talk with classmates or play a game; a chance to work with a friend, choose the place to do your work or work with certain equipment or materials; special privileges like helping in another classroom, running errands or doing special housekeeping tasks; time for a movie or story. (Note: Reading to kids can be a fantastic and enjoyable experience regardless of the age of the students!)

- Withdraw the privilege or positive consequence as soon as a misconduct occurs. Keep your tone and body language as neutral as possible. (A statement like "This isn't working" can help you intervene decisively without attacking or criticizing.)

- Whenever possible, invite the student to reclaim his privilege or possession as soon as the misbehavior ceases: "You may return to the group as soon as you can control your talking," "You can continue playing with this game as soon as you finish cleaning up the area you just left."

- If correcting his behavior will not give the student immediate access to the privilege or possession, let him know when it will be available again: "Please return to your seats. Let's try (working together) again tomorrow," or "Please put the puzzle back on the shelf until you finish your seatwork."

- Provide support, feedback, guidelines and limits to help, but leave the responsibility for the student's behavior with the student.

- If instruction and activities would help in areas such as problem solving, social interaction, or handling anger and frustration, for example, save them for a non-crisis setting. Likewise, if you feel that you and your students could benefit from the administration or support staff (counselor, school psychologist, social worker), invite them to conduct or participate in these activities. These individuals may also be available to discuss particular problems and help you brainstorm possible win-win solutions, and will be especially helpful when you can provide documentation and don't attempt to dump the responsibility for the problem on them.

- In problem-solving activities and discussions, keep coming back to win-win: "How can we both get what we want?

Intervention Strategies:

Productive Student Behavior

Description: Cooperative, positive or desirable student behavior which a student is currently exhibiting or has already demonstrated.

Intervention Strategy: Positive Reinforcement, Recognition

Goal: Maintaining existing behavior, improving likelihood of behavior recurring independently.

Process: Two-step process that connects the student's positive choice to positive outcomes.

Step 1: *Describe* the positive behavior: "You put all the science materials away."

Step 2: *Connect* the behavior to what's in it for the student: "Now you can go on to the next activity."

Note: Outcome (step 2) must be need-fulfilling for the student.

Connection to Boundary: Relates back to boundary expressed before behavior occurred. For example, if you promised dismissal after students line up quietly, once they do as you've asked, you allow the positive consequence promised in the boundary to occur. Experiencing the privilege or positive outcome as a result of their cooperation strengthens (reinforces) the students' cooperative behavior. (If no boundary was used—or necessary—to elicit the cooperation, you can still reinforce the behavior by connecting it to a positive outcome. This action communicates conditions in implicit or unexpressed boundaries.)

Caution: Avoid praise that connects the student's self-worth to his or her choice or those that reinforce people-pleasing: "I like the way . . .," "I really like you when . . .," "You're so good when . . ." or "You make me happy when . . ." Focus on the student's behavior and how the cooperative choice benefits the student, not you!

Intervention Strategies:

Non-Productive Student Behavior

Description: Neutral or non-disruptive student behavior that is nevertheless off task (that is, student is not doing what you've asked or assigned, but is not preventing teaching or learning from occurring elsewhere).

Intervention Strategy: Motivating with meaningful positive outcomes; offering choices to accommodate students' needs for power and autonomy (within limits that protect their need for safety and security).

Goal: Eliciting cooperative, constructive behavior from student

Process: Connecting low-probability behavior (what you want) to high-probability behavior (what the student wants): "If your work is done by noon, you can help out in the kindergarten." "As soon as you clear your desks and we can watch the video." "You may work together as long as you don't disturb anyone."

Note: To be effective, motivator (outcome) must be meaningful and need fulfilling to the child.

Connection to Boundary: The motivating statement *is* the boundary, connecting what the students want to what you want and expressing the conditions, terms or limits under which they can have or do what they want.

Intervention Strategies:

Counter-Productive Student Behavior

Description: Negative or disruptive student behavior that is interfering, in some way, with the teaching or learning process.

Intervention Strategy: Removing or withholding privileges or positive consequences; holding students accountable for their behavior.

Goal: Stopping the negative behavior *and* encouraging more cooperative choices; building responsibility, accountability and self-management.

Process—dealing with misbehavior due to uncooperative choices, lack of self-control: Interrupting disruptive or destructive behavior. Withdrawing positive consequences until students change their behavior (or until another time when the students have another chance to behave more cooperatively), or until students correct, repair, restore or replace materials or areas damaged or disarranged. Insisting or requiring that the students change their behavior in order to gain (or regain) access to meaningful outcomes or privileges. Accepting the students even though you do not accept their behavior. Leaving the door open for the student to stop and replace negative behaviors: "You can have the book back as soon as you both agree on how you'll share it."

Note: Many misbehaviors can be *avoided* by getting students attention before giving clear directions or instructions ahead of time, by making sure adequate materials and resources are available, by practicing transitions and building independent work habits, by making sure that assignments challenge students and yet allow for achievement and success for everyone, and by physical proximity (moving around the room to see how everyone is doing) and eye contact. Further, minimizing reactions whenever possible, especially to negative attitudes, validating students' feelings or reality, and maintaining a sense of humor can avert many problems.

Note: If a misbehavior or potential misbehavior is due to lack or misunderstanding of directions, *interrupt* the behavior: "Stop" or "Freeze." Give additional information or directions, or suggest more acceptable options, especially if the desired behavior hasn't been requested, clarified or practiced beforehand: "Stop. We don't pour paint in the trash can. Pour the paint in the sink and run the water until you can't see the paint anymore."

Connection to Boundary: Boundaries offer conditional access to positive outcomes (privileges, meaningful activities, for example). As long as students behave in ways that respect the conditions of the boundary, they retain the privilege the boundary promises. As soon as those conditions are violated, the privilege is removed. Keep in mind that removal of positive consequence depends on availability of positive consequence, which is why a reward-oriented, win-win environment makes this process possible and effective.

Caution: Follow-through requires constructive action. Once previously-announced limits have been violated, withdraw privileges *immediately*. Avoid warnings and reminders after the fact. Do not ask for excuses ("why"); instead, simply restate the boundary (or ask what the student plans to do to correct the situation). Avoid punishing, giving advice or solutions, or taking responsibility for the student's problem.

Activity

Date_____

What kinds of misbehaviors have occurred recently in your classroom?

In what way did these behaviors interrupt the teaching or learning process?

What limits, if any, had been previously specified to prevent such misbehaviors from occurring?

What else might you do to avoid similar future incidents?

What options do the students have for resolving or correcting these behaviors on their own?

What other options might you make available for similar future incidents?

In what ways have you been able to:

Isolate what was bothering you and avoid reacting to behaviors that were not actually disruptive?

Stay calm and minimize your reaction?

Mentally separate the student from the behavior, attacking the behavior without attacking the student?

Deal specifically with the behavior, regardless of the morality of the behavior, previous indents, or the personality behind the misconduct?

Back off and shift to a more positive approach if you felt yourself moving toward no-win or win-lose?

Stay responsible for your actions and words?

Remove a privilege or meaningful consequence as soon as the misconduct occurred?

Maintain a neutral tone of voice and a non-aggressive body posture?

Leave the door open for the student to return to the positive consequence (participation, using particular equipment, access to a privilege, for example)?

Leave the responsibility for the student's behavior with the student?

Keep coming back to win-win?

What have you done to avoid the following negative reactions?

Punitive response (any task, look, word, or behavior intended to hurt or get back at the student)?

Praising unrelated or previous behaviors to try to get the student to cooperate (or stop misbehaving)?

Ignoring misconduct that violate your safety, rights or needs, or those of any of your students?

Lecturing, moralizing or attempting to talk the student into cooperating?

Calling on another teacher or administrator to handle your students' negative behaviors?

Delaying intervening (by removing a privilege) by using warnings or reminders?

Asking for, accepting or making excuses for misbehavior (asking "why")?

Reacting or getting involved in situations which the students are resolving non-disruptively on their own.

Participating in no-win, power struggles; disempowering a student, backing a student into a corner.

Which of the above negative responses have been most difficult for you to avoid?

How have your efforts at developing a win-win classroom environment, focusing on meeting student needs (personal, academic, learning style) and providing a variety of positive options and consequences affected the incidence of negative and disruptive student behaviors?

How have these efforts contributed to your own growth, wellness and enjoyment of your work?

In what ways have your students shown growth in:

Meeting their needs for attention, recognition and belonging non-disruptively?

Finding non-disruptive means of dealing with anger and frustration?

Finding non-disruptive means of getting their control needs met?

Interacting positively with other students?

Respecting and accommodating your boundaries?

What are your plans to further enhance your growth—and your students' growth as well—in these areas?

Working The System

18

Building and Maintaining a Support Network

Parents tend to be far more enthusiastic and positive in their support when they feel informed and included, when they feel welcomed in our classrooms, and when their interest in their children's well-being is respected.

Naturally, up to this point we have focused on relationships between teachers and their students. Yet teaching can sometimes leave us feeling isolated from everyone *except* our students. It's important to remember that each of us is also a part of an adult school community that includes administrators, support staff, other teachers and parents. Even if our contact is infrequent, the quality of these relationships can have a very real impact on our attitude, performance, mental health and sense of belonging. With support from the adult community, even the most difficult students seem less challenging; lack of support can make us feel completely alone. And negative relationships with other adults can make life miserable, even with an ideal class.

Building a support network involves consciously connecting with other adults—not just for solving problems, but also for feedback, encouragement and renewed perspectives throughout the year. It means using the same win-win objectives and behaviors that work with children to prevent and resolve conflicts with other adults. And it means being there for others as a resource as well.

This task requires some groundwork. Exploring your school community—the one that exists outside your classroom—is essential. Who's out there? What does each resource have to offer? At what point do they want or expect to be included? What sort of approach works best with each? How much background work do you need to do to make it more likely that they'll be willing to help? What can you do to make their help more meaningful and effective? Which of their needs can you accommodate to minimize conflict at work?

Parents and guardians, for example, can provide a great deal of support and reinforcement. For the most part, they want to know what's happening in school, how their children are doing and how they, the parents, can help. They tend to be far more enthusiastic and positive in their support when they feel informed and included, when they feel welcomed in our classrooms, and when their interest in their children's well-being is respected. Unfortunately parent-teacher relationships rarely attain their maximum potential. Often both parties complain of a lack of contact unless there's a problem. If this has indeed been the case with the parents of your students, imagine how effective a more positive approach can be!

Get acquainted early in the year, either by note, phone, in-school conferences, welcome meetings or home visits. Keep first meetings positive. Make a point of keeping in contact on a regular basis. An occasional note or newsletter can keep parents informed about new projects, activities, policies and objectives, and provides a showcase for students' contributions. Parents are especially likely to read newsletters that have been prepared by their children or include work, stories, poems, puzzles or drawings made by their kids.

Checklist-type progress reports can tell a parent or guardian about the specific strengths and positive behaviors the child exhibited that week. These weekly reports, which need not take more than five or ten minutes to complete for an entire class, communicate your interest in and commitment to their child's success.* Even if your usual correspondences never seem to get home, somehow these "good notes" manage to get there.

If you teach several classes, weekly progress reports may not be practical. Select one or two classes you feel would benefit most from parent support and send reports home with the students in those classes. One middle school vice-principal told me that he made a point to call the parents of each child in his school at least one time each semester, just to say something positive. He kept a list of the entire student population; as he spoke to teachers and heard or observed something positive about a student, he would make a note and call the parent that evening. He insisted that even with a large student population, this was entirely feasible, and took no more than about ten minutes a night.**

You can wait for something special to happen to send a note home, but make sure you send one for each child in the class. Try to communicate on a regular basis, weekly if possible, but at least once every two or three weeks. (Checking off names of students on a roll sheet as you send notes home will help you avoid missing those quiet or less "visible" students.) These messages are appreciated, not only by the parents, but also by the students and administration as well. The notes tend to build good home-school relationships and invite regular, positive parent involvement.

Once this pattern of communication has been established, you'll probably find parents much more supportive and open when a problem arises (approaching a parent in the context of frequent and positive prior contacts is quite different from approaching a parent only to report that something is wrong.) Nonetheless, your attitude, goals and overall approach are important. Your efforts will be far more effective if parents do not end up feeling defensive, protective, shamed, anxious, angry or resentful.

If you call parents to let them know about a problem, state that as the purpose of the call, describe the incident without anger or judgments, and inform them of your goals and plans for solving the problem. You might also want to ask if they have any ideas or suggestions. Above all, avoid blaming, unloading or asking them to solve the problem for you. This is between you and the student. You undermine your professionalism, accountability and personal responsibility when you try to make this their problem as well. It's one thing to let a parent know that a problem came up, in fact it's important that we keep them informed about incidents that could affect a child's performance or success in school. However, parents rarely appreciate being called as a punishment for their child's misbehavior, nor do they enjoy being asked to scold or punish their child for a behavior that they did not witness. (Paradoxically, I have found that the more responsibility teachers are willing to take for the problems they encounter with their students, and the less they demand that the parents intervene, the more supportive the parents are—especially in classrooms in which systematic, positive contact with parents comprises a regular part of the teacher's routine.)

If a student is experiencing difficulty, either with the work or social behavior, or if the student is demonstrating behaviors that are interfering with his potential success in school, get in touch with the parents right away. Don't

Even if your usual correspondences never seem to get home, somehow these "good notes" manage to get there.

Parents rarely appreciate being called as a punishment for their child's misbehavior, nor do they enjoy being asked to scold or punish their child for a behavior that they did not witness.

---

*For more details about building positive home-school relationships with newsletters and progress reports, see *Being a Successful Teacher*, Bluestein, J. Torrance, CA: Fearon Teacher Aids, 1988.

**The vice-principal said that his calls to parents averaged less than 20 seconds each. He would simply call to say something like, "Hey, I was talking to your child's Spanish teacher today and I heard that he's been doing just great with his grammar exercises. I thought you might want to hear that." He shared that the parents quickly understood that he had many other calls to make and didn't have time to chat—he simply wanted to pass on a positive comment he had heard.

allow yourself to be placed in the embarrassing position of having to explain why you didn't contact the parents until the behavior became enough of a problem to affect the student's grades, progress or placement.

In all instances, keep relationships and interactions professional. Focus your discussions on the child's behavior—not character. Avoid judgments about personalities or values and avoid mentioning other students, parents or professionals.

School administrators are also valuable resources and can make the difference between a great year and one fraught with obstacles. Here again, your willingness to take responsibility for conflicts with or between students will work in your behalf. One of the most common complaints from administrators is that teachers rely on them to take care of their discipline problems. Many principals resent being called on to punish students, especially for things like chewing gum, talking, being unprepared for class, behaving disrespectfully or acting out as the result of the teacher's negative or hurtful behavior.

But even if your principal enjoys playing disciplinarian, you will not be well served by relying on him or her to take care of misbehaviors. For one thing, it's nearly impossible for someone outside the actual incident to intervene in a fair, meaningful, related or win-win manner. Sending a child to the principal's office, therefore, tends to be a win-lose, punitive option that rarely has anything to do with the misbehavior, is intended to hurt or retaliate and, at the very least, conveys a lack of acceptance of the student.

Further, referring misbehaving students to the principal communicates—to the administration, staff and the students themselves—that we are unable to resolve our own conflicts, and it also models a dependence on someone else to fix our problems for us. If we want to get the student out of the room in order to defuse or break up a conflict, the office may be a fine place for the student to go to calm down, but beyond requesting the use of that space for that

specific purpose, the principal need not be involved in the intervention nor resolution. (If the principal cannot resist getting involved, you and the student will probably be better off asking the student to go to another classroom, the library, the hall or some place nearby.)

Again, assume responsibility for what goes on in your classroom. Invite your principal to observe, make recommendations, point you to the best resources, clarify available options or help you brainstorm solutions. If you feel that the principal could be helpful in some way, approach him or her with a plan. Be specific about the problem, your objective and what the administrator can do to help. When you attempt to resolve problems on your own, administrators are far more likely to be supportive when you really need them.

Finally, make sure the office gets a copy of anything you send home (such as announcements, newsletters or general correspondences). Administrators also appreciate documentation. Keep track of any parent contacts, incidents with students or student achievement, diagnoses, placement and progress. In doing this, you are also protecting the administrator. If you are sending individual progress reports, as suggested above, let the principal know what you're up to. It's also a good idea to inform him or her of special plans or events you have scheduled. The fewer surprises that end up in the office, the more supportive the administrator will probably be.

The support staff, particularly the school psychologist, counselor, health care resource and social worker, can also provide a tremendous amount of assistance during the year. They, too, are far more receptive and helpful when approached to assist—not *solve* the problem for you. If you approach a support staff member to help with a particular student, be specific about the problem as well as how you want that person to help.

In general, you will probably seek the assistance of these staff members with regard to individual students. The more information you can provide, the more help you are likely to receive. Keeping track of student performance and behavior with a variety of data-collection techniques can provide you with valuable documentation. A student file containing work samples, interest inventories and anecdotal records (brief notes describing a students' language, performance, interests, behaviors, strengths or interactions, for example, usually with regard to some specific incident or observation) will present a more detailed and objective picture of students than grade sheets and opinions.*

Such information can also be critical for generating administrative or parental support for special testing, help or placement. Collecting a variety of data about a student can help administrators and other staff members make decisions about what they can do or recommend to help. A thick, diverse student file also adds to your professionalism and is far more likely to get positive results than simply telling the school psychologist that "Adrian is driving me nuts."

Other teachers can be valuable resources in a number of ways. In addition to providing ideas for activities, materials and instructional techniques, they can also serve as models for teaching and discipline strategies. Other teachers may be willing to observe you and provide feedback for specific skills you're trying to develop. They can give you helpful background on specific students as well as some perspective on problems you encounter. They can also be great allies for projects that involve a grade level, department or the entire school, or anything that requires administrative or community support.

You will probably have far more contact with other teachers than any of the other resources mentioned previously, so you have a great deal to gain by building strong relationships with this segment of your support network. If you are new to a staff, you may not be as familiar with existing relationships, power structures and traditions. It may take a while to determine who is willing to share materials, who is interested in your ideas, and who is most

likely to offer encouragement, acceptance and support when you're having a bad day. There will also be times that require cooperation from other teachers simply so that you can do your job effectively, such as the need to schedule the use of certain equipment or to cooperate on a project too large for you to handle alone.

Other personnel, such as the cafeteria staff, school secretary and custodian will appreciate your efforts at building and maintaining a positive relationship. These individuals are essential members of the school community who can make a great difference in the quality of your life at school.

Finally, the community itself is full of resources—people and places—that can enrich your instruction, provide background information or lead you to a wealth of materials. The professional community, including teacher resource centers, professional libraries, colleges, universities, various educational organizations, and, of course, the Internet can likewise contribute to your personal and professional growth.

As in any relationship, the basics apply. We will always fare better when we treat others the way we wish to be treated, when we take the time out to show our appreciation, when we are willing to ask directly for what we want and when we are willing to give in return. The same win-win characteristics that apply in the classroom apply to professional adult relationships as well.

Yet getting students to cooperate is slightly different from generating cooperation from other adults. In any teacher-student relationship, the teacher is ultimately accountable for the classroom's emotional climate, the criteria for acceptable behavior and for the methods chosen to encourage positive student behavior. Peer relationships, even those in which one adult has greater power or seniority, aren't nearly as clear-cut.

Too often, teacher stress and burnout involves problems with other adults, and problems will arise from time to time wherever

Collecting a variety of data about a student can help administrators and other staff members make decisions about what they can do or recommend to help.

The same win-win characteristics that apply in the classroom apply to professional adult relationships as well.

---

*For more information about data collection tools and strategies, *Being a Successful Teacher*, Bluestein. Torrance, CA: Fearon Teacher Aids, 1988.

170

Learning when and how to respond can save you from personal feelings of anger, frustration, powerlessness or self-righteousness, and can also help you avoid ending up on the receiving end of suspicion, alienation or hostility.

Successful relationships require a belief in your power to influence your life and make choices about your own behavior.

people are working together. Learning when and how to respond can save you from personal feelings of anger, frustration, powerlessness or self-righteousness, and can also help you avoid ending up on the receiving end of suspicion, alienation or hostility.

When something comes up, be direct. Many people dance around a problem, never getting close enough to actually resolve it. Consider Mr. Gordon, who is angry at Mrs. Hartz. He tells Mr. Sanchez, Miss Rodgers, and Mrs. Chasler; he mentions it to the principal, the custodian, his wife, and the cat. He tells everyone *except* Mrs. Hartz. Complaining does not solve his problem. In fact, it may even compound whatever was wrong in the first place, especially if it gets back to Mrs. Hartz.

People perpetuate conflict by complaining rather than confronting, addressing or even acknowledging—and they do so for a number of reasons. Sometimes they secretly hope that someone else will solve the problem for them. (Is this why Mr. Gordon mentioned it to the principal?) Some people avoid communicating because they believe in the existence of clairvoyant connections ("Well, she should have known!") or to avoid a perceived risk ("She'll throw a fit." "She won't like me"). Very often, people shy away from a direct approach because they don't believe (or don't want to believe) that they have the power to change things.

Successful relationships don't mean that you never have any problems with people. But they do require a belief in your power to influence your life and make choices about your own behavior. This fact becomes especially clear in the language and tone you select when you do confront someone directly.

When you encounter a problem in which someone else's behavior is keeping you from doing or enjoying your job, the first response is often reactive. It's hard to be objective when the noise from next door hinders your teaching or when someone is using equipment you reserved, even though these events are probably not personal assaults. When, for example, you find that Mrs. Patton is using the VCR, and the only

other time it will be free before you must return the video is when your students will be in another class, your initial reaction may be somewhat emotional: "Can't she read the schedule?"

Beyond experiencing the initial feelings, as with your interactions with students, you have several options. If you slip back into a powering or authoritarian approach, you might confront Mrs. Patton and demand that she shut off the VCR immediately. After all, you have the schedule on your side. But regardless of how justified you are, you have just backed the other teacher into a win-lose situation, and it can cost you plenty, even if you win. This powering approach considers only your needs; it's likely to create hostility, resentment and strong resistance with someone who might otherwise have tried to work out the problem. Even if you get the equipment, is it worth the emotional strain and future stress on your relationship?

The possibility of making a scene—or an enemy—can lead to the opposite win-lose scenario. In this instance, you decide to not mention it, either because it probably wouldn't do any good or it would just create greater problems. In the meantime, your need for the VCR falls by the wayside. You may tell yourself, "It's just easier" to shelve your plans, but it's a safe bet that your cowardice will leave you feeling resentful and victimized, feelings that will surely express themselves in negative ways, both internally and interpersonally. The why-bother approach is an adequate response as long as you can live with the consequences of not bothering—quietly and happily. But a victim stance often masks the same "how dare she" feelings that prompted a power approach. It will probably manifest as sniping, complaints, helplessness or manipulation to see if Mrs. Patton will relent out of pity or guilt.

Then again, you can try a win-win approach. In this case, you actively and assertively take responsibility for meeting your own needs while considering the needs of another person. By saying to Mrs. Patton, "I think we have a problem; I signed up to use the VCR this period," you are simply describing the situation. You have stated the problem without attacking Mrs. Patton. You have also side-stepped any issues of emotion or morality. "I don't see any other time the VCR will be free before the video goes back. Is there some way we can work this out?" This statement gives the other teacher additional information, allows her to comment and puts you both in a position to cooperate.

As a more serious example, consider the noisy class next door that's disturbing you and your students. In the same way, this problem can be approached with words and tones that will neither destroy the other teacher's credibility as an instructor nor invalidate her worth as a person. Describe the problem, directly and privately, in terms of your own needs: "I'm about to give a test to my class and need a bit more quiet, please," or "We're having a hard time hearing the movie." You have respectfully taken responsibility for your needs and for what is disturbing you. You have simply asked for what you want, without attacking, criticizing or asking her to defend her standards, tolerances or teaching behaviors. And by keeping the focus on the situation, you have made your request without attempting to make her responsible for your feelings or your state of mind.

As in teacher-student relationships, the best way to resolve a problem with other adults is to prevent it from occurring in the first place. It helps if you're good at anticipating, but even more important is the realization that people rarely understand implicitly what you want, need or think until you let them know. We're all creatures of our own experiences and everyone's experiences are unique. This means that what may be incredibly obvious, logical and right to you may never enter someone else's head.

Suppose, for example, that you and Ms. Bender plan to combine your classes for a special project. In the past, you have observed that she seems to favor certain children. To avoid this from happening in the work you are doing together, you can tell her, before the activity takes place, that it is important to you that everyone has a chance to share opportunities, materials and responsibilities.

This statement probably won't cause Ms. Bender to restructure her value system, although she may think twice before she assigns particular jobs to favored children—at least while you're around. Even if your request makes absolutely no dent in her behavior, you have the privilege of knowing that you've done your best with what you can control—your own behavior.

Anticipation and simple courtesy can help avoid problems arising from assumptions that no one has conflicting needs or that no one cares. Ask ahead of time if neighboring teachers will be bothered by a noisy activity in your room after lunch. Find out when the library will be free for your students to use next week. Establishing a strong support network and consistently modeling win-win behaviors in your adult relationships might even help your colleagues become more considerate of your needs and how you might be affected by their plans and the choices they make.

One final thought: Even if you have your interpersonal and conflict-resolution skills in order, you may run into problems if the administration is not supportive of your 21st century intentions. Although the absence of administrative support can sometimes degenerate into a no-win situation, certain attitudes and behaviors will give you a much better chance of minimizing resistance. Attempt to build your win-win environment within the confines of school policies. Keep the office informed about your policies and practices. Avoid soap-boxing and maintain a high degree of professionalism. Avoid judging other teachers' approaches and policies that differ from your own. Keep in touch with the parents and build as much support as you can there. Take responsibility for solving problems with students. If you do all of these things and get results—especially if those results are documented—you'll certainly make yourself a smaller target. If you aren't causing problems for the administration, even a significant difference in philosophy and approaches to motivation can avoid drawing fire from above.

As in teacher-student relationships, the best way to resolve a problem with other adults is to prevent it from occurring in the first place.

People rarely understand implicitly what you want, need or think until you let them know.

Activity

Date_____

What have you done to build support relationships with the following groups of people?

Administration:

Support staff:

Other teachers:

Parents:

Other school staff:

Other community resources:

How have the relationships you've established contributed to your mental health?

Administration:

Support staff:

Other teachers:

Parents:

Other school staff:

Other community resources:

In what ways have you involved the following people in your discipline program?

Administration:

Support staff:

Other teachers:

Parents:

Other school staff:

Other community resources:

What have you done to maximize the ability of these individuals to help—without making them responsible for solving the problem for you?

In what ways have these people contributed to a win-win classroom environment?

Administration:

Support staff:

Other teachers:

Parents:

Other school staff:

Other community resources:

Activity

Date_____

Think about a situation in which your needs were in conflict with the needs of another adult (in school or out). Regardless of how you actually approached or resolved the conflict, use the following questions to explore the various dimensions of the situation and the possibilities involved:*

Your needs (what you wanted):

Their needs (what they wanted):

The conflict (how their needs interfered with yours):

Your initial feelings or reactions:

Describe the powering (you win, they lose) options you considered or might have considered:

Describe the probable short-term outcomes of your implementing these solutions:

Describe the probable long-term outcomes of your implementing these solutions:

What would have been the probable outcomes of simply ignoring the problem?
   Short-term:

   Long-term:

List any other people you talked with about this problem before you actually confronted the other person involved:

What was the purpose of these discussions:

In what ways did these discussions help you (or the situation)?

In what ways did (or could) these discussions create new problems?

---

*You may want to use some of these questions in your discussions and activities on conflict resolution and relationship building with your students.

How long did this problem exist before you actually confronted the person directly?

If your approach was not immediate, what held you back?

Brainstorm a variety of possible win-win solutions in which you and the other person could eventually manage to get what you each wanted. (If that is not practical or possible—say, you're both fighting over the last piece of candy—how can you resolve the conflict in the best interests of all concerned?)

What are the probable short-term outcomes of the win-win solutions you suggested?

What are the probable long-term outcomes?

In what way did your actual approach consider the needs and feelings of the other person?

Describe the other person's response:

In what ways (or to what degree) were you successful at preventing the situation from becoming a no-win experience?

In what ways are you satisfied with the way you handled your feelings about this problem?

In what ways would you have like to have behaved differently?

In what ways are you satisfied with the way the situation was resolved?

If the problem was not resolved to your satisfaction, how could it be better?

Describe any new problems created by the solution.

How can the new problems—or your dissatisfaction with the solution—now be resolved in the best interests of all involved?

How do you plan to handle similar conflicts in the future?

19

Taking Care of Yourself

If teaching only involved content planning and presentation, it would still be an extremely demanding job. But consider the paperwork that requires secretarial skills, the movement and organization that calls for management expertise, the emotional needs that oblige a teacher to serve as a counselor, or the "boo-boos" that demand the role of nurse. Every facet of teaching, as fulfilling and enriching as it may be, can also be stressful and exhausting, both physically and emotionally.

As if these demands weren't enough, the common habit of setting unrealistic expectations for ourselves can be terribly stress-producing in itself. Becoming a great teacher is a developmental process that doesn't always jibe with our self-expectations. Even if we've been teaching for years, as long as we're committed to excellence, we'll always be looking for new tricks to try and new ways to grow.

One of the greatest things about teaching is the fact that there is always something new for us to deal with: different groups of students each year, changes in programs and equipment, different grades or subjects to teach, or research, ideas and innovations that we encounter for the first time. Even after years of teaching, a lesson or topic that has always proved reliable, successful, inspiring or fun can inexplicably fall flat. Any time we try something new, or face a different group of kids, we can run into problems that would have been impossible to anticipate.

Maintaining a positive focus is critical to our mental health, as well as our ability to perform and continue to grow. While such a focus certainly enhances relationships with students (and others), our ability to see the positive elements of our own teaching behavior can sometimes be the difference between a lesson that bombs and the end of a career!

During my first year, one of my professors from the university came out to observe in my classroom. He and I had worked together in the past; I had a great deal of respect for this man and it was very important to me that he be impressed with my work. (Back then, I was far more vulnerable to other people's opinions of me than I have been in recent years!) Of course he came in on a day when everything possible was going wrong. The copy machine had broken and one of my handouts wasn't ready. The students didn't understand my instructions and did the activity incorrectly. My emergency plans flopped when I attempted to show a filmstrip and the bulb burned out on the third frame. When I finally got the kids' attention at the end of the period, one of the blinds let go and dropped with a crash.

By the time the students left, I was in shambles. I sat and sobbed, offered my resignation, and made secret plans to apply to dental school or marry someone very rich instead. I even started cleaning out my desk and suggested that he try to find a replacement who could actually teach. I had a very bad case of the

"I can'ts" and he listened and nodded patiently.

Finally, he got up and said, "You know, your flag looks great!"

I stopped, stunned. My flag? I couldn't even reach the flag without a ladder.

"That's a good start," he said. "We'll work on the rest. Don't worry, you'll be fine. You've got everything you need to be a great teacher. You just need a little more practice. I'll see you next week." After which he gave me a hug and he left.

Now here was a person able to look beyond the "mistakes," some of which I could have managed better, others that were completely out of control and impossible to predict, to the one thing I hadn't messed up. My flag looked great! Once I recovered, I started noticing that my flag actually did look pretty good. And then my focus started to shift: The materials I had prepared were done well; the filmstrip I had selected had been interesting, applicable and well-sequenced. I might not have seen the other successes if he had mentioned them, but the comment about the flag certainly got my attention!

I can. Maybe.

Not terribly illustrious beginnings, I'll admit. But the lesson was not lost on me, even if it did take a while to surface.

This example illustrated another danger of coming from an industrial-era background that reinforced achievement over efforts, product over process, and perfection over everything else. No wonder "looking good" and impressing authority (product) seemed more important than seeing the opportunities in each experience to become a better teacher (process)! The emphasis on performance and appearance distracts us from truly valuable opportunities to see failures or mistakes simply as a chance to reevaluate goals and objectives and look for different approaches or more effective strategies. It is this very tendency that so emphatically interferes with our ability to model responsibility, either by shifting blame to outside events (so we don't have to change our own behaviors that aren't working) or by adopting an attitude of despair (so that there's no point in trying to change.) It's also easy to see how a priority, in which our appearance supersedes our actual effectiveness, can lead us to being extremely arrogant or extremely hard on ourselves. Both are based in denial—one of our vulnerability, the other of our capability; and both deny our need to continually grow and develop as professionals.

In sorting through this experience, I also realized that if I wanted to focus on my students' strengths and abilities, I would have to learn to do so for myself. This was only one aspect of self-care. Another was learning to detach when necessary—not only from self-destructive or difficult students, but also from the demands of the job.

Because the planning and preparation of lessons, activities, materials, and environments can consume so much time—especially during the first few years of a teacher's career, in a new setting or at a new grade level—it's not uncommon for hobbies, recreational reading or other outside interests to shift to a lower place on a teacher's priority list. Teaching requires a great deal of giving on many levels. True, there can be a great deal of satisfaction in putting out so much time, creativity and physical and emotional energy. However, many teachers reach the end of the day with little to give back to themselves.

Teaching tends to attract helpers and nurturers. Although it's not always the case, most teachers identify heavily with the progress and performance of their students. We don't want to see people we care about fail—especially if we believe that their failure reflects on us. While these feelings may seem natural and caring, they may also create very negative consequences, for both us and the students. For example, when our professional identity and feelings of success are tied up in the choices our students make, our focus can shift from success orientation for the sake of the students to rescuing them from failure for the sake of ourselves. When our ability to feel successful depends on other people's behaviors,

The emphasis is on performance and appearance distracts us from valuable opportunities to learn from our mistakes.

Many teachers identify heavily with the progress and performance of their students. We don't want to see people we care about fail—especially if we believe that their failure reflects on us.

appearance, values, attitudes or approval, we expend the majority of our energy trying to control the choices they make. If our sense of our teaching self is too closely connected to our students' behavior and achievement, we may become resentful and punitive when our sincerity and commitment don't generate the kind of enthusiasm and cooperation from our students we need in order to sustain our sense of adequacy. It's easy to see how our attachment to certain specific outcomes can lead us far from our win-win objectives and indeed create the exact kinds of stress and conflict we're trying to avoid.

One of the most important skills in self-caring is learning to separate things we can change, control or influence from those we can't. Unfortunately, some of the most frustrating experiences in our lives come from events we can't do much about. We get moved to a grade we didn't want to teach. Our normal ride to work takes twice as long because of a two-year construction project. The parents of our students don't read to them (or perhaps are guilty of more serious neglect).

True, we can transfer to a new school or go back and get a degree in architecture. We can leave the house two hours early to avoid rush hour or buy a home closer to where we work. We can make home visits and start a home literacy education project in our spare time. There are always options and alternatives in any situation, but the more removed something is from our direct control, the greater the discrepancy between the energy we'll need to effect change and the amount of change our energy will actually produce. Hard work and few results is a great recipe for frustration and burnout—outcomes we can avoid when we choose, instead, to channel our efforts in a high-impact direction and make constructive choices about the things we can control.

If we've learned anything about win-win interactions, we know that students—along with everyone else—fall in that great grey area between those things that are completely out of

When our ability to feel successful depends on other people's behaviors, appearance, values, attitudes or approval, we expend the majority of our energy trying to control the choices they make.

We can, as we have seen, take care of everything under our control and still have things go wrong.

our control (like the weather) and those that we control completely (like how often we floss). Throughout this book we have seen how the behaviors, attitudes and language we choose in interacting with our students can make it more likely that they will behave in a certain way, but at no time do we actually control them.

So when we run into disappointments—lessons that fall flat, students who drop the ball, administrators who simply can't see the beauty in what we were trying to do—it's tempting to lump them all into one pile of evidence that can discredit us as instructors. Not necessary. We can, as we have seen, take care of everything under our control and still have things go wrong.

Somewhere between beating ourselves up for our failures and becoming completely indifferent is a very loving place called "letting go." This is that nice middle ground at which we realize that regardless of our efforts, the final outcome is often beyond our control. We sometimes come to this place when we've tried everything and realized that our attempts to control others have endowed us with more responsibility, self-righteousness, anger and stress than we can comfortably bear.

Every now and then we will run into students who appear committed to their own destruction or invalidation, children whose self-concepts are so low or so fragile that they feel safest when they constantly attract chaos or create continual opportunities to fail. Some students expend a great deal of energy trying to convince us that they aren't worth the bother. Others can spend an entire year hiding behind mistrust—of us as well as their own potential for success—regardless of our devotion and encouragement. In many instances, our love, acceptance, faith, patience and persistence will win out.

However, when our efforts fail, or when they create additional problems, either for the individual we're trying to support, ourselves or the rest of the class, it helps to remember that the ultimate responsibility for changing self-defeating behaviors and attitudes lies with the person who practices them (child or adult). We can provide a safe and nurturing environment in which this kind of healing can occur. We can make success possible. We can offer caring, acceptance, respect and opportunities to make positive choices and experience the true empowerment of which the student may be capable. We keep on trying—and we give ourselves credit for trying. And we also let go. We disengage from results over which we have little control: now not only is the student still worthwhile and valuable despite his beliefs and behavior, so are we.

Our professional self-concept can be rather fragile at times. If the bulk of our experiences have been with factory-era authority relationships, we have years of practice judging ourselves against other people's standards and reactions. If approval from others is a high priority, we become extremely vulnerable to the power-oriented teacher who doesn't sanction our methods, the parent who wanted his child in a different fourth grade or the fact that the other social studies teacher is twenty pages ahead of us. Learning to hear, respect and operate from our own, internal vision, guidance or standards promises a great deal of freedom, however doing so may require some relearning and refocusing, as well as letting go of old beliefs that no longer work for us.*

Taking care of yourself also means identifying which challenges deserve your time and attention and determining whether or not you need to get involved. For example, it's easy to allow classroom attitudes, where most things *are* your business, to become school attitudes, where many things are not. Wherever you teach, you will find people who work differently from you. And while at times, you may find the differences annoying, your involvement is not called for unless the other adult keeps your approach from working.

There will be occasions when you believe that another teacher's behavior is unprofessional, destructive or hampering student success. I'm often asked, in workshops and interviews, what to do about other teachers who are not committed to win-win principles or relationships. I typically respond, "Nothing." If that teacher wants new ideas or suggestions for making changes in order to achieve more positive goals, and she comes to you for help, by all means share what you've got. But I have found that people are generally resistant to suggestions that require major changes in their belief systems or behaviors until they are either curious or dissatisfied enough to be receptive to this information. People who are invested in *not* changing, either because they firmly believe in what they're doing or because they aren't ready to question beliefs they've always held, will certainly see your best intentions to "help" as controlling and invasive. Until they are open to the possibility of doing things differently, even the most inquisitive will simply be looking for an opportunity to vent or complain. (You'll be able to tell when this happens by how often they counter your suggestions with "Yeah, but . . ."). Further, your assistance may not be welcome, even when it's requested, if your response is not the one the other person wants to hear.

The more win-win your orientation becomes, the more sensitive you'll become to other people's win-lose approaches. Most of us sincerely want to keep people from hurting one another and it will be a matter of conscience at which point you become involved. Too often, however, it's just a judgment call: one person's teaching style is another person's hurtful behavior. That line can be pretty fine. I recommend extreme caution in making other people's attitudes, beliefs or behaviors your business. The cost of unsolicited intervention,

The ultimate responsibility for changing self-defeating behaviors and attitudes lies with the person who practices them (child or adult).

People are generally resistant to suggestions that require major changes in their belief systems or behaviors until they are either curious or dissatisfied enough to be receptive to this information.

Your assistance may not be welcome, even when it's requested, if your response is not the one the other person wants to hear.

---

*Control issues, approval-seeking, rescuing and the desire to manage what other people think of us are among the topics discussed in greater detail in Melody Beattie's *CoDependent No More* (New York: Harper-Hazelden, 1987) as well as other resources on codependency. Although the term originated in work with families of alcoholics and has unfortunately often been overused, misapplied and misunderstood, the dynamics of codependency can occur in any situation and are especially common in the helping professions. Therefore, the behavioral characteristics associated with codependency put many educators, counselors, directors and administrators at risk. (See chart at end of chapter.)

particularly when it comes in the form of judgments or criticisms, can be high. Little growth is likely to occur in an atmosphere of suspicion, resentment or defensiveness. Often, the best way to help someone move forward is to simply move forward yourself. Your success and self-confidence will be far more inspiring than your advice or admonitions.

The same holds true when you encounter situations in which, for example, two colleagues are in conflict with one another, a friend is having problems with the principal or you are working with someone who can't quite get it together. Situations like these can engage you almost by accident.

Whether you're hooked by conflicting values or just trying to help, whenever you jump into a situation that does not truly concern you, you risk creating additional stresses and problems for yourself. Taking responsibility for these kinds of problems, even when your help is desired and appreciated can take a tremendous toll on your energy and goodwill. Few things in life are more exhausting—physically, emotionally, psychologically or spiritually—than the pressure of feeling as though the whole system would fall apart if it weren't for you.

Healthy interdependence requires boundaries: You can be supportive of another teacher and still recognize where this responsibility begins and ends. Listening, accepting, acknowledging, modeling, reflecting, providing information and materials, and helping that person think through possible solutions may help—when you are willing and able—without assuming responsibility for the problem. These strategies neither attack others nor do they attempt to impose your value system on them. Further, these behaviors offer alternatives to rescuing or "fixing" others, which frees you to be there for them without becoming enmeshed or assuming the burden of their conflicts. Remember, the best help is often letting others solve their own problems.

Learning to detach is especially important if you ever become involved in a no-win

situation. If you have been unable to resolve a conflict to your satisfaction, the next step may involve arbitration. If Mrs. Patton is unwilling to work with you to settle the problem with the VCR, you might propose, "I understand that the schedule was developed to avoid problems like these. Would you prefer to work this out with the building committee?" Notice that this statement is not intended as a threat—you have simply presented another option.

Unfortunately, when you turn a problem over to someone else, you almost always turn over the responsibility for a solution to that person as well. The advantage is that the third party can usually see things more clearly and objectively and may suggest options that didn't occur to either of the parties involved. The disadvantage is that a mediator may well solve the problem as quickly and conveniently as possible (or in terms of what is most need-fulfilling to him or her), with less regard to the specific needs of both parties. Finally, an outside person may have difficulty remaining objective, avoiding power decisions or sticking with relevant issues. There is always the chance that the third party will make things worse, so select your arbitrator cautiously.

Sometimes persistence can overcome a seemingly no-win situation. Even with the support of your principal, custodian, and the students' parents, it may still be hard to convince repair services that you and your students really need to have the heater fixed. When that office recognizes that they will no longer be bothered by three calls a day once the heater works, you are more likely to get results. Be pleasant if you choose to be persistent and, if possible, always make a point of telling the other people involved what's in it for them to cooperate.

Unfortunately, you may not be able to directly resolve every problem with another individual. Such a no-win situation may arise from a loss of perspective or a personality conflict. For example, Mr. Collins was scheduled to be observed by Miss Willard, the principal, who came by the class when the teacher was presenting an activity designed to reinforce a particular reading concept. Miss Willard was concerned that his activity was not in the teacher's guide and asked that he use the guide exclusively.

Under protest, Mr. Collins did use the guide, almost word for word, in his planning. He then came under attack for being unoriginal. Mr. Collins was clearly caught up in a no-win power struggle. He told Miss Willard that he was getting conflicting messages from her. "I'm trying to follow your suggestions, but it seems that I can't do anything without being criticized. Is there something I'm not understanding?" Miss Willard responded that he was being too sensitive. When pressed to elaborate her expectations, she refused further discussion.

What options does Mr. Collins have? He may try several different approaches, depending upon his need for approval, his tenure and mobility within the system, his self-assurance, his career goals, and his sense of humor. He may choose to enlist parents, colleagues and the union to fight. He might continue to persuade the principal to give him more specific information—or at least attempt to understand his approach. He might agree with Miss Willard to her face and devote his energy to beating or side-stepping the system for as long as he can get away with it. He may go with the flow to try to keep Miss Willard off his back.

But considering the deliberate lack of support and intent to undermine this teacher's confidence, Mr. Collins may not be in for a long-term relationship with Miss Willard. In such a painful no-win situation, seeking a position elsewhere may be the most emotionally cost-effective option.

When our jobs—for whatever reasons—become a stressful bundle of obstacles and conflicts, we may need to reevaluate whether the payoffs and benefits adequately offset the negative aspects of the work. The times we are most vulnerable to burnout, fatigue, depression and poor self-concept are times when no other options seem available (low sense of personal empowerment).

One of the most powerful behaviors we can engage in for our own self-protection is the conscious act of exploring options: a different grade level, another school (or district), arbitration, a year off to finish the degree or the pursuit of an entirely different career. Consciously choosing to stay in a situation in which we are well aware of the challenges, lack of support or other, more negative realities can also eliminate constant disappointment and an exhausting sense of being victimized. Sometimes it can help relieve some of the pressures in even the most negative situations to simply realize that we're not trapped—we just haven't found a more satisfying option yet.

In any teaching situation, there are a number of things we can do to take care of ourselves. Self-care starts with a belief in its legitimacy. Traditional factory-era upbringing often promotes self-sacrifice and denounces self-care, confusing it with selfishness. But self-care is not the same as selfish! Selfishness either fails to consider the needs of others or simply disregards them. This is not the case with self-caring behavior, which leaves plenty of room for caring and giving, but in a way that will not leave us feeling depleted, violated or angry.

Self-care involves our ability to meet our own needs. Of all the ingredients of healthy and positive relationships, it is perhaps the most important, for lacking an ability to take care of ourselves will inevitability compromise the quality of any relationship we have with others. Self-care reduces the chances that we will feel resentful, self-righteous or disempowered—feelings which often result from self-sacrifice—and enhances the quality of love and care you can give others.

Self-care continues with a belief in our own deservingness, acknowledging that it is not just for other people. (Have you ever noticed how many adults who are truly committed to helping children learn how to appreciate their own worth have a hard time doing the same for themselves?) Until we believe we deserve to be

Sometimes, we may need to reevaluate whether the payoffs and benefits adequately offset the negative aspects of our work.

One of the most powerful behaviors we can engage in for our own self-protection is the conscious act of exploring options.

Self-care starts with a belief in its legitimacy.

treated with respect, for example, modeling self-respect and maintaining boundaries necessary to communicate our insistence to others will certainly be quite difficult. And it's equally challenging to honestly promote self-caring choices to children if we have a hard time appreciating what we see in the mirror or making constructive choices in our own behalf.

One of the best ways to take care of ourselves is to avoid or minimize our exposure to negative people, information or influences. This can be tough! Start by noticing how you feel after you're around certain people or experiences. For example, does more than a few moments' contact with certain people leave you feeling drained or depressed? Do you find certain kinds of music uplifting or energizing while others make you edgy or downhearted? Do you walk out of the teachers' lounge some days wondering why you ever went into this profession?

Any person or experience can have an impact on our energy.* On days that you find watching the news or reading the paper to be devastating, switch channels or turn to the comics. Watch for that sense of obligation to spend time with someone who tends to be toxic and exhausting for you to be around, just because that person cares about you or needs you to be there. Learn to say no, even at the risk of rejection or criticism. (Do you really want someone who does not respect you, your boundaries or your right to take care of yourself actively involved in your life? Give yourself permission to attract and be with people who truly accept and value you, and who don't endlessly impose their agendas and disappointments on you.) Read or listen to inspiration material, either exclusively or in between more disquieting information.

Learn to say no, even at the risk of rejection or criticism.

Sometimes the best way to avoid a potential conflict is to simply agree with the other person.

We also need interests and diversions in our lives besides teaching to give us balance and perspective.

Learn how to ignore or defuse criticism from others. You have a right to your enthusiasm, dedication, commitment, optimism, values and beliefs, without having to defend them and without being subjected to ridicule, judgments or put-downs. Sometimes the best way to avoid a potential conflict is to simply agree with the other person. Watch what happens when you respond by saying something like "You could be right," "No kidding!" or "I appreciate your concern," and then changing the subject or walking away, which communicates that you don't care to discuss the issue further. (Note that we're talking about criticism, not reasonable requests to cooperate. There's a difference between "Please turn down the music," and "I can't believe you let your kids listen to music that loud!")** This strategy is certainly less stressful, time consuming and wearing than becoming defensive, making excuses, trying to interpret what the other person is really saying, or explaining yourself to secure the other person's approval. Unless the strategies you use in your classroom interfere with someone else's teaching, it really is no one's business why you allow your students to sit where they want for certain activities, offer choices about work sequence or materials, or spend an extra week on the Civil War.

We also need interests and diversions in our lives besides teaching to give us balance and perspective. Activities that are also stress-reducing can serve us best. Being good at what we do comes easier when we're in shape physically and mentally. Taking a class in our field, pursuing a hobby, practicing relaxation techniques, exercising, reading some exciting fiction, listening to motivation tapes, or learning something we've never done before

---

*For more information about, self-care, particularly as it applies to physical well-being, read *Anatomy of the Spirit* by Caroline Myss, Ph.D. (New York: Harmony Books, 1996). This outstanding book also addresses maintaining (and reclaiming) one's energy (or spirit), healing and releasing old hurts, and the willingness to change.

**Recognize, however, that many people are more comfortable criticizing and judging than they are asking for what they want. Regardless of how you interpret their comments or respond, the point here is to not get hooked emotionally, to whatever degree that is possible.

can help us develop as vital, dynamic and well-rounded people.*

Learn to set goals for yourself to reaffirm your sense of "I can." Goal setting acknowledges your power, potential and capability, not to mention your optimism. Unfortunately, many people rarely get beyond wishing, which lacks the determination and commitment involved in setting goals. Wishing may be a great way to start, but conscious, active goal setting and planning will get you where you want to go much more quickly and reliably.

Be specific and concrete about your goals. Use numbers, names and dates. Write out your goals: it strengthens your commitment, as well as the probability that you'll realize them. Record them positively and affirmatively, perhaps beginning with the words "I can . . ." or "I will . . ." Go back to your list of goals from time to time to see how much you've accomplished. Acknowledge the progress you've made and continually update and revise your list with new goals.

If you are working in a particularly supportive environment, you may be getting a good bit of positive feedback about the work you're doing. Unfortunately, it's likely that you don't get many strokes from the people you work with (who, incidentally, probably need them just as badly). It's certainly reasonable to ask for positive feedback, especially when you can be specific about the kinds of information that would be helpful to you. Whether or not you get the support you need, you certainly increase the odds by asking for what you want. Better yet, you can make a habit of recognizing and appreciating others—for your own sake as well as theirs—however don't take this route unless you can do so without an agenda or expectation for getting something back in return.

Regardless of the quality of the support networks you build, the bottom line in responsibility for self-care is "self." Fortunately, even in an extremely negative, nonsupportive environment, you can still draw upon support from within. Learn to offer recognition and feedback to yourself. This behavior is a great way to practice focusing on the positive and will help you perceive a failure or mistake as an impetus to help you refine or set new goals for yourself.

To pat yourself on the back, use the same process my professor employed: looking for what you did right. If you've ever found yourself lying awake in bed at night, agonizing over the bulletin board you haven't changed in five months, the papers you still haven't graded or the laundry you forgot to take out of the washer last Tuesday, you're a great candidate for this strategy.

Put a little datebook, journal or a pen and pad next to the bed. Tonight and every night, before you shut your eyes, take a few seconds to make a list of at least three things you did right that day—regardless of the results or anyone else's reaction—or three things for which you feel grateful. Fill the page if you can. The only rule is that you can't qualify what you write or use the word "but." Simply put down what you did well, what you tried for the first time, what you appreciate about yourself or your life, or what you feel good about . . . Even if it's only "my flag looked great."

Educators at Risk**

Characteristics of educators at risk:**

• feels personally responsible for a student's successes and failures

---

Wishing may be a great way to start, but conscious, active goal setting and planning will get you where you want to go much more quickly and reliably.

Go back to your list of goals from time to time to see how much you've accomplished.

Take a few seconds to make a list of at least three things you did right that day—regardless of the results or anyone else's reaction—or three things for which you feel grateful.

---

*If you're feeling extremely stressed out, depressed or stuck, if you have difficulty feeling deserving of self-caring choices (or feel guilty when you set boundaries or say "no"), if you feel particularly vulnerable to other people's judgements or opinions of you, or if you feel tempted to engage in negative or self-destructive behaviors, please consider joining a support group, talking to a counselor or taking advantage of your employee assistance program if one exists. Find a place, preferably outside of your immediate work world, where it will be safe to explore and express your feelings, restructure belief systems, seek alternative behavior patterns and rethink your goals and direction.

**From a handout originally entitled "Codependency in the Classroom." In searching for a more generic title, I've borrowed the idea of "Educators at Risk" from Orville Dean, educator and consultant, in Medina, Ohio.

- measures personal success by student behavior and achievement, or by approval from others
- has an overwhelming need to avoid conflict and generate approval from others (which can manifest as attention-seeking, maintaining status quo, or even rebelliousness)
- compromises student needs to avoid "rocking the boat," either with administrators, parents, or other students
- believes that the job would be easier to perform if only the students, their parents, the administration, and/or "the system" would change
- has difficulty setting and maintaining boundaries between self and other people
- has difficulty setting and maintaining boundaries between self and job
- deals with discipline problems by shaming, blaming, complaining, manipulating, ignoring, or dumping them on someone else
- feels threatened by another teacher's progress or success
- feels as though "things would completely fall apart if it weren't for me."
- swings from chaos, helplessness, and victimization to moral superiority and self-righteousness
- often rescues students by ignoring misbehavior, offering inappropriate second chances, or failing to impose previously-stated consequences
- protects a student from failure or negative consequences in an effort to feel successful, valuable, or powerful
- over-identifies with, and even adopts, another person's feelings
- appears to be "fine" and "in control"
- probably denies that any of the above are personally relevant

These patterns can ultimately interfere with a teacher's ability to:

- interact with students without violating their self-worth
- interact with school staff effectively
- meet students' academic and learning-style needs
- behave consistently within the framework of his/her own values
- feel worthy and successful
- detach from the job
- take care of himself or herself

Other contributing factors:

- a tradition of dysfunctionality (which now feels "normal")
- a scarcity of healthy, functional role models
- the lack of a healthy, functional system to support people trying to operate in healthy, functional ways.
- the very human tendency to resist change

Some assumptions on reducing risk factors:

- It is possible to adopt healthy patterns of behavior, even in unhealthy and unsupportive environments.
- The "system" is not likely to change all by itself, nor is it likely to take care of (or support) a teacher's needs regardless of that teacher's enthusiasm, instructional skills, dedication, or good intentions.
- Change happens best in supportive environments; Teachers tend to function effectively, grow professionally and personally, and avoid stress and burnout when they can create a support network for themselves, either in or out of school—preferably in both environments.
- Change is most effective when individuals take responsibility for their own growth, rather than attempting to change or blame others.
- Change is most effective when encouraged rather than coerced.
- As individuals change, the system will change.

Activity

Date_____

On the next few pages, identify the things you already do well. Select categories that apply to your interests and to your life, such as: Planning and Organization, Instruction, Interpersonal Skills, Hobbies, Taking Care of my Body, Relaxation, Driving, Housekeeping, Sports, Personal Appearance, or whatever is meaningful and important to you. There's space for seven different categories—feel free to duplicate these pages and add more! Start with who and where you are and only write good stuff! Note: The harder this activity is for you to do, the more you need to do it!

Category: _____

Category: _____

Category: _____

Category: _____

Category: _____

Category: _____

Category: _____

Using the same or different categories, now identify *goals*—new behaviors you would like to achieve at some point. Be as specific as possible and start each goal statement with the words "I can . . ." or "I will . . ." (For example, instead of saying, "I want to spend less time working at home on planning and paperwork," write, "I can leave school empty-handed by 4:00 twice a week." Instead of expressing your desire to lose a few pounds, write, "I can get into my grey pants again.") Make more copies of these pages if necessary.

Category: _____

Category: _____

Category: _____

Category: _____

Category: _____

Category: _____

Sanity Savers

Make a list of things you can do to relax, relieve stress, release negative feelings and gain perspective. What do you enjoy doing? What makes you feel happy and alive? Brainstorm ideas you can go back to after a long day. Note: the best "sanity savers" are those that do not depend on another person's availability or cooperation. Also, please avoid listing alternatives that are ultimately self-destructive or those that will hurt someone else. Use extra paper if you'd like; continue to revise and add to this list.

Gift Certificate

A gift certificate can be a sanity saver for someone else you care about. It offers your support and will probably make you feel pretty good, too. Duplicate the certificates below and fill in with the name of the person and what you're willing to do for him or her.

Some possibilities:

Coverage of one recess duty, a six-pack of your favorite soft drink, grading of one test (one class, no essay), a double-dip ice cream cone after school, a new student-made bulletin board courtesy of my class, dinner at my house, use of my class's computer for one full afternoon, one hour of grunt work (such as laminating, filing, cutting or cleaning), a new poster for your room, a surprise brown-bag lunch, a break while I invite your class to watch a movie with mine, a copy of my "Emergency Activity" file, a puppet show for you and your class performed by my class, help washing your car, the return of your library books, one evening of house (dog or baby) sitting, an hour's sanctuary for any one student you are about to blow up at, a partner for racquetball (or tennis, aerobics, jogging or

---

Gift Certificate

This certificate entitles

_____

to

_____

_____

Signed: _____

Self-recognition

Starting today, use a calendar, datebook or blank tablet to do this activity for one month. Keep it on your desk to be the last thing you do before you leave school, or next to your bed to be the last thing you do before you go to sleep. For each day, write down at least three things you did great, or three things you're grateful for! Do not qualify or use the word "but." Stay positive. You're doing fine!

Post-assessment

Chances are, if you've made it this far, you've considered some new ideas, practiced new strategies, and reflected on the process. If you've been working through the ideas and activities in this book for a few weeks, you might want to take another look at the pre-assessment at the beginning of this book. As with the earlier assessment, select the statement that most closely resembles your own beliefs or attitudes.

Compare your responses to your pre-test choices. Although you may notice several differences immediately, many of the goals suggested in this book require changes that need time and practice before they truly feel integrated. Check back again in another few months or even a year and take this survey again. Use your answers to focus on new goals for growth.

Date_____

Reflection

Areas of greatest growth:

What I'd like to improve or work on next:

Best wishes for success with your process and happiness in your work.

Appendix: Implications for Administrators

Consider yourself fortunate if you are working with teachers who are already committed to a win-win discipline approach, such as the one described in this book. They will make your job much easier.

For most of us, the word "discipline" conjures up thoughts of reactive and controlling measures for dealing with student misbehavior. However, the 21st century model of discipline proposed in this book is an ongoing, proactive set of behaviors used to create a cooperative environment which minimizes the likelihood of negative, disruptive behavior. (This positive discipline process can occur in any group—a classroom, department, building or district.)

Consider yourself fortunate if you are working with teachers who are already committed to a win-win discipline approach, such as the one described in this book. They will make your job much easier. These are teachers who assume responsibility for handling misbehaviors that occur in their classrooms. They will see you as a resource, not a rescuer, and will be far less likely to request that you solve their discipline problems for them. In contrast, teachers who use typical win-lose strategies frequently find those techniques frustrating and ineffective for managing conflicts with students, parents or other teachers, and may frequently ask that you intervene.

Implementing successful changes in the classroom takes time and effort.

The attitudes of win-win teachers are generally more positive than their authoritarian counterparts; they and are also able to provide an atmosphere that encourages growth and learning without the stress and external control typical in a win-lose classroom. By focusing on the connections between choices and outcomes, these teachers help students take responsibility for their actions and behaviors. As a result, their students are more likely to exhibit initiative, independence, self-management and an awareness of others' needs than students in a

A win-win focus involves rethinking, relearning and retraining, and could take some teachers a number of years to fully implement.

win-lose classroom, who often do only what is required to get by or stay safe. Win-win teachers are also clear about their limits and boundaries, and secure enough to encourage empowerment among their students.

Yet, *21st Century Discipline* can be quite a challenge for any teacher unfamiliar with win-win management models. To generate their commitment, these teachers first need to learn how *21st Century Discipline* can pay off for them. As often occurs in the life of an administrator, your job will involve selling these ideas to them, giving them good enough reasons to want to change what, in many instances, will be deeply ingrained habits and ideas.

If necessary, start with staff members who are most open to change, perhaps those who have already demonstrated a commitment to win-win objectives, if not the actual skill to reach them. Allow their successes to be the invitation and inspiration for others. These teachers will need information about effective adult behaviors for achieving a variety of interactive goals. Your support will encourage them to take risks and try new approaches and will help build confidence in developing new techniques. Keep in mind that implementing successful changes in the classroom takes time and effort. A win-win focus involves rethinking, relearning and retraining, and could take some teachers a number of years to fully implement.

Beware of the difficulties inherent in attempting to *require* across-the-board attitude changes or even implement any particular discipline program school- or district-wide. Be especially wary of programs that offer quick fixes or simple formulas for managing or reacting to children's behavior, regardless of the amount of pressure you feel from your community or staff.* Relationship building—the key to minimizing discipline problems—is a process. Since so many of the changes necessary

---

*At the end of this chapter are two lists which include characteristics of positive, healthy *21st Century Discipline* classroom relationships and a checklist of specific behaviors which can reflect or create these characteristics. Feel free to use the checklist as a goal sheet for yourself and your staff, to communicate to parents the kind of relationships your school is committed to building or to evaluate the characteristics and recommendations of any discipline programs or approaches being researched or considered.

in making a transition from industrial-age beliefs and behaviors to those of an information-age model occur at a very personal level—and on a very individual basis—you probably won't have much success attempting to mandate the change or trying to establish *21st Century Discipline* as a uniform discipline code. (Adults aren't much different from kids when it comes to being told what to do, especially if such mandates include directives about how to feel or what to tolerate!) Work with your core group and anyone who cares to join in and focus your energies on creating a school climate in which 21st century, win-win interactions are likely to emerge.

The strategies described in this book also apply well to adult relationships. This may translate to letting go, or to sharing some of your authority to involve teachers in decisions you may have previously made alone. Empowered teachers, those who feel they have input in decisions that affect them, have a greater stake in—and are more likely to commit enthusiastically to—the success and welfare of the organization.

As an administrator, begin to think of new ways to motivate, empower, value, inspire and build commitment with your staff, perhaps by:

- giving them opportunities to suggest topics and resources for inservice and staff development programs
- presenting options for scheduling, room assignment or grade level
- trying to accommodate staff members' needs for input and choice when making administrative decisions that concern them
- providing the most direct channels possible for access to supplies, resource personnel and yourself
- modeling the beliefs, behaviors, language patterns and attitudes you would like your teachers to adopt
- discouraging dependence or victim behavior by helping teachers explore and evaluate available options (rather than solving problems for them)

- offering acceptance, feedback and support while encouraging teachers to solve their problems themselves
- resisting the habit to get in the middle of—and taking responsibility for—squabbles between kids and teachers, even if that's always been your job
- refusing to punish students for infractions you did not witness
- helping teachers resolve conflicts with other staff members or parents without assuming responsibility for the solution of the problems
- encouraging the development or creation of a reward-oriented school environment; helping teacher find ways to increase the number of positive options they can offer to students
- providing resources or support necessary to help teachers develop success-oriented instruction and routines (make success possible for students at a variety of ability levels)
- being visible in non-conflict arenas; visiting every classroom, as often as possible, to offer feedback or just help out
- finding something positive to say about every member of your staff
- making time to regularly acknowledge the contributions your staff members make (including casual, informal verbal or written messages of recognition and appreciation)
- encouraging (not requiring) your staff to do the same for one another
- using motivators and rewards to show appreciation, recognize special achievements or just break up routines
- identifying and changing negative, reactive school policies
- maintaining regular and positive communication with the community
- taking care of yourself; learning to let go, delegate, set and maintain boundaries

As you model cooperative interactions with students, parents and staff, you will set the tone for the entire school. The payoffs for you and the other adults in your building are considerable. But in terms of learning, behavior and self-concept, the real winners are the students.

Relationship building is the key to minimizing discipline problems.

Work with your core group and anyone who cares to join in and focus your energies on creating a school climate in which 21st century, win-win interactions are likely to emerge.

Characteristics of Healthy, Positive Adult-Child Relationships

Use this information and the checklist that follows to evaluate patterns in your current relationships with children and adults. If you have implemented (or are considering) a specific discipline, self-esteem or instructional model, does it encourage relationships in which the following are true?

Proactivity

The ability to recognize and, whenever possible, accommodate the student's need for unconditional love and acceptance, safety, belonging, success, limits, fun, recognition and control (power), without allowing anyone else's needs to be violated. Anticipating; doing before (there is a problem); letting the student know limits or conditions ahead of time. Alternative to reactivity.

Win-win

The ability to get one's needs met without violating anyone else, particularly with regard to empowering a student without disempowering oneself. The ability to resolve and prevent conflict by sharing power within an authority relationship. The ability to offer choices within limits to encourage cooperation instead of obedience and people-pleasing. Alternative to win-lose (powering or permissiveness).

Success Orientation

The ability to help a student succeed by giving clear directions, setting boundaries, offering opportunities to choose and negotiate, requesting age-appropriate behaviors and responses, accommodating curricular and learning style needs, giving opportunities to self-manage and staying in present time (teaching according to a student's current needs, not anticipated demands of other teachers or grade levels in the future). Alternative to unrealistic expectations, misunderstandings, instruction or environments poorly matched to student's needs, and "set ups" for failure, passivity or rebelliousness.

Positivity

The ability to differentiate the child's worth from his or her behavior. The ability to focus on what the child is doing right and building on strengths. The ability to create a reward-oriented environment in which consequences are positive outcomes and incentives received or experienced as a result of cooperation. The ability to communicate positively (using promises instead of threats, or reward instead of punishment, for example). The ability to maintain a sense of humor. Alternative to negativity and punitive orientation.

Eliminating Double Standards

The ability to interact and communicate with a child in ways that would be acceptable to an adult. The willingness to maintain consistency between one's own behaviors and those expected of the student. The ability to respond to a student's behavior in similar ways as would be inspired by the same behavior if it were demonstrated by an adult. The willingness to accept the fact that students require meaningful, positive outcomes for their efforts, just as adults do.

Boundaries

The ability to connect what you want with what the student wants in positive ways. The ability to motivate and reinforce cooperative behavior with outcomes other than adult approval or avoidance of negative adult reactions (shaming, criticism, abandonment). The willingness to withhold positive consequences until the student has held up his end of the bargain. The ability to immediately intervene breaches in conditions or limits of a boundary, avoiding warnings, delayed consequences, punishment, or praise.

Supportiveness

The ability to respond to a student's problems or feelings with acceptance, support and validation. The willingness to provide outlets for a student's feelings that will allow the student to externalize the feelings (get them out) without hurting himself or others. The ability to help the student seek solutions to problems without enabling, fixing, dismissing or judging the child's problems or feelings. The ability to resist adopting a student's feelings or take responsibility for the solutions to her problems, either directly solving the problems or giving advice or solutions ("shoulds").

Integrity

The ability to maintain congruence between personal values and behavior. The ability to hear and respond according to inner guidance and personal values. The ability to act within personal value system despite potential or actual criticism from others. The willingness to make decisions based on what is best for a particular student or group of students, rather than simply, automatically following tradition. The ability to withstand judgment, criticism and ridicule if necessary, without becoming defensive, apologetic or reactive. The willingness to maintain documentation to support decisions, when necessary.

Responsibility

The ability to take responsibility for feelings, without attempting to make others responsible. The ability to express feelings in non-hurtful ways. The ability to depersonalize and resolve conflict. The willingness to maintain regular, positive contact with students' parents. The ability to work with administrators, support staff and parents without projecting blame or expecting (or demanding) that they take responsibility for solving problems you may be having with a particular student or group.

Self-Care

The ability to identify personal needs and feelings, set boundaries, take time for self, self-validate and get help when necessary. The ability to distinguish between self-care and self-ishness. The ability to feel deserving of self-caring behaviors and decisions. The ability to use mistakes and failures as opportunities for new goals, strategies or growth. The ability to utilize support resources while maintaining responsibility for solving one's own problems. The ability to self-forgive.

Checklist

Proactivity:

___ I focus on prevention—not reaction.

___ I attempt to meet student needs in healthy, constructive ways.

Win-Win:

___ I can motivate cooperative behavior without powering, threatening, humiliating or using conditional approval.

___ I am more interested in encouraging cooperation than obedience, even though the outcome behaviors usually look about the same.

___ I want to empower my students within limits that do not disempower others.

___ I use my authority to set limits, offer choices, and decide what is and is not negotiable.

Success Orientation

___ I give clear directions.

___ I set clear, pro-active and win-win boundaries.

___ I attempt to meet student curricular needs.

___ I attempt to accommodate student preferences and learning styles.

___ I give students opportunities to self-manage.

___ I stay in the present.

Positivity:

___ I can separate my students' behavior from their worth.

___ I state boundaries as promises rather than threats.

___ My classroom is reward-oriented.

___ I think of consequences as the positive outcomes for cooperation or completion.

___ I look for the positive (what the student is doing right) and build on that.

___ I try to maintain my sense of humor.

Avoiding Double Standards:

___ I model the kinds of behavior I would like my students to exhibit.

___ I avoid talking to students in ways I would not talk to adults.

___ In terms of motivation, I recognize that students desire (and deserve) to experience meaningful outcomes as a result of the behaviors they choose, just as adults do.

___ I avoid making a big deal over issues and incidents that involve my students just because they aren't adults.

Boundaries:

___ I offer students a variety of meaningful positive consequences to motivate or encourage cooperative behavior.

___ I can recognize positive student behavior without reinforcing dependence and people-pleasing.

___ I avoid giving warnings, as well as delayed or meaningless consequences. (When a student misbehaves, I am willing to withdraw privileges immediately.)

___ I avoid asking for excuses. (I am willing to withhold privileges and rewards until students come through on their end regardless of their excuses.)

___ I have built in some proactive flexibility (such as requiring 95% of all homework assignments, rather than 100% or giving students until the end of the day to get work finished) so I can accommodate occasional problems that may arise without compromising my boundaries.

Supportiveness:

__ I recognize that students can't always "leave their feelings at the door," and I do not demand that they do so.

__ I can accept a student's feelings even if I don't understand or agree with them.

__ I have a variety of healthy outlets for students to use to get their feelings out (or be listened to) without creating problems for themselves or others.

__ I will listen and validate without giving advice, dismissing the problem, or interfering with the feelings.

__ I ask rather than tell to help students find solutions to problems without giving them answers or advice about what they should do.

Integrity:

__ I make choices based on my values and my students' needs regardless of possible reactions from others.

__ I am able to deal with criticism without becoming defensive, apologetic or reactive, and without explaining in order to secure approval for what I'm doing.

__ I maintain regular, positive contact with parents.

__ I minimize potential conflict with documentation and communication.

Communication:

__ I avoid using my feelings as a way to control or change others.

__ I take responsibility for solving problems that arise in my classroom.

__ I communicate positively and responsibly with parents.

__ I use administrators, support personnel and parents as resources without attempting to make them responsible for my problems.

__ When I slip up and say or do something hurtful, I take responsibility for my behavior (rather than blaming it on something the student has done).

__ When I make a mistake or fail to keep my word, I avoid making excuses and apologize make things right.

__ I am able and willing to ask for what I want directly.

Self-care:

__ I model a commitment to personal growth.

__ I know how to set boundaries and am willing to do so to take care of myself.

__ When things get to be too much for me, I am willing to reach out for help without making others responsible for my feelings or state of mind.

__ I have developed a strong support network and am willing to use it.

__ I minimize or avoid contact with negative, toxic people and experiences.

__ I can use my mistakes and errors as opportunities for new learning rather than as excuses for beating myself up.

__ I have a variety of outlets and resources outside of the classroom for personal enrichment, relaxation, stress management and fun.

__ I acknowledge what I'm doing right and give myself space to grow and keep getting better!

About the Author

Dr. Jane Bluestein is a world-renown author and educator, with nearly 30 years' experience in the field of eduction. A dynamic and entertaining speaker, she has presented hundreds of keynote and training programs world-wide for educators, counselors, administrators, health care professionals, parents and other community members who enjoy her down-to-earth speaking style, practicality and great sense of humor. She is a sought-after media and talk-show guest, including numerous appearances as a guest expert on *National Public Radio, TalkNews Television,* and *The Oprah Winfrey Show.*

Dr. Bluestein is the author of *Being a Successful Teacher, Rx: Handwriting,* and the award-winning *Mentors, Masters and Mrs. MacGregor: Stories of Teachers Making a Difference.* She has also written several books for parents, including *Parents in a Pressure Cooker; Parents, Teens & Boundaries: How to Draw the Line;* and *The Parent's Little Book of Lists: Do's and Don'ts of Effective Parenting.* Her latest project is a co-authored book entitled *Daily Riches: A Journal of Awareness and Gratitude.* Her articles and interviews have appeared in dozens of magazines, journals and newsletters throughout the world.

Formerly a classroom teacher, crisis-intervention counselor and teacher training program coordinator, Dr. Bluestein currently heads Instructional Support Services, Inc., a consulting and resource firm that distributes resources for educators and parents, and provides staff development and parent training programs worldwide.

Dr. Bluestein can be reached at the following:

Jane Bluestein, Ph.D.

President

Instructional Support Services, Inc.

1925 Juan Tabo NE, Suite B-249

Albuquerque, NM 87112-3359

1-800-688-1960 • 505-323-9044

Fax 505-323-9045

E-mail: jblue@wizrealm.com

http://www.janebluestein.com

Bibliography: Products and Resources

The books listed in this section include resources that were referenced in the text of *21st Century Discipline* as well as materials on related topics, including instruction and mentorship, behavior and classroom management, success and achievement, motivation, goal setting, decision making, thinking and study skills, teaching and learning, brain-compatability, problem solving and getting along, learning styles, special needs, at risk and prevention (failure, drop out, substance abuse, violence), character development and self-worth, as well as resources for parents, self-care and personal development.

Adderholdt-Elliott, Miriam. *Perfectionism: What's Bad about Being too Good?* Minneapolis: Free Spirit Publishing, 1987.

Akin, Terri, Gerry Dunne, Susanna Palomares and Dianne Schilling. *Character Education in America's Schools.* Torrance, CA: Innerchoice Publishing, 1995.

Albert, Linda. *Cooperative Discipline.* Circle Pines, MN: American Guidance Service, Inc., 1996.

Algozzine, Bob. *Teacher's Little Book of Wisdom.* Merrillville, IN: ICS Books, Inc., 1995.

Arends, Richard I. *Learning to Teach.* New York: Random House, Inc., 1998.

Arkin, Elaine Bratic, and Judith E. Funkhouser. *Communicating About Alcohol and Other Drugs: Strategies for Reaching Populations at Risk.* Rockville, MD: U.S. Department of Health and Human Services, Office for Substance Abuse Prevention, 1990.

Arthur, Richard, with Edsel Erickson. *Gangs and Schools.* Holmes Beach, FL: Learning Publications, Inc., 1992.

Beattie, Melody. *Codependent No More.* New York: Hazelden/Harper and Row Publishers, Inc., 1987.

Benson, Peter, Judy Galbraith, and Pamela Espeland. *What Kids Need to Succeed.* Minneapolis: Free Spirit Publishing, 1995.

Benson, Peter L., Judy Galbraith, and Pamela Espeland. *What Teens Need to Succeed: Proven, Practical Ways to Shape your own Future.* Minneapolis, MN: Free Spirit Publishing, 1998.

Bernstein, Daryl. *Kids Can Succeed.* Holbrook, MA: Bob Adams, Inc., 1993.

Bloom, Benjamin S., editor. *Taxonomy of Educational Objectives, Handbook I: Cognitive Domain.* New York: Longman, 1956.

———. *Taxonomy of Educational Objectives, Handbook II: Affective Domain.* New York: David McKay Company, Inc., 1964.

Bleuer, Jeanne, Susanna Palomares and Garry Walz. *Activities for Counseling Underachievers.* Torrance, CA: Innerchoice Publishing, 1993.

Bluestein, Jane. *Being a Successful Teacher.* Torrance, CA: Fearon Teacher Aids (Frank Schaffer Publishers), 1989.

———. *Book of Article Reprints.* Albuquerque, NM: I.S.S. Publications, 1995.

———. *Mentors, Masters and Mrs. MacGregor: Stories of Teachers Making a Difference.* Deerfield Beach, FL: Health Communications, Inc., 1995.

———. *The Parent's Little Book of Lists: Do's and Don'ts of Effective Parenting.* Deerfield Beach, FL: Health Communications, Inc., 1997.

———. *Parents, Teens & Boundaries: How to Draw the Line.* Deerfield Beach, FL: Health Communications, Inc., 1993.

———. *Rx: Handwriting: An Individualized, Prescriptive System for Painlessly Managing Handwriting Instruction.* Albuquerque, NM: I.S.S. Publications, 1980.

———. "Secrets of Successful Mentorship," article reprint. Albuquerque, NM: I.S.S. Publications, 1995.

Bluestein, Jane, and Lynn Collins. *Parents in a Pressure Cooker.* Rosemont, NJ: Modern Learning Press, 1989.

Bluestein, Jane, Judy Lawrence and SJ Sanchez. *Daily Riches: A Journal of Gratitude and Awareness.* Deerfield Beach, FL: Health Communications, Inc. 1998.

Borba, Michele. *Esteem Builders.* Torrance, CA: Jalmar Press, 1989.

———. *Home Esteem Builders.* Torrance, CA: Jalmar Press, 1994.

———. *Staff Esteem Builders.* Torrance, CA: Jalmar Press, 1993.

Bosch, Carl. *Bully on the Bus.* Seattle: Parenting Press, 1988.

———. *Making the Grade.* Seattle: Parenting Press, 1991.

Bradshaw, John. *Bradshaw on: The Family.* Deerfield Beach, FL: Health Communications, Inc., 1988.

Branden, Nathaniel. *The Power of Self-Esteem.* Deerfield Beach, FL: Health Communications, Inc., 1992.

———. *The Six Pillars of Self-Esteem.* New York, Bantam Books, 1994.

Brown, Les. *Live Your Dreams.* New York: Avon Books, 1992.

Budd, Linda S. *Living with the Active Alert Child.* Seattle: Parenting Press, 1993.

Caine, Renate Nummela and Geoffrey Caine. *Education on the Edge of Possibility.* Alexandria, VA: Association for Supervision and Curriculum Development, 1997.

———. *Making Connections: Teaching and the Human Brain.* Menlo Park, CA: Addison-Wesley, 1994.

Caine, Geoffrey, Renate Nummela Caine and Sam Crowell. *MindShifts: A Brain-Based Process for Restructuring Schools and Renewing Education.* Tucson, AZ: Zephyr Press, 1994.

Callahan, James J. *Walls.* Merchantville, NJ: Callahan Associates, 1993.

Cameron, Julia, with Mark Bryan. *The Artist's Way.* New York: Putnam, 1992.

Canfield, Jack. *Self-Esteem in the Classroom.* Santa Barbara: Self-Esteem Seminars, 1989.

Cantor, Ralph, Paul Kivel, and Allan Creighton. *Days of Respect.* Alameda, CA: Hunter House, 1997.

Clark, Jean Illsley, and Connie Dawson. *Growing up Again.* San Francisco: Harper & Row, Publishers, 1989.

Cole, Jim. *Thwarting Anger.* Novato, CA: Growing Images, 1985.

Covey, Stephen R. *The Seven Habits of Highly Effective People.* New York: Simon & Schuster, 1989.

Cowan, David, Susanna Palomares, and Dianne Schilling. *Conflict Resolution Skills for Teens.* Torrance, CA: Innerchoice Publishing, 1994.

———. *Teaching the Skills of Conflict Resolution.* Spring Valley, CA: Innerchoice Publishing, 1992.

Cox, Fran and Louis Cox. *A Conscious Life: Cultivating the Seven Qualities of Authentic Adulthood.* Berkeley: Conari Press, 1996.

Crary, Elizabeth. *Children's Problem-Solving Series* (6 books). Seattle: Parenting Press, 1996.

———. *Dealing with Feelings Series* (6 books). Seattle: Parenting Press, 1994.

———. *Kids Can Cooperate.* Seattle: Parenting Press, 1984.

Creighton, Allan, with Paul Kivel. *Helping Teens Stop Violence.* Alameda, CA: Hunter House, 1992.

Daleo, Morgan Simone. *Curriculum of Love.* Charlottesville, VA: Grace Publishing, 1996.

Davis, Joel. *Mapping the Mind: The Secrets of the Human Brain and How it Works.* Secaucas, NJ: Carol Publishing Group, 1997.

Delisle, Deb, and Jim Delisle. *Growing Good Kids.* Minneapolis: Free Spirit Publishing, 1996.

Dennison, Paul E. and Gail E. Dennison. *Brain Gym.* Ventura, CA: Edu-Kinesthetics, Inc., 1996.

Dennison, Susan. *Creating Positive Support Groups for At-Risk Children.* Torrance, CA: Jalmar Press, 1997.

Drew, Naomi. *Learning the Skills of Peacemaking.* Torrance, CA: Jalmar Press, 1995.

Dryden, Gordon, and Jeanette Vos. *The Learning Revolution.* Torrance, CA: Jalmar Press, 1994.

Dunn, Kenneth, and Rita Dunn. *The Educator's Self-Teaching Guide to Individualized Instruction.* New Jersey: Parker Publishing, Co., 1975.

Duvall, Lynn. *Respecting our Differences.* Minneapolis: Free Spirit Publishing, 1994.

Dyer, Wayne W. *What Do You Really Want for Your Children?* New York: Avon Books, 1985.

Elchoness, Monte. *Why Can't Anyone Hear Me?* Ventura: Monroe Press, 1989.

———. *Why do Kids Need Feelings?* Ventura: Monroe Press, 1992.

Espeland, Pamela, and Rosemary Willner. *Making the Most of Today.* Minneapolis: Free Spirit Publishing, 1991.

Faber, Adele, and Elaine Mazlish. *How to Talk so Kids can Learn.* New York: Rawson Associates, 1995.

The Faculty of New City School. *Celebrating Multiple Intelligences.* St. Louis: New City School, Inc., 1994.

Finney, Susan. *Together I Can.* Spring Valley, CA: Innerchoice Publishing, 1991.

Fisk, Lori, and Henry Clay Lindgren. *A Survival Guide for Teachers.* New York: John Wiley & Sons, Inc., 1973.

Fogarty, Robin. *Brain Compatible Classrooms.* Arlington Heights, IL: SkyLight Training & Publishing, 1997.

Folkers, Gladys, and Jeanne Englemann. *Taking Charge of My Mind and Body.* Minneapolis: Free Spirit Publishing, 1997.

Fox, C. Lynn. *Let's Get Together.* Torrance, CA: Jalmar Press, 1993.

Fox, C. Lynn, and Shirley E. Forbing. *Creating Drug-Free Schools and Communities.* New York: HarperCollins, 1992.

Fox, Matthew. *The Reinvention of Work.* New York: Harper Collins, 1994.

Garfield, Charles. *Peak Performers.* New York: William Morrow & Co., 1986.

Gerrard, Tamara L. *Com-Packs: Kids' Committees for Integrated Learning.* Albuquerque, NM: I.S.S. Publications, 1987.

Ginott, Haim. *Between Parent & Child.* New York: Avon Books, 1956.

———. *Teacher and Child.* New York: Avon Books.

Glenn, H. Stephen, and Jane Nelsen. *Raising Self-Reliant Children in a Self-Indulgent World.* Rocklin, CA: Prima Publishing & Communications, 1988.

Goleman, Daniel. *Emotional Intelligence.* New York: Bantam Books, 1995.

Goodlad, John I. *A Place Called School: Prospects for the Future.* New York: McGraw-Hill, 1984.

Gootman, Marilyn E. *When a Friend Dies.* Minneapolis: Free Spirit Publishing, 1996.

Gordon, Thomas. *L.E.T.: Leader Effectiveness Training.* Toronto: Bantam Books, 1980.

———. *T.E.T.: Teacher Effectiveness Training.* New York: Peter H. Wyden Publishers, 1974.

Hannaford, Carla. *Smart Moves: Why Learning is Not All in Your Head.* Arlington, VA: Great Oceans Publishers, 1995.

Harmin, Merrill. *Strategies for Active Learning.* Edwardsville, IL: Inspiring Strategies Institute, 1995.

Heacox, Diane. *Up From Underachievement.* Minneapolis: Free Spirit Publishing, 1991.

Hipp, Earl. *Fighting Invisible Tigers.* Minneapolis: Free Spirit Publishing, 1995.

Hoffman, Carol. *Reaching and Teaching the Kids Today.* Rosemont, NJ: Modern Learning Press, 1996.

Holt, John. *How Children Learn.* New York: Dell Publishing Company, Inc., 1967.

Howard, Pierce. *The Owner's Manual for the Brain.* Austin, TX: Leornian Press, 1996.

Hunt, D. Trinidad. *Learning to Learn.* Kaneohe, HI: Elan Publishing, 1991.

Hyland, Bruce, and Merle Yost. *Reflections for Managers.* New York: McGraw-Hill, 1994.

Jacobs, Thomas A. *What Are my Rights? 95 Questions and Answers about Teens and the Law.* Minneapolis, MN: Free Spirit Publishing, 1997.

Jensen, Eric. *Brain-Based Learning.* San Diego, CA: The Brain Store, 1996.

———. *Brain Compatible Strategies.* San Diego, CA: The Brain Store, 1997.

———. *Completing the Puzzle: The Brain-Compatible Approach to Learning.* San Diego, CA: The Brain Store, 1997.

———. *Introduction to Brain-Compatible Learning.* San Diego, CA: The Brain Store, 1998.

———. *The Learning Brain.* San Diego, CA: The Brain Store, 1995.

———. *Super Teaching.* San Diego, CA: The Brain Store, 1998.

Johnson, Kendall. *School Crisis Management.* Alameda, CA: Hunter House, 1993.

———. *Trauma in the Lives of Children.* Alameda, CA: Hunter House, 1989.

Jones, Frederic H. *Positive Classroom Discipline.* New York: McGraw-Hill, 1987.

———. *Positive Classroom Instruction.* New York: McGraw-Hill, 1987.

Joyce, Bruce, and Marsha Weil. *Models of Teaching.* Englewood Cliffs, NJ: Prentice-Hall, Inc., 1980.

Kaufman, Gershen, and Lev Rafael. *Stick Up for Yourself.* Minneapolis: Free Spirit Publishing, 1990.

Kehayan, Alex. *Partners for Change.* Torrance, CA: Jalmar Press, 1992.

Kincher, Jonni. *Psychology for Kids.* Minneapolis: Free Spirit Publishing, 1995.

Kivel, Paul, and Allan Creighton. *Making the Peace.* Alameda, CA: Hunter House, 1997.

Kotulak, Ronald. *Inside the Brain: Revolutionary Discoveries of How the Mind Works.* Kansas City, MO: Andrews McMeel Publishing, 1997.

Kozol, Jonathan. *Illiterate America.* Garden City, NY: Anchor Press/Doubleday, 1985.

———. *Savage Inequalities: Children in America's Schools.* New York: Crown Publishers, 1991.

Kroen, William C. *Helping Children Cope with the Loss of a Loved One.* Minneapolis: Free Spirit Publishers, 1994.

Krueger, David W. *What is a Feeling?* Seattle: Parenting Press, 1993.

Laborde, Genie Z. *Influencing with Integrity.* Palo Alto: Syntony Publishing, 1983.

Laik, Judy. *Under Whose Influence?* Seattle: Parenting Press, 1994.

Lalli, Judy. *Make Someone Smile.* Minneapolis: Free Spirit Publishing, 1996.

Lazear, David. *Seven Ways of Teaching.* Arlington Heights, IL: SkyLight Training & Publishing, 1991.

Lee, Dorris M., and Joseph B. Rubin. *Children and Language.* Belmont, CA: Wadsworth Publishing Company, 1979.

Lewis, Barbara. *The Kid's Guide to Service Projects.* Minneapolis: Free Spirit Publishing, 1995.

Lewis, Barbara A. *What do you Stand For? A Kids Guide to Building Character.* Minneapolis, MN: Free Spirit Publishing, 1998.

Lewis, Byron, and Frank Pucelik. *Magic of NLP Demystified.* Portland: Metamorphous Press, 1990.

Liebig, James E. *Merchants of Vision.* San Francisco: Berrett-Koehler Publishers, 1994.

Lillard, Paula Polk. *Montessori Today.* New York: Schocken Books, 1996.

Linney, Jean Ann, and Abraham Wandersman. *Prevention Plus III: Assessing Alcohol and Other Drug Prevention Programs at the School and Community Level.* Rockville, MD: U.S. Department of Health and Human Services, Office for Substance Abuse Prevention, 1991.

Loomans, Diane and Karen Kolberg. *The Laughing Classroom.* Tiburon, CA: HJ Kramer, Inc., 1993.

Markova, Dawna. *How Your Child is Smart.* Berkeley: Conari Press, 1992.

———. *The Open Mind.* Berkeley: Conari Press, 1996.

Markova, Dawna and Anne R. Powell. *Learning Unlimited: Using Homework to Engage Your Child's Natural Style of Intelligence.* Berkeley, CA: Conari Press, 1998.

Marston, Stephanie. *The Magic of Encouragement: Nurturing Your Child's Self-Esteem.* New York: Pocket Books, 1990.

Maslow, Abraham H. *Toward a Psychology of Being, second edition.* New York: D. Van Nostrand Company, 1968.

McCutcheon, Randall. *Get Off My Brain: A Survival Guide for Lazy Students.* Minneapolis: Free Spirit Publishing, 1985.

McDaniel, Sandy and Peggy Bielen. *Project Self-Esteem.* Torrance, CA: Jalmar Press, 1990.

McGinnis, Alan Loy. *Bringing out the Best in People.* Minneapolis: Augsburg Publishing House, 1985.

McMurchie, Susan. *Understanding L.D.* Minneapolis: Free Spirit Publishing, 1994.

McLaughlin, Cathrine Kellison. *The Do's and Don'ts of Parent Involvement: How to Build a Positive School-Home Partnership.* Torrance, CA: Innerchoice Publishing, 1993.

Miller, Alice. *Banished Knowledge.* New York: Doubleday, 1985.

———. *For Your Own Good: Hidden Cruelty in Child-Rearing and the Roots of Violence.* New York: Farrar, Straus & Giroux, 1983.

———. *Thou Shalt not be Aware: Society's Betrayal of the Child.* New York: New American Library, 1986.

Mitchell, Craig, with Pamela Espeland. *Teach to Reach.* Minneapolis: Free Spirit Publishing, 1996.

Moawad, Bob. *Whatever it Takes: A Journey into the Heart of Human Achievement.* Edmonds, WA: Compendium Publishing, 1995.

Moberg, Randy. *TNT Teaching.* Minneapolis: Free Spirit Publishing, 1994.

Moorman, Chick, and Dee Dishon. *Our Classroom: We Can Learn Together.* Saginaw, MI: Personal Power Press, 1983.

Moorman, Chick, and Nancy Moorman Weber. *Teacher Talk: What it Really Means.* Saginaw, MI: Personal Power Press, 1989.

Montessori, Maria. *Childhood Education.* New York: New American Library, 1949.

Muller, Wayne. *Legacy of the Heart: The Spiritual Advantages of a Painful Childhood.* New York: Simon & Schuster, 1992.

Munson, Patricia J. Winning *Teachers, Teaching Winners.* Santa Cruz: Network Publications, 1991.

Murray, Margo. *Beyond the Myths and Magic of Mentoring.* San Francisco: Jossey-Bass Inc., 1991.

Myss, Caroline. *Anatomy of the Spirit.* New York: Harmony Books, 1996.

Naisbitt, John. *Megatrends: Ten New Directions for Transforming our Lives.* New York: Warner Books, Inc., 1982.

———. *Megatrends 2000.* New York: William Morrow & Co., 1990.

Naisbitt, John, and Patricia Aburdene. *Re-Inventing the Corporation.* New York: Warner Books, 1985.

Nelsen, Jane. *Positive Discipline.* New York: Ballantine Books, 1987.

Ohme, Herman. *101 Ways for Teachers to Motivate Students.* Palo Alto: California Education Plan, 1991.

————. *"Learn How to Learn" Study Skills.* Palo Alto: California Education Plan, 1986.

Osborn, D. Keith, and Janie Dyson Osborn. *Discipline and Classroom Management.* Athens, GA: Education Associates, 1977.

Packer, Alex. *How Rude! The Teenagers' Guide to Good Manners, Proper Behavior and Not Grossing People Out.* Minneapolis, MN: Free Spirit Publishing, 1997.

Palomares, Susanna. *All About Me.* Spring Valley, CA: Innerchoice Publishing, 1991.

Palomares, Susanna, Sandy Schuster and Cheryl Watkins. *The Sharing Circle Handbook.* Spring Valley, CA: Innerchoice Publishing, 1992.

Payne, Lauren Murphy. *Just Because I Am.* Minneapolis: Free Spirit Publishing, 1994.

Payne, Lauren Murphy, and Claudia Rohling. *We Can Get Along.* Minneapolis: Free Spirit Publishing, 1997.

Peck, M. Scott. *The Road Less Traveled.* New York: Simon & Schuster, 1978.

Perkins, David. *Smart Schools: Better Thinking & Learning for Every Child.* New York: The Free Press/Simon & Schuster, 1992.

Peters, Thomas J., and Robert H. Waterman, Jr. *In Search of Excellence.* New York: Warner Books, 1982.

————. *Thriving on Chaos: Handbook for a Management Revolution.* New York: Alfred A. Knopf, 1987.

Peterson, Jean Sunde. *Talk with Teens about Feelings, Family, Relationships and the Future.* Minneapolis: Free Spirit Publishing, 1995.

————. *Talk with Teens about Self and Stress.* Minneapolis: Free Spirit Publishing, 1993.

Pipher, Mary. *Reviving Ophelia: Saving the Selves of Adolescent Girls.* New York: Ballantine Books, 1994.

Racosky, Rico. *dreams+action=Reality.* Boulder: Action Graphics Publishing, 1996.

Radencich, Marguerite, and Jeanne Shay Schumm. *How to Help your Child with Homework.* Minneapolis: Free Spirit Publishing, 1997.

Redenbach, Sandi. *Autobiography of a Drop-Out: Dear Diary.* Davis, CA: Esteem Seminars Publishing, 1996.

————. *Self-Esteem: The Necessary Ingredients.* Davis, CA: Esteem Seminars Publishing, 1991.

Rogers, Spence and Shari Graham. *The High Performance Toolbox: Succeeding with Performance Tasks, Projects and Assessments.* Evergreen, CO: Peak Learning Systems, 1997.

Rogers, Spence, Jim Ludington and Shari Graham. *Motivation & Learning: A Teacher's Guide to Building Excitement for Learning & Igniting the Drive for Quality.* Evergreen, CO: Peak Learning Systems, 1997.

Romain, Trevor. *Bullies are a Pain in the Brain.* Minneapolis, MN: Free Spirit Publishing, 1997.

Rosenfeld, Lawrence B. *Human Interaction in the Small Group Setting.* Columbus: Charles E. Merrill Publishing Co., 1973.

Rutter, Virginia Beane. *Celebrating Girls.* Berkeley: Conari Press, 1996.

Schaef, Ann Wilson. *Co-dependence: Misunderstood, Mistreated.* San Francisco: Harper and Row Publishers, Inc., 1986.

————. *When Society Becomes an Addict.* San Francisco: Harper & Row, 1987.

Schilling, Dianne. *50 Activities for Teaching Emotional Intelligence. Level I: Elementary School.* Torrance, CA: Innerchoice Publishing, 1996.

————. *50 Activities for Teaching Emotional Intelligence. Level II: Middle School.* Torrance, CA: Innerchoice Publishing, 1996.

———. *Getting Along: Activities for Teaching cooperation, Responsibility, Respect.* Torrance, CA: Innerchoice Publishing, 1993.

Schilling, Diane, and Gerry Dunne. *Understanding Me.* Spring Valley, CA: Innerchoice Publishing, 1992.

Schilling, Dianne and Susanna Palomares. *Helping Teens Reach their Dreams.* Torrance, CA: Innerchoice Publishing, 1993.

Schmuck, Richard A., and Patricia A. Schmuck. *Group Processes in the Classroom.* Dubuque: Wm. C. Brown Co. Publishers, 1975.

Schriner, Chris. *Feel Better Now.* Torrance, CA: Jalmar Press, 1990.

Schumm, Jeanne Shay, and Marguerite Radencich. *School Power.* Minneapolis: Free Spirit Publishing, 1992.

Schwallie-Giddis, Pat, David Cowan and Dianne Schilling. *Counselor in the Classroom: Activities and Strategies for an Effective Classroom Guidance Program.* Torrance, CA: Innerchoice Publishing, 1993.

Senge, Peter. *The Fifth Discipline.* New York: Currency Doubleday, 1990.

Shalaway, Linda. *Learning to Teach.* Cleveland: Edgell Communications (Instructor Books), 1989.

Silberman, Charles. *Crisis in the Classroom.* New York: Random House, 1970.

Silberman, Mel. *Active Learning: 101 Strategies to Teach Any Subject.* Boston: Allyn & Bacon, 1996.

Sousa, David A. *How the Brain Learns.* Reston, VA: NASSP, 1995.

Sutton, Marcia. *In Harmony: Resolving Stress.* Albuquerque, NM: Harmony Publishing, 1988.

Tobin, L. *What Do You Do with a Child Like This? Inside the Lives of Troubled Children.* Duluth, MN: Pfeifer-Hamilton Publishers, 1991.

Vitale, Barbara Meister. *Free Flight: Celebrating Your Right Brain.* Torrance, CA: Jalmar Press, 1986.

———. *Unicorns Are Real.* Torrance, CA: Jalmar Press, 1982.

Waas, Lane. *Imagine That.* Torrance, CA: Jalmar Press, 1991.

Williams, Linda K., Dianne Schilling and Susanna Palomares. *Caring and Capable Kids: An Activity Guide for Teaching Kindness, Tolerance, Self-Control and Responsibility.* Torrance, CA: Innerchoice Publishing, 1996.

Winebrenner, Susan. *Teaching Kids with Learning Difficulties in the Regular Classroom.* Minneapolis: Free Spirit Publishing, 1996.

Wright, Esther. *Good Morning Class—I Love You!* Torrance, CA: Jalmar Press, 1989.

———. *The Heart and Wisdom of Teaching.* San Francisco: Teaching from the Heart, 1997.

———. *Loving Discipline A to Z.* San Francisco: Teaching from the Heart, 1994.

Youngs, Bettie B. *Goal Setting for Young Adults.* Torrance, CA: Jalmar Press, 1995.

———. *Problem Solving Skills for Children.* Torrance, CA: Jalmar Press, 1995.

———. *Stress Management for Administrators.* Torrance, CA: Jalmar Press, 1993.

———. *Stress Management for Educators.* Torrance, CA: Jalmar Press, 1993.

Glossary

All-or-Nothing Thinking

Sometimes called dualism or black-and-white thinking, this term refers to a belief that certain events or situations can only be one way or another. Examples might include: "Either I'm in control, or my students are in control," or the belief that a student (or idea) is either good or bad.

Anecdotal Records

These records may be little more than a sentence or two written on an index card or a scrap of paper and kept in a students file, and often reflect observations a teacher makes and wishes to track or remember. Teachers using more comprehensive and inclusive methods of record keeping (such as portfolios of student work and writing samples, goal sheets, profiles and inventories, for example), find that anecdotal records can contribute essential or crucial information about individual students.

Boundaries

A statement that expresses our needs, requirements or limits, as well as the positive outcomes of respecting those needs, requirements or limits. Unlike most rules, boundaries consider the needs of both the person expressing the boundary and the person or people the boundary might affect.

Consistency

Refers especially to the degree of congruence we can demonstrate between our goals (or beliefs) and our behaviors, and between the behaviors we desire from others and those we are willing to practice ourselves (modeling).

Enabling

Anything that undermines the process of following through on a boundary, such as excusing (excuse-making or asking for excuses), warnings, threats, meaningless negative consequences, or denying that a problem exists, is an example of enabling.

Expectations

Refers to the picture we create in our mind of how certain things should be or how certain individuals should behave.

Factory-era

Working in a factory required certain types of skills, attitudes and behaviors in order to operate productively, and it was the job of the schools to train children with these skills, attitudes and behaviors so that they could successfully function in this factory environment.

Follow Through

When we've set a boundary or otherwise made the availability of a meaningful positive outcome dependent on certain criteria, following through means that we only allow students access to the positive outcome when they've fulfilled their part of the bargain (met the criteria we've established and communicated).

Interaction Patterns

Refers to behaviors that an individual will demonstrate repeatedly in certain situations which involve others.

Lose-Win

A permissive form of win-lose power dynamics in which the person in authority is reluctant to express needs and limits, follow through (maintain boundaries), or hold others accountable for their behavior.

People-Pleasers

Individuals who place primary importance on the needs and reactions of others in making choices, sometimes (or often) at the expense of their own needs.

Positive Reinforcement

This term is used to refer to any positive feedback or outcome that increases the likelihood of a particular behavior reoccurring.

Recognition

Recognition allows us to avoid the implicit value judgments often present in praise. Rather than connecting the worth or goodness of a student to the student's choices, recognition focuses on behavior, and connects the outcomes of a student's choices to the choices themselves.

Relationship Building

The foundation of *21st Century Discipline*, and critical to creating an environment conducive to learning and remembering. The focus on building relationships is based on the premise (supported by current brain-based learning research) that commitment, risk-taking and even the most basic levels of participation require a certain level of emotional safety in order to occur. This emotional safety is a product of certain interaction patterns, interactions that occur in relationships, in this case, between teachers and students.

Responsible Cooperation

Refers to a positive or cooperative behavior response that is not motivated by either the need for someone's approval or by the fear of someone's rejection, impatience, anger (or other negative reaction).

Self-care

This term refers to the ability to meet one's own needs without hurting, disturbing or depriving anyone else.

Self-Esteem

Self-esteem is critical component of a healthy sense of self. It includes a perception not only of personal worth or value, but also of an ability to meet one's needs, the confidence to handle life's challenges, and the power to influence the course of one's own life.

Stuffed Feelings

This term, common in counseling and therapeutic environments, refers to emotions that are repressed or stuffed. The act of stuffing feelings can result from a fear of others' reactions to the feelings (including the possibility of shaming, impatience, discounting, attacking, or ridicule), a fear of losing control, or a desire to avoid the discomfort of the feelings themselves.

Success-oriented Focus

The intention that allows teachers to select content, procedures, methods, materials, grouping arrangements and other options necessary for every student in the class to experience success. This focus attempts to balance curricular goals with student needs and experiences, rather than simply proceeding through the curriculum regardless of students' readiness.

Win-Lose

A powering approach to resolving conflicts based on the belief that only one person (or group) can win or have power in a given conflict situation.

Win-Win

A cooperative approach to resolving conflicts in which the needs of everyone involved are considered and respected, if not actually accommodated.

Date_____

Notes

Date_____

Notes

Date_____

Notes